PRESIDENTIAL TRANSITION IN HIGHER EDUCATION

(Friday)

January 13, 2006

For a valued colleague
who does not need this
book – but who could
have written it himself –

with our best wishes –

[illegible]

J. Martin

PRESIDENTIAL TRANSITION IN HIGHER EDUCATION

Managing Leadership Change

James Martin, James E. Samels & Associates

The Johns Hopkins University Press *Baltimore & London*

Printed in the United States of America on acid-free paper

Johns Hopkins Paperbacks edition, 2006
9 8 7 6 5 4 3 2 1

The Johns Hopkins University Press
2715 North Charles Street
Baltimore, Maryland 21218-4363
www.press.jhu.edu

The Library of Congress has cataloged the hardcover edition of this book as follows:

Martin, James
Presidential transition in higher education : managing leadership change / James Martin, James E. Samels & Associates.
p. cm.
ISBN 0-8018-7934-5 (hardcover : alk. paper)
1. College presidents—United States. 2. Universities and colleges—United States—Administration. 3. Organizational change—United States. 4. Educational leadership—United States.
I. Samels, James E. II. Title.
LB2341.M294 2004
378.1'11—dc22

2003024782

ISBN 0-8018-8377-6 (pbk. : alk. paper)

A catalog record for this book is available from the British Library.

Contents

Foreword

When I was a college student a half-century ago, I read an article about an Ivy League president who spent much of the summer sailing, his favorite hobby. Today most college and university presidents wouldn't dare leave their office for more than a few days.

Presidents now munch power breakfasts, often work seven days a week, and stay up most evenings hosting potential donors or writing remarks for tomorrow's address. Never before have campus presidents been so busy and besieged.

As the United States has become a knowledge-based society, colleges and universities have moved from the polite periphery to the incubating center, and their presidents have become major, carefully selected executives. The work, the pay, and the difficulties of the job have all ballooned. More than two dozen university presidents currently earn more than $500,000 a year, and several receive nearly $1 million annually if one includes a free house and a few servants, abundant fringe benefits, money from corporate board memberships, and a limousine. Two recent surveys estimate that roughly one-fourth of all presidential spouses are also paid, from $5,000 to $75,000 a year. As former Harvard president Derek Bok asked in print recently, "Why should any college president make twice as much as the president of the United States?"

The search for these paragons of academic leadership and fund-raising has led to the creation of nearly thirty firms that help colleges find a new president, and more than half of all academic institutions now employ them—for fees ranging from $100,000 to $500,000. And after a new president is chosen, she or he is presented to the world with appropriate pomp and solemnity in an inauguration ceremony that usually costs from $50,000 for small colleges to as much as $250,000 for large universities.

Clearly, the search for, the selection of, the announcements surrounding, and the introduction of the new barons of brainpower to the campus community have assumed a larger import in academic life. So this book by more than a dozen experts on presidential transition is significant. Readers will find a marvelous trove of information and experienced counsel inside its covers. The book's impresarios, one a professor and former provost, the other a lawyer and education consultant, have a knack for writing and researching about unconventional cutting-edge issues in higher learning. They have also prudently employed an excellent copy editor to smooth out the uneven prose, always a concern when a book consists of a collection of essays by numerous contributors.

What I found particularly absorbing are the identification of several trends and the rich emphasis on all the details of presidential transitions. You will learn that the time that most presidents serve is now shorter, that there are many more female presidents, that a growing number of schools use an interim president until they can locate a proper successor or fix an internal tangle, and that perhaps as many as one-fourth of all thirty-nine hundred U.S. colleges and universities in any year are preparing for a presidential change, are in the midst of one, or have just selected a new president. As for details, there is advice on what to do when a president dies suddenly, on how to deal with the voracious media and sunshine laws, and on what presidents should and should not do in their first months at the new institution. There are even guru-like bits such as the caution that presidents ought not to resign in less than five years but find good reasons to stay more than ten.

The volume is a profoundly practical and wonderfully instructive book that trustees, senior faculty and staff, education officials, and others, including lay persons curious about the inside working of academe, all should read to their profit.

GEORGE KELLER

Preface

Presidential Transition in Higher Education is a theory-based, practitioner-oriented handbook to managing presidential transitions strategically and proactively. Although a number of national higher education associations have suggested the need for such a resource in recent years, this is the first comprehensive examination of the transition process from the earliest, often confidential, considerations of the outgoing president and members of the board to the conclusion of the new president's "honeymoon," however long or short. Collectively, the chapters of this volume advocate a new model of "transition management," which approaches the principal elements of the experience with a coordinated, constructive, and strategic intent.

The 2000 edition of *The American College President,* issued by the American Council on Education, notes that half of all presidents in both the public and the private sectors in 1998 had served for fewer than five years. ACE's research reveals that the average tenure for all presidents at specialized public institutions, for instance, was only 5.2 years. Continuing review of ACE's data, along with information being considered by the American Association for Higher Education, the American Association of State Colleges and Universities, the Council of Independent Colleges, and the Harvard Seminar for New Presidents, to name just a few of the participants involved in this national conversation, has formed the background to this volume.

As presidential tenures grow shorter, as the average age of all presidents pushes toward sixty, and as various sectors of the higher education community begin to claim openly that their leadership structure is in some form of "crisis"—almost 50 percent of all community college presidents are planning to retire within the next six years, for example—presidential transitions now exert an impact in shaping institutions well beyond the straightforward choice of their next leaders.

The first four chapters of *Presidential Transition* address the changing role of the presidency in American higher education along with the pressures that are causing chief executive officers to leave their positions early, and often unhappily. Other chapters review key aspects of how to conduct a successful presidential search; however, this volume is not, principally, a guide to the executive search process or an extended study of the presidency. There are numerous volumes in print that focus specifically on these issues. Rather, we provide advice about best practices for an institution and its core constituencies to utilize during a presidential transition as they attempt to achieve strategic institutional objectives in and beyond that process.

The text is divided into three parts: "Context," "Action," and "Key Issues." Part I offers four broad views into the contemporary college and university presidency in the context of the book's theme of managing transitions more strategically. In chapter 1, James Martin and James E. Samels assess the impact of both familiar and some surprising new reasons for presidential turnover and outline key reasons why a comprehensive resource on presidential transitions is needed now.

Chapter 2 comprises a set of candid comments by Vartan Gregorian on the limitations and opportunities in a contemporary presidency. Gregorian speaks from his perspectives as former president of Brown University and current chief executive of the Carnegie Corporation to explain how the American college and university presidency has changed dramatically even from perceptions of less than a decade ago. He examines why presidential migration has increased at institutions of every size and classification, as well as how the impact of turnover influences all areas of operation, from internal governance to external advancement.

Steven Muller, former president of the Johns Hopkins University and now professor in that university's Paul H. Nitze School of Advanced International Studies, is also well positioned to describe (in chapter 3) the pressures placed on contemporary presidents, the reasons some choose to leave, and the reasons others should leave. With almost 20 percent of the women and over 25 percent of the men already serving as presidents at the time of their transition to a new presidency, a number of the traditional reasons associated with turnover may no longer apply. Muller examines the underlying causes for the current wave of presidential migration and offers recommendations both for presidents and for their institutional communities.

Chapter 4 considers the primary statistical evidence available nationally on presidential migration and offers new explanations for this trend. In his chapter "Passing the Baton: Leadership Transitions and the Tenure of Presidents," Arthur Padilla, a professor of business management and higher education researcher at North Carolina State University, updates a number of the standard conclusions reached in recent editions of ACE's *American College President,* as well as those provided by Michael D. Cohen and James G. March in *Leadership and Ambiguity: The American College President.* In doing so, Padilla delivers a fresh look at familiar numbers by applying a new statistical tool called "survival analysis."

He proposes several new theories about when and why chief executives are leaving, based on this tool.

Part II, "Action," focuses on best practices for the presidential transition process at institutions of any size, regardless of whether the institutional community saw this change on its horizon or not. It opens with a chapter on the board's integral involvement in every transition and discusses how the board can most effectively be positioned. William A. Weary, president of Fieldstone Consulting, Inc., and author of several publications for the Association of Governing Boards of Universities and Colleges, brings the roles of trustees, and their chair, into clearer focus by defining a best practices approach to their involvement in the transition, including a set of parameters that define the points at which "how much" becomes "too much."

Chapter 6 describes a proactive model for presidential transition when the process has been carefully and collegially planned, runs smoothly, and demonstrates structured collaboration among all parties. After attending the Harvard Seminar for New Presidents, Patricia Stanley, then the incoming president of Frederick Community College in Maryland, used her new perspective to initiate a collaboration with Lee John Betts, her predecessor, to design and implement a transition template that their community characterized as thoughtful and memorable, and one that can be applied to private institutions and larger universities as well.

E. K. Fretwell Jr., former chief executive officer at the State University of New York at Buffalo; the University of Massachusetts; the University of North Florida; and the University of North Carolina, Charlotte, addresses a dramatically different set of transitional circumstances in chapter 7. Fretwell focuses exclusively on best practices for an institution facing a turnover, usually sudden, that it did not foresee. What must a community *additionally* accomplish in its transition when its president departs unexpectedly for a "better offer," when the board terminates the chief executive, or when the campus leader dies or becomes seriously disabled virtually overnight? In these situations even a flexible, consensus-driven transition plan may have little value or may fail outright. To address the crisis raging on the doorstep, Fretwell, a seasoned president and interim president, presents a specific action plan for institutions to use in turning unforeseen negative circumstances into opportunities for institutional stabilization and future planning.

In chapter 8 the focus moves away from the corner offices of executive and board authority to discuss how successful transitions can empower all of a community's core constituencies by liberally sharing information and resources with those who are sometimes left out, such as student leaders, middle managers, alumni, and local business and civic leaders. Nancy L. Zimpher, chancellor of the University of Wisconsin—Milwaukee, has researched the literature on community leadership in the context of transition and developed a checklist of factors that gauge a higher education institution's health during and following executive turnover. Zimpher also offers a set of related transition guidelines for effective relations with state chancellors, coordinating boards, and legislative delegations.

Part III, "Key Issues," assembles the primary factors determining the success of most transitions and examines them in a collective context. Chapters 9 and 10 confront the rise of executive search firms and their role in and impact on presidential migration. Jean A. Dowdall, former president of Simmons College and now a vice president with Educational Management Network/Witt/Kieffer Executive Search Consultants and a columnist on these issues for the *Chronicle of Higher Education Online,* provides an overview of the use of executive search firms in higher education, a practice that the editors of the ACE *American College President* study confirm occurs in 41 percent of all searches and 60 percent of the searches conducted at public doctorate-granting institutions. Half of all new presidents hired between 1995 and 1998 came to their positions via a search firm, whereas for presidents recruited before 1985, the level was only 16 percent, according to ACE. Dowdall explains in her chapter why an institution should, or should not, consider an outside firm.

For chapter 10, Thomas H. Langevin and Allen E. Koenig, both former college presidents and the creators in 1992 of the national Registry for College and University Presidents (the leading clearinghouse to provide interim executive leadership to higher education institutions), define what an *interim* president is and is not, how that position differs significantly from an *acting* chief executive's job, and the principal factors a college or university should weigh in deciding whether such a transitional leader is its best choice in the short term. Having placed more chief executives in interim positions than any other organization over the past decade, Langevin and Koenig have coordinated the narrative of their chapter with that of Dowdall's in order to provide a collective overview of the roles of search consultants in presidential transitions.

The directive for presidential transitions in chapter 11 is blunt: *leaks kill.* John Ross, a senior higher education public relations specialist and coauthor of a major study from the Council for Advancement and Support of Education, *Public Relations and the Presidency: Strategies and Tactics for Effective Communications,* outlines a set of best practices for all campus leaders to follow with the media during the uncertainties of a leadership transition. As George Keller has observed, "leaks can kill a successful presidential transition process" when word escapes early about the field of finalists or when a search team's unofficial, preliminary vote is circulated during a delicate round of negotiations.[1] Ross addresses these possibilities and also the fact that effective public relations must extend beyond the turnover and well into the start of the new administration.

In Chapter 12, "Weathering the Storm: Institutional Advancement during a Presidential Transition," Charles Brown, director of medical giving at Stanford University's Medical Center, outlines the complexities and challenges of continuing to raise funds during the transition process. From alumni relations to state and federal policy, turning over a chief executive officer rearranges everything in an institutional advancement office, and Brown provides a set of careful guidelines for institutional development personnel to consider when confronted by a high-profile leadership change.

Chapter 13, "Shaky Ground in Troubled Times: The Legal Framework of Presidential Transitions," provides a set of legal guidelines to manage all of the principal parties involved in the transition, emphasizing throughout the key concept that the college or university counsel will typically represent the president and the board in almost every aspect of their collective decision making, except during a transition, when presidents are advised to retain their own attorneys. Consistent with the design of other chapters in this section, Samels and Martin focus their legal best practices on the benefits of a proactive, strategic approach to presidential departures and arrivals.

Chapter 14 offers advice on an aspect of presidential transition that has generally been overlooked: the president's spouse. Whether from the male or the female perspective, the many and interlocking roles of the president's spouse have been little explored in the literature on American higher education. This oversight only places in bolder relief how important a spouse now is to the success of an executive transition beyond the familiar and stereotypical outreaches almost every institution feels compelled to make. Scottie Trebon, spouse of Thomas J. Trebon, president of Carroll College, has served as a coordinator of the Spouses Task Force for the Council of Independent Colleges, one of the most effective national higher education organizations to maintain this kind of formal network. Collaboratively the Trebons offer perhaps the first detailed model for the constructive involvement of presidential spouses during their own transitions.

In the concluding chapter, "Knowing the End of the Beginning: A Conceptual Approach to Presidential Transition," two priorities are addressed: a methodology and flowchart to approach the overall transition experience conceptually, and the benchmarks that determine when the transition finally ends. More specifically, the authors provide a model that harmonizes the overlapping perspectives of the departing president, the incoming president, and the institution as a whole. The chapter concludes with a set of twelve indicators marking the points at which the presidential *transition* becomes the next *presidency.* The book closes with a bibliography of pertinent readings on presidential turnover.

The authors would like to thank key individuals for making this study possible. Numerous current and former presidents who provided invaluable support are credited in endnotes. For those who are not quoted directly in these chapters, we offer thanks a final time for their courage, forthrightness, and good humor. We would also like to thank our editor at the Johns Hopkins University Press, Jacqueline Wehmueller, for her patience and candor in helping us to form her thoughtful suggestion into a finished narrative. Arlene Lieberman of Samels Associates, Attorneys at Law, again provided key research for the chapter on legal frameworks, and Kate Drezek did the same for the concluding chapter. Finally, we would like to thank Catherine Jacquet, our editorial assistant for this project, for her skill and commitment in combining drafts and late-breaking developments into a completed book.

We dedicate this volume to our children, from oldest to youngest, Max Samels, Gabrielle Samels, Nicholas Martin, and Rory Martin, as we are sure that there will be at least one president—and two transitions—among them.

J. M.
J. E. S.

I

Context

CHAPTER ONE

A New Model of Transition Management

James Martin and James E. Samels

Transition, turnover, migration: whatever people on campuses may be calling it, the increasingly frequent departures of presidents, together with an inability to find adequate pools of qualified candidates to replace those who are leaving, are unsettling and reshaping the culture of American higher education. For the first time, college and university leaders are openly noting the similarities between the frequency of a presidential search and that of a regional accreditation visit. Both now occur every five years or so, and campus leaders have learned that it is wise to keep track of all key documents related to both processes, because they will most likely be needed again in a matter of months by one strategic planning team or another.

As John W. Moore and Joanne M. Burrows explain in their recent study for the American Association of State Colleges and Universities (AASCU), *Presidential Succession and Transition: Beginning, Ending, and Beginning Again,* "The presidency at American colleges and universities is increasingly a revolving door. . . . The frequency with which the college presidency turns over today makes the subject of presidential succession and transition important to those who are concerned about the welfare of our institutions of higher learning and those women and men who serve in the office of president."[1]

In fact, the presidential transition process has achieved a critical mass and become a focused subject of research within the past five years, as various studies have been initiated at AASCU, the American Association for Higher Education, the American Association of Community Colleges, and the Council for Christian Colleges and Universities. This process has also received a heightened emphasis in the American Council on

Education's *American College President* survey and the work of the Harvard Seminar for New Presidents.

Presidential transitions reshape institutions in numerous ways. As this concept has become better understood, campus stakeholders have begun to see that the overall process can be managed more effectively and intentionally to leverage institutional resources in the achievement of strategic objectives. Moore and Burrows confirm this early in their study: "Presidential transitions involve more than simply searching for a new president. They are complex processes with implications that extend far beyond those typically acknowledged by presidents, boards of trustees, or campus constituencies."[2] As noted at several points in this narrative, treating the broader complexities and uncertainties of the complete process more intentionally from the outset has become a new model of "transition management."

The Rising Impact of Declining Tenures: The New College Presidency

Why are so many American college and university presidents leaving their positions earlier than they anticipated they would, and with a sense of dissatisfaction? There are challenges now facing presidents whether they lead major research universities, large community colleges, or small religiously affiliated institutions that are gradually driving many of them to leave their positions without looking back. While some will debate, even argue, that the college presidency is stronger and more vital than ever in the constellation of American career choices, after speaking formally and informally with approximately one hundred and fifty current and former presidents for this chapter, we have little doubt that the position and the career are no longer what they once were.

James L. Fisher, Martha W. Tack, and Karen J. Wheeler offer this background observation in their 1988 volume *The Effective College President:* "The college presidency has been the subject of endless conversation, investigation, and analysis in higher education since the beginning of the 1950s,"[3] and while some still testify to the unending satisfactions in a presidency (such as a recent retiree from a nationally prominent liberal arts institution, who said: "I've often joked that if my fairy godmother had created the perfect job for me, she could not have done better than the presidency of Colorado College"),[4] more often we are now reading testimonies that document the burdens and sacrifices in the position, such as these two critiques, the first from 1993, the second from 2002:

> The academic presidency is increasingly beleaguered. . . . The ever-increasing multiplicity of expectations from group and individual stakeholders has taken its toll on the president's ability to provide academic leadership.[5]

> The American college presidency [is] an increasingly demanding position that chews up the best in higher education.[6]

When we read these and other comments like them, it seems clear that key aspects of the presidency, which has been researched in earnest for the past half century or more, became rougher and more unstable during the 1990s.

One reason for this may be the dual losses of power and authority. One of the most influential recent studies of the presidency, *Renewing the Academic Presidency: Stronger Leadership for Tougher Times,* was published by the Association of Governing Boards of Universities and Colleges in 1996. Early in that volume, its editors highlight a telling comment by Robert Rosenzweig, former president of the Association of American Universities: "University presidents operate from one of the most anemic power bases in any of the major institutions in American society." The editors continue: "The trustees of corporate, philanthropic, medical and non-profit organizations encourage their chief executives to make decisions and act on them. Academic presidents, often lacking the clear lines of authority they need to act effectively, are compelled to discuss, negotiate, and seek consensus."[7]

A second, more subtle reason for increasing presidential departures appears to be the timing of the appointment for many younger candidates. Michael D. Cohen and James G. March in their influential report for the Carnegie Commission on Higher Education, *Leadership and Ambiguity: The American College President,* explain that chief executives who receive their appointments before they turn forty-five face a special set of disappointments later in life: "These individuals, presumably the most articulate, aggressive, competent, and lucky of the presidents, have little chance of retiring from their office or of moving from their job to a better one. They will eject themselves, or possibly be ejected, from the best job they will ever have at a time when they see their own capabilities as impressive."[8]

As presidents spend greater percentages of their time off campus raising friends and funds, many of the traditional understandings held both by the president and by her or his community about the principal roles of the institution's leader can fracture, leading to a generation of absent, less engaged chief executives. Exacerbating these tensions is the fact that there still do not appear to be simple, nationally recognized standards and methods to orient new presidents to the complexity and changing nature of their undertakings. Judith Block McLaughlin, lecturer on higher education at the Harvard University Graduate School of Education and chair of the Harvard Seminar for New Presidents, agrees: "The presidential leadership transition is an intense experience, which has serious ramification for the success of the president's tenure. Second, far too little explicit attention is given to this period of entry. Ironically, although considerable time is spent orienting new students to our institutions, little thought is devoted to designing an orientation or entry process for our senior leadership."[9]

McLaughlin's observation, following interviews with hundreds of college presidents over a fifteen-year period, supports the contention in every chapter of this volume that there is now a critical need to *manage the presidential transition process more effectively and strategically.* Focusing on the community college presidency as just one of several needy constituencies, the national higher education press now routinely refers to a "crisis" for community colleges seeking presidents: "There was a day when you would get 70, 80, 90, well over 100 applicants, half of whom would have the full-range of qualifications you were looking for," comments David B. Wolf, executive director of the Western Association of Schools and Colleges Accrediting Commission for Community and Junior Colleges.[10] Yet, as of 2002, even the number of *applications* for positions was closer to fifty.[11]

With the projected rate of retirement among current community college presidents at almost *50 percent* by 2007, and upwards of 90 percent of all current chief executive officers having come to the position via the old-fashioned method of ascending through the ranks of their own institutions,[12] there is a pressing need to think more clearly and comprehensively about how future presidents are identified, what will be expected of them, and how they can be guided most effectively through the presidential transition process.

Thomas Gamble, district president of Brevard Community College in Florida, has begun to openly advocate training programs that target business leaders of the top five hundred companies in the country in order to interest them in becoming college presidents.[13] Toward this end, the American Association of Community Colleges surveyed its member presidents in 2001 regarding the status of their jobs and future plans. It discovered that presidents believe their roles have changed greatly over the past several decades. Many presidents responded that there was "a lack of understanding from the public and other institutions of the overwhelming nature of the job." They also reported that they "were unprepared for the level of politics involved, the fundraising, the budgeting and amount of relationships they are expected to build throughout their tenure."[14]

These examples of a "new" college presidency demonstrate how it is less and less like the "old" college presidency of fifty years ago. Yet, debates still break out in the academic press where one sees the assertion that "things have not changed that much," that it is simply a matter of perspective or degree. Perhaps examining in more detail some of the greatest pressures now placed on presidents will convince at least some skeptics that the leaders of our college and universities are steadily becoming more like corporate CEOs in their roles and responsibilities—and that campuses can *benefit* from this broad transition.

The Pressures on College Presidents

As fewer and fewer candidates apply for the position, as its power base becomes more anemic, and as many new appointees are not lasting long enough even to complete one regional accreditation cycle, the pressures on presidents to leave often emerge with the first board agenda. Ann Korschgen, Rex Fuller, and John Gardner inquired in a 2001 issue of the *AAHE Bulletin,* "Is the fact that many presidents serve less time at a single institution than the probationary periods for most of our untenured assistant professors a good thing?"[15] The author of chapter 4 in this volume, Arthur Padilla, concluded in 2000 when applying astatistical technique called "survival analysis" to update Cohen and March's 1974 research on presidential tenures "that the average tenure of presidents and chancellors of Research I universities is declining markedly. . . . In fact, not since the 1960s have presidential tenure averages been at such low levels among the major American universities." He continued: "Average total tenures of the recent cohorts of presidents are at historically low levels, in spite of the vigorous economic conditions in the 1990s that would tend to lengthen presidential tenures. . . . The presidency at major American universities is increasingly entered through a revolving door."[16]

Once in the position, the president must serve as a "juggler-in-chief, expected to meet an endless stream of individual needs and special demands within and outside the institution."[17] As the late Daniel Perlman, former president of Suffolk and Webster Universities, wrote with a tinge of regret in "Paradoxes of the Presidency," "Scholarship and teaching are the arenas in which most presidents have previously gained satisfaction and rewards. . . . Yet, curriculum and student life issues are matters that are most often delegated by the president." Perlman's characteristic humor came through in a second comment: "Nowhere in the library does one learn what it feels like to be a public figure. Nowhere in the quiet of the laboratory does one learn what it feels like to be attacked or cheered."[18]

In our conversations with approximately one hundred and fifty presidents during the past four years, we noted that the following five reasons were the most powerful forces driving worthy candidates into other lines of work:

1. *The pressure to raise extraordinary amounts of money.* Presidents told us that by a factor of four or five, fund-raising challenges formed the greatest pressure in their professional lives. Even Vartan Gregorian, now CEO of the Carnegie Corporation, carefully set limits on this area of responsibility when he accepted the presidency of Brown University fifteen years ago, saying at that time, "Brown cannot do everything well, so it has to concentrate on those areas that are proven to be excellent. . . . Fund-raising will be an important component of my job, naturally, but not *the* most important. No amount of money will give a university direction."[19]

Among the 2,380 respondents to the American Council on Education's 2000 edition of the National Presidents' Study, the most common wish for more training was in the areas of fund-raising and financial management.

2. *The pressure to do more with less.* Having raised more money than they ever thought possible, many new presidents have then learned the hard, unexpected lesson that those same funds must immediately be spent on a legion of unsolved financial questions that they inherited and which desperately need significant infusions of cash. As Carol Lucey, president of Western Nevada Community College, acknowledges, "The greatest pressure by far relates to budget. Simply put, there are never enough resources to meet the community's expectations, no matter how one manages them."[20] Debra Murphy, president of Nichols College, a small, private business school in Dudley, Massachusetts, translates this same challenge into the vocabulary of her campus: "In fact, our community now *expects* to achieve more with less. Less resources, not more, are the starting point for all of us to accomplish more as an institution."[21]

3. *The pressure to decide about distance education.* By *distance education,* we mean the broad constellation of information technology–related instructional and programmatic decisions that presidents, provosts, and members of the faculty now need to make regarding the future of their institutions. One proof of this pressure is the trend among some colleges nationally, such as northern New England's Goddard and Vermont Colleges, to close their high-cost, high-profile undergraduate resi-

dence programs in order to reassign resources to lower-cost, low-residency, distance-education-based graduate programs. This is simply one option that colleges with "traditional" missions are considering as they search for their best chances for long-term survival.

A continent away in the summer of 2002, *Universitas 21*—a consortium of seventeen universities from Asia, Australia, Europe, and North America—announced that it would begin to sell online degrees internationally. While faculty unions in five countries have protested participation in the enterprise and its goals of "collaboration and commerce," Thomson Learning, a major academic publisher and co-owner of the consortium, is plunging forward with a confidence based in the twin statistics of a $111 billion higher education market outside the United States and 32 million potential students to be served in that market worldwide.[22] Even if a college or university has offered only a few partial courses online to date, the "distance education decision" will loom large in the next several master-planning cycles at higher education institutions of every size and category.

4. *The pressure to compete with and outperform for-profit competitors.* As the momentum to create new community colleges fades in every sector of the nation, the strongest driver of innovation—and competition—in American higher education has become for-profit colleges. Whether via "necklaces" of low-profile, postsecondary training schools ringing major cities up and down the two coasts, or ubiquitous "corporate universities" springing up in literally hundreds of companies from Motorola to Dunkin Donuts, for-profit competitors have also changed the priorities and timelines of presidential transitions.

The authors of an article titled "Capital Gains: Surviving in an Increasingly For-Profit World" confirm that "first-time presidents of nonprofit colleges are generally unprepared for the rapidly evolving market forces that exert a profound impact on their colleges. . . . According to the American Association of Colleges and Schools of Business, top-tier business programs at not-for-profit institutions saw an 11% drop in their market share for baccalaureate degrees from 1992–1997. In the same period, enrollments at for-profit business schools soared by 180%."[23]

Even more tellingly for new presidents, the editor of *Executive Summary: 1999 Survey of Corporate University Future Directions* notes the following trend: "The number of corporate universities has increased dramatically over the last 10 years—from 400 in 1988 to more than 1,600 today, including 40% of Fortune 500 companies. Assuming the current pace of growth, the number of corporate universities will exceed the number of traditional universities by the year 2010, if not sooner."[24]

Pressures on Presidents

- To raise extraordinary amounts of money
- To do more with less
- To decide about distance education
- To compete with and outperform for-profit competitors
- To overcome deprofessionalization

5. *The pressure to overcome deprofessionalization.* As far back as 1968, Christopher Jencks and David Riesman described the dangers for presidents of a seemingly irreversible process: "Today's college and university presidents . . . usually start out as members of the academic profession. When they become administrators and have to deal more often with non-academicians, they inevitably become somewhat deprofessionalized."[25] That passing comment by two authors studying other issues thirty-five years ago was prescient in its assessment of the presidency. In fact, the position has become less attractive, less desirable, and less prestigious to more, rather than fewer, of its possible aspirants.

At least one-fifth of the presidents polled by the American Council on Education for its 2000 survey believed that they did not have a clear understanding of an important aspect of the job or their new campus at the time they accepted the position. Daniel Perlman, with equal portions of fascination and dismay, acknowledged, "It also seems paradoxical to me that the threshold preparation for a presidency is the world of scholarship, in which the essential experience is doing research and writing in a library or laboratory, often alone, when, instead, the position requires the skills of a political leader, corporate executive, and evangelist."[26]

Moving from the deprofessionalization of the traditional presidency to new linkages with corporate CEOs, considered in the next section, there is a final pressure to confront. As Harold T. Shapiro, former president of Princeton, argues, "universities are too complex and face too many constituencies for a president to be [their] moral arbiter."[27] In an era of corporate scandals unprecedented in their magnitude at companies like Enron, WorldCom, and Global Crossing, the American population is clamoring for leadership characterized not simply by skill and courage but, as importantly, by a moral integrity missing at a growing number of international brand names. Many college and university presidents may perceive this pressure as the strongest one of all.

Presidents as Higher Education CEOs

Over the past half-century, the designation CEO has gradually become synonymous with college or university president, to the chagrin of many who believe that this represents one of the most visible proofs that higher education has lost its bearings and fallen prey to a ruthless corporate mind-set. For many, in fact, the title "president and CEO" has become one of the principal lightning rods to galvanize anti-administration sentiment among faculty members. The prevalence of this title has also begun to shape the way candidates approach the presidential transition process and think about the position itself. Pressure on a president can produce higher, even extraordinary, performance. However, as often indicated in our interviews, pressure also produces departures. Thus, as higher education presidents behave more like nimble, fleet-footed industry CEOs, this mind-set also carries new strategies for leaving, and accepting, presidencies.

William Rezak, former president of the State University of New York College of Technology at Alfred, spoke for many higher education leaders in his 2000 article "Leading Colleges and Universities as Business Enterprises." Rezak argued that "college and University CEOs must perform a sophisticated balancing act as they try to allocate scarce resources to programs attractive to students and to employers of graduates. During the last 20 years, American business and industry have faced a similar dilemma, under pressure to reduce costs, maintain profit margins, and compete successfully for market share in a global economy. The companies that survived and thrived can serve as role models for colleges and universities."[28] In a few short paragraphs, Rezak cut through much of the fear and timidity college leaders continue to demonstrate about acting decisively—not to be confused with unilaterally—within higher education governance systems. In fact, this kind of decisiveness is increasingly needed among college and university executives during a transition process, whether they are called presidents or CEOs.

Are college presidents actually higher education CEOs? In retrospect, the weight of the corporate experience and training of many higher education trustees has gradually made itself felt more persuasively over the past several generations, in part through publications from their influential national organization, the Association of Governing Boards of Universities and Colleges, and through the major reengineering and professional training activities of thousands of American companies, all of which have challenged colleges and universities to act more like corporations—and their leaders to act more like CEOs. In fact, the author of a 1996 study of the organization of academic institutions believes that they are complex "in ways in which even such a huge corporation as General Motors is not."[29] With a multiplicity of goals forming their missions, rather than simply the goal of maximizing profit over time, higher education enterprises need increasingly mobile and assertive leadership to compete—and many are getting it from presidents who view themselves as a new kind of campus CEO. As a result, many schools have become much more market-sensitive and keyed in on the competitors in their cohort nationally and internationally.

Market forces have "invaded the academy" in the minds of many, and growing numbers in this group are also coming to believe that these same forces are actually helping institutions to improve themselves.[30] Whether as new age CEO or not, higher education presidents may now include conquering the market and outperforming competitors as pressures of the position.

And what does this bode for the presidential transition process? Current presidents are going to leave more quickly, new presidents are going to arrive more quickly, and both ends of this transaction will be held to closer scrutiny and higher standards of accountability. Finally, both executive search consultants and interim presidents will be employed with rising frequency as institutional stakeholders come to believe that the search process, as a strategic opportunity, has become an end in itself and can best be managed by professionals who have made it their careers.

Comings and Goings: New Skills for Presidents in Transition

According to research published by the Association of Governing Boards, "Not since the tumultuous events of the late 1960s—the Vietnam War, racial strife, and campus demonstrations—have presidents leaving office expressed such high levels of physical and emotional exhaustion."[31] Add to this data another somewhat surprising statistic: there are 45 million Americans between the ages of 35 and 44, the key launching cohort for new presidencies, but only 37 million Americans between the ages of 25 and 34.[32]

By 2010 American colleges and companies will both face the most severe shortage of leaders in several generations. Resource-challenged higher education institutions will surely come in second or third in attracting new leadership when forced to compete with larger, more powerfully financed corporate and governmental recruitment operations as the baby boom generation passes from active service into retirement. For those who are leading our colleges and universities at that point, new skills will be needed to survive and prosper.

As one example, presidents will craft their own transitions more consciously. William C. Gordon left the presidency of the University of New

Mexico in 2002 after only four years, although he had spent almost twenty-four there as a faculty member and academic administrator, to serve as the provost at Wake Forest University. In planning his transition, Gordon was guided by the candid realization, "It's a matter of waking up one morning . . . and saying, 'How much do I have to bring to this, in this particular place?' I've always felt that presidents of major universities really have a limited period of time when they can be maximally effective."[33]

Presidents will still need to know how to interpret a balance sheet and give an effective speech well into the future, but there are also several new skills that were identified during our interviews, which form a new script for departing and arriving leaders.

Master technology choices. This initial skill is not to be confused with mastering new technologies, which also accompanies an effective presidency. Put differently, presidents who do not personally and professionally grasp the implications, from a leadership perspective, of the technology choices that they must make will not succeed over the long term. F. Warren McFarlan, a professor at the Harvard Business School since 1973, has worked with scores of presidents and corporate leaders. When asked to predict the long-term role of technology, he described how leaders are trained at Harvard Business School: "In our Advanced Management Program, 50% of all classes are about information technology in one form or another. Fifty percent—that's where the intellectual content of the world has gone. . . . We're not in a 100-meter dash. We're in a marathon. If you don't die of a heart attack on the first lap around the track, there will be more laps to run."[34]

Produce partnerships. Ten, or even five, years ago, presidents needed to be able to "design partnerships." Today, presidents in transition will be judged by the partnerships they have *produced,* not designed, with other colleges, corporations, and for-profit learning organizations. Fluid and changeable strategic alliances, in contrast to a full merger, which is static and irreversible, represent a new way to leverage limited resources more creatively through collaborations with competitors. Wise presidents realize that starting with a single successful programmatic partnership with a mission-complementary learning organization can lead to a broad-based, long-term joint venture that saves millions of dollars in individual marketing, recruitment, and faculty professional development costs.

Vanquish adversaries. This "skill" provoked strong responses from a good percentage of the presidents interviewed. Many agreed, in retrospect, that it was imperative upon starting in a new position to trust one's instincts, to define a new power base, and to separate adversarial colleagues, no matter how high-ranking, from the institution, *even if one had been advised against doing so.* Michael Riccards, former president of St. John's College in New Mexico, Shepherd College in Virginia, and Fitchburg State College in Massachusetts, spoke for a number of chief executive officers when he declared, "The presidency today has less and less of a power base; the job is too 'constituency-driven.' New presidents must build a power base immediately that is independent of anyone and everyone on campus. They should not be afraid to trust their instincts and fire people earlier in their presidencies."[35]

Build a brand. Presidents in transition need to know how to build and manage a distinctive brand for their institutions—and for their own careers—within weeks of arrival. While some critics still claim that brand-building is simply a subset of spin doctoring and gradually extinguishing the last vestiges of what was real about campus life, brand formation has become a more complex and valuable skill than many in higher education grasp. While thousands of presidents have played amateur admissions officers at their colleges and universities over the past century, sometimes simply meddling, sometimes offering true vision, and though hundreds of schools have tangibly improved their quality and market positions, only a few undeniable *brands* have emerged in American higher education over that same period. Duke University, Rhode Island School of Design, and Notre Dame University are examples.

Building a brand remains a more powerful process than simple admissions proficiency. Brand building is predicated on two factors: teamwork and personal conviction. Presidents may receive much of the credit in retrospect for an enduring institutional brand, but insiders realize that powerful brands arise out of a community's commitment to persist in strengthening the institution's name and reputation even when that school may be suffering a serious downturn in enrollment, positioning, or fund-raising.

Although many continue to fear and resist, higher education is now viewed as a "commodity to be purchased by a consumer in order to build a 'skill set' to be used in the marketplace."[36] And whether they agree or disagree with this trend, many presidents now realize that a successful transition involves moving beyond the basic marketing of their institutions to focus on developing durable "hooks of quality" into the public consciousness about their college—and their own leadership styles.

New Skills for Presidents in Transition

- Master technology choices
- Produce partnerships
- Vanquish adversaries
- Build a brand
- Seek selective excellence
- Value bricks and clicks
- Leverage mentoring networks
- Ensure entrepreneurial advantage

Seek selective excellence. Some have queried how closing a program or denying a colleague tenure is a skill. In building institutional and personal brands, producing partnerships, and positioning their colleges and universities relentlessly in the marketplace, effective presidents will note institutional weaknesses during their transitions and return to address them at the appropriate moment. Before starting his presidency of Brown in1988, Vartan Gregorian acknowledged, "Brown cannot do everything well, so it has to concentrate on those areas that are proven to be excellent. . . . That is one of the attractions that brought me here—that Brown is not afraid to take a chance."[37]

Many presidents view themselves as builders and creators, rather than as price-watchers and cost-cutters; however, on many campuses, more must be accomplished with less, and chief executives realize that since their appointment at a new institution may not even last to the next comprehensive accreditation visitation, their survival and success depend on treading the thin gray line between institutional expansion and the need to eliminate dated, resource-draining programs along with the faculty who support them.

Value bricks and clicks. In the early 1990s, when Ronald Remington served as president of Great Basin College in Elko, Nevada, with a huge student recruitment area, he saw that it was critically important to build a cohesive campus infrastructure, that is, "bricks," in order to provide Great Basin's almost five thousand students with a sense of educational focus amid the vast Nevada territory. As a result, Great Basin added twelve new buildings during Remington's eleven years as chief executive officer.

Then as president of the Community College of Southern Nevada in Las Vegas, with more than 32,000 students and a projection of between

40,000 and 50,000 students within the next decade, Remington viewed a different kind of campus "expansion" as his first priority:

> Great Basin College has one of the largest student catchment areas in the West, 45,000 square miles, and there was a need to construct a campus culture. New buildings were a primary source of institutional focus and pride. The construction of the highly visible Campus Bell Tower, in fact, was a significant experience. At the Community College of Nevada in Las Vegas, we are huge, almost 33,000 students and growing extremely fast, and our infrastructure is far more complex. Technology is our new "mortar" because it allows us, more than buildings could, to meet virtually, to provide students with expanded learning resources, and to achieve our mission more effectively in key areas of operation and outreach.[38]

In this case, new construction was not seen as a questionable expense and reflective of a dated approach to college life; Remington's two presidencies, in fact, epitomize the need to balance "bricks" with "clicks" in helping institutions fulfill their educational missions.

Leverage mentoring networks. College and university presidents have always, to some degree, networked politically, socially, and strategically; the new skill for presidents today is leveraging these networks, often via the Internet, more intentionally and strategically and, when a needed network does not exist, simply inventing it. Even then, the number of customized networks that presidents in transition now can access is not the point; rather, it is the instinctive ways in which presidents leverage them as elements of a presidency just ending, or just beginning, that marks their power in shaping new styles of executive leadership.

Several years into his fifteen-year presidency at Greenville College in Illinois, during the 1980s, W. Richard Stephens noticed that there was a troubling lack of professional interchange and networking opportunities among the leaders of small midwestern Christian colleges. His next step was simple and had lasting impact: he worked with a small group of colleagues to found the Council for Christian Colleges and Universities. The CCCU, now with its own Web site and more than 150 intentionally Christian institutions around the world, provides an ongoing menu of leadership training, focused professional development programs, and lifelong resources to help its membership transform lives through scholarship and service.

The previously mentioned Institute for New Presidents at Harvard University has established itself as arguably the premiere mentoring network for chief executive officers over more than fifteen years of intensive, residency-based summer programming. The American Council on

Education's National Identification Program (ACE-NIP) has also carved a solid niche in the national mentoring landscape. However, whether it is the continuing, quiet success of the relatively small Council for Christian Colleges and Universities or the higher-profile influence of ACE-NIP and the New Presidents Seminar at Harvard, the simple proliferation of these opportunities should not be confused with any kind of skill. Instead, it is the open and straightforward interweaving of institutional and individual advancement during the transition process and into a new presidency that reflects a purposeful management of media and resources not seen in previous periods of American higher education.

Ensure entrepreneurial advantage. This final skill gathers aspects of the previous seven into a new approach to presidential leadership and its role in institutional growth and positioning. Ensuring entrepreneurial advantage challenges presidents to manage greater percentages of their own transitions by shaping activities like brand refinement, strategic alliances, and student consumer quality surveys even before their official arrivals.

Our interviews have confirmed that most presidents want to be described as entrepreneurs and want their institutions to be considered "nimble," "adaptable," and "strategic." Thus, one can view new "weekend colleges," e-learning programs, licensed testing centers, outsourced services, "policy" institutes, and a return to highway billboard advertising, all issuing, sometimes simultaneously, from the desks of new presidents as they follow through on promises to their trustees, students, and faculty. Similar to the expectation that new leaders will not only design but also produce institutional partnerships, this final skill should not be viewed simply as devising isolated solutions in the executive offices. Rather, overall entrepreneurial advantage must be "ensured" by the transitioning presidents almost immediately, as community stakeholders make it clear in multiple ways that their new chief executive has been appointed, ultimately, to *deliver.*

Having served for twenty-eight years as founding president of the University of Medicine and Dentistry of New Jersey, an institution that now garners more annual research dollars than its neighbor, Princeton University, while managing five campuses, three teaching hospitals, and the largest enrollment of any state medical and dental school in the nation, Stanley Bergen was surprisingly humble upon being asked how he consistently "ensured" entrepreneurial advantage for UMDNJ over three decades in one of the most competitive regions for educational choice in the country: "Instinct and practicality are more important than any great vision in developing an entrepreneurial advantage for your institution. Too many administrators do not trust their instincts and do not act pragmatically when they should."[39]

The Need for Effective Transition Management

Pressures on presidents, as noted previously, produce departures, and this trend, combined with a documented decline in the number of candidates even to apply for presidencies nationally and a broadening of career opportunities for candidates in the corporate and for-profit education sectors, has intensified the need for effective executive transition management models.

In this context, presidential transitions also need to be managed more effectively because the *price* of a transition experience has grown so significantly in terms of lost work hours, altered relationships, and distraction from mission. As Richard Ingram, president of the Association of Governing Boards of Universities and Colleges, explains, institutions can "lose enormous momentum" in planning, fund-raising, and staff productivity. "You potentially can cause some of your best people to think about whether they want to stay. . . . There are enormous institutional costs, many of them not really anticipated by boards of trustees. When boards face up to the real costs, they are, in the end, appalled."[40]

Almost thirty years ago, Cohen and March identified these same costs in *Leadership and Ambiguity: The American College President:* "We think that a career system that places these kinds of pressures on presidents is relatively costly in terms of lost leadership. It is also costly in terms of the corruption of the lives of presidents and those around them. . . . We can imagine improving the situation by changing presidential beliefs or by changing the system."[41]

As the process of leadership transition began to be studied as an end in itself during the 1990s, and as the costs associated with losing and gaining leadership have become more defined, volumes such as this one have identified the need for *all* participants, not simply the candidates themselves, to think through the transition process more deeply and to a point beyond the appointment of the next president. In this way the transition experience can transcend individual candidates and address larger uncertainties facing the institution.

As a college or university manages the uncertainties of its leadership transition more effectively, it becomes an institution more intentional in its systems, administration, and mission. With these clarifications, it is also more effectively positioned both to compete for a declining pool of qualified presidential candidates and to collaborate with complementary institutions in the development of strategic alliances to enhance teaching and learning.

Conclusion: Toward a More Intentional Institution

Steven Muller, former president of Johns Hopkins University, noted several years ago in an essay entitled "The University Presidency Today: A Word for the Incumbents": "To most, the president remains an office rather than a person, a symbol more than a reality. . . . the president as a person is far less evident than before."[42] Seeing that their communities perceive them less as individuals and more as a leadership *type,* some presidents have consciously fashioned their candidacies into smoothly polished entities with no rough edges or points of vulnerability, as reflected in these two comments from 2001–2:

> Like politicians, today's higher education candidates usually fare best if they are articulate, photogenic, and skilled in the art of self-promotion. Campaigns for presidential appointments call for carefully prepared resumes, glossy photos, speeches, and other public appearances. . . . And, of course, sartorial correctness is a given. The goal is to look like the college president from central casting.[43]

> The leadership profile that has become the staple of most presidential searches is now so well honed that the nets are almost never cast beyond an accustomed range. . . . Most finalists are from within the academy, most are white males with Ph.D.s, most are already presidents or provosts, and most have carefully constructed resumes denoting successful careers of meeting challenges and avoiding catastrophes.[44]

With significantly smaller slates of increasingly polished, politically astute candidates to consider, it becomes easy to see how presidential search committees must become more intentional and more vigilant as they exercise the responsibilities delegated to them.

Building on a comment by Judith Block McLaughlin that "just as there is no one generic community college, college, or university in the United States, neither is there a generic presidency,"[45] we would add that there is also no generic presidential transition. Each is permanently shaped by the thousands of factors that have made the institution and its history singular. However, uniqueness does not excuse an institution for botching its transition, and few schools can afford the current bill for recovery costs in personnel, curriculum, and retention.

Why, finally, are so many presidents leaving their positions early and unhappily? Sylvan Lashley, well into his second decade as president of Atlantic Union College in Massachusetts, offered this blunt rationale: "Presidents are departing in droves because their basic role has changed from academic leader and strategic director to 24-hour provider. This change foments cognitive dissonance and intellectual burn-out as presidents move further away from their main customers in the stretch to close the gap between rising consumer expectations and decreasing resources."[46] In part, it is also because presidential search and transition processes have become so public-relations-driven, niche-based, and constituent-controlled. As the former president of an Arizona university observed in 2002, "In our fast-paced information age, higher education needs 'thinkers in chief' of the caliber of those who in previous generations had the talent and the courage to help invent entirely new models of higher education. . . . The selection processes now in vogue are not giving us those kinds of leaders."[47]

Or, as candidly described by the senior vice president with overall responsibility for a recent presidential transition at one of New Jersey's largest universities: "It's all about ego, money and turf, and presidents have to be very bold and run like hell to stake out their vision, and then work like hell to hold that vision as others become involved in their presidency."[48] Many of those now leading colleges and universities are coming to recognize that an effective transition process is far more difficult to manage than most higher education guidebooks and resource manuals ever acknowledge, because while presidents, ultimately, come and go, *how* they come and go has a profound effect on the institution and largely determines the difference between extended periods of failure and success.[49]

CHAPTER TWO

Presidents Who Leave, Presidents Who Stay: A Conversation with Vartan Gregorian

Vartan Gregorian and James Martin

Presidential transitions at institutions in all categories are increasingly in the national news. What is the greatest pressure on college and university presidents today, and why are presidents leaving their positions more quickly than in the past?

First, all institutions expect too much from their presidents, and the presidents, instead of moderating those expectations, go along with them. They often know that their college or university is not a B+ institution about to become an A institution. Rather, it is a B– institution, possibly on the way to becoming a B institution; but in order to please all campus constituents, presidents continue to talk as if the college is *almost there.*

Second, presidents struggle between two cultures, the academic culture and the corporate culture. Some presidents become like Janus with two faces. To the faculty and students, they portray themselves as struggling on their behalf against the Philistine board. To the board, they pose as martyrs who are being tortured by tenured faculty and radicals. With alumni, they talk about the old days and sports because they are neutral. However, sooner or later, a crisis emerges and the two cultures have to face each other. In the process, community members discover that the president, instead of serving as a bridge between the two cultures, has been trying to use one against the other in order to protect his or her territory.

Finally, I have been surprised at how many presidents do not know the history of the institutions they are joining. The most recent National Presidents Survey by the American Council on Education confirms that one-fifth of new presidents are claiming, soon after arrival, that they did not understand something about the job or the institution when they accepted the position.[1] Transitioning presidents need to ask for all current external evaluations, such as regional accrediting reports, because trustees and faculty often conceal those weaknesses, and the presidential transition process needs to provide a new chief executive with easy access to critical information of this kind.

What are the most essential aspects of leadership that a college or university president must display upon beginning or concluding a transition in the year ahead?

The defense of educational standards of faculty, because without great faculty there can be no great universities. We now have two sets of cultures and two sets of organizations: horizontal and vertical. The last true horizontal organization remaining in the world is not the church, the unions, the government, or the military. The university is the only true horizontal organization left, and it frustrates many board members who are corporate individuals because it is very difficult for them to understand that all organizations are not vertical.

From Bologna on, faculty have always felt that the university was theirs. They do not think of themselves as employees; rather, they view themselves as the leaders of the university. So, in 2003, one has to understand what moves institutions, and it is not money or structure. It is values. Presidential leadership, particularly during a transition experience, has to stand for values, yet it also has to convey a readiness for change along with the continuity of those values.

Stephen Muller, former president of the Johns Hopkins University, wrote an essay several years ago entitled "The University Presidency Today: A Word for the Incumbents." In it, he commented that contemporary college and university chief executives are an "office rather than a person, a symbol more than a reality."[2] *Do you agree?*

I do not fully agree with those observations. Presidents *are* symbols, but they must also be leaders. Leaders can always hire managers, but managers rarely hire leaders. Before World War II, colleges and universities typically chose an English professor or historian as president. This trend continued, more or less, until the Vietnam conflict. During that period, colleges and universities suddenly realized that conflicts were not simply in the "outside world"; they were also within their institutions, and those institutions were sociologically, intellectually, and organizationally unprepared to meet them. Trustees and presidents had not been prepared to deal with student and faculty activists.

After the 1960s, we thought of universities as conflict places, and in turn, we thought we needed constitutional and labor lawyers as presidents to mediate contending forces. During the recession of the 1970s, colleges and universities turned to scientists for leadership in the hope that their scientific know-how could secure their institution's share of national resources and governmental influence. Presidents now had to be savvy politicians, as well.

In the 1980s, much more money was available to campuses, and institutions identified presidents who could and would raise funds for them. Private and public universities used to relying on governmental sources suddenly found out they were in major competition, unlike the 1940s or 1950s. Everybody was going to every source, it seemed. Private colleges were seeking public money, and public universities began searching for private funding. During this period, presidents needed to defend their institutions externally while managing the allocation of unprecedented amounts of money internally.

In the 1990s, a new question about college and university presidents emerged: institutions asked, now that we have amassed this new wealth, what kind of president should lead us? Economists were then greatly in demand to preserve each school's resources. Today, I believe that presidents in transition need to arrive with an agenda of what they want to accomplish, and once they have accomplished it, to stay no fewer than five years and no more than ten. I stayed at Brown for nine years.

The late Daniel Perlman, former president of Suffolk and Webster Universities, once wrote an article entitled, "Paradoxes of the Presidency," in which he observed that although most college and university presidents were originally, and often principally, trained in areas of curriculum development and student mentoring, these are two of the first areas new presidents delegate upon arrival.[3] *Do you agree that this is a "paradox" of a higher education presidency?*

My three priorities at Brown were *faculty, students,* and the *library.* Those are the three that make a university a university. The curriculum was central to our enterprise, and I had doubts about Brown's curriculum at that time. So the first thing I did was to form a committee to review the transcripts of an entire class, for its four years, recording what they really took, not what was required. I was very pleased to find out that those students took mathematics and history and English language and literature because they wanted to, not because they were required.

When I was president, we added 265 university-wide courses in general education. I also served as an adviser to nine randomly picked students and taught freshmen and seniors because I wanted to set that example, as well. I did not use teaching assistants: teaching assistants should be assisted in finishing their Ph.D.'s. I do not believe these constitute "paradoxes" of a college or university presidency.

What can presidents do to keep the rising costs of higher education affordable in order to provide access to the greatest number of citizens?

Access is the most important issue in America, because access is a means to provide equal opportunity. However, it should not be seen in isolation; it is a key aspect of our nation's cultural framework. The press tends to let forty or fifty of our most expensive colleges and universities serve as the norm. As a result, it is rarely reported that tuition at many state colleges and universities is not thirty thousand dollars or more per year and that many of these institutions, perhaps more than a thousand, can offer ample fellowship support and provide equal opportunity from day one. This kind of access needs to be presented to the public more thoughtfully.

I have recommended the development of a simple handbook for families that could be published on the Internet and that would provide them with easy answers to questions about access to higher education. This resource would list colleges and universities in categories according to cost. So if a family earns seventy-five thousand dollars per year and can only afford a contribution of a few thousand dollars for the education of a daughter or son, a group of institutions fitting that economic profile would be readily referenced. This would provide a great service to the American people.

The danger I see in our future is that state colleges and universities are going to reach a point of becoming essentially semiprivate institutions by being forced to incorporate fund-raising activities in their missions. Also, if a great number of lower-cost colleges and universities decide to raise their tuitions and become closer in price to the major private universities, then we will have a problem.

Finally, we need to find ways to publicize the fact that there are several *billion* dollars in fellowship and scholarship money available in our country that many students and families know nothing about. This information needs to be shared with them more systematically and effectively.

Philip G. Altbach, the J. Donald Monan, SJ, Professor of Higher Education at Boston College and editor of International Higher Education, *wrote in one of the recent issues of that journal that education is no longer seen primarily as "a set of skills, attitudes, and values required for citizenship and effective participation in modern society. Rather, it is increasingly seen as a commodity to be purchased by a consumer in order to build a 'skill set' to be used in the marketplace."*[4] *Do you agree, and what implications does this have for college and university presidents in transition?*

There is a cultural disconnect in the United States and elsewhere around the world at this time. On the one hand, our entire educational system tells us that we value education for the sake of education and that we value character. At the same time, popular culture has become materialistic enough to force us to speak in terms of "what you have" rather than "who you are." In some instances, people have been able to address both issues in a liberal education. The challenge is how to preserve values, because when one receives a liberal arts education, it is only an introduction to learning.

I also find it intriguing that most of us continue to believe that one can become educated in three or four years despite the fact that this model has remained unchanged for over three centuries. In fact, many students cannot learn it all in this short a time. Students must also learn more clearly what they do not know during this process. Critical thinking skills and adaptability are the two keys, but instead of emphasizing them, recruiters emphasize immediate marketability, conveniently omitting that in a person's lifetime he or she will have at least six or seven different jobs. And we, as presidents, sometimes have perpetuated this confusion by not differentiating between a job and a career. They are not identical. I often cite the example of New York waiters and waitresses who are actually actors and singers. Waiting on tables is their job, not their career. However, if you travel to Vienna, the waiters in that city's grand hotels consider their work to be both their job *and* their career. They take great pride that this is what they have chosen to do.

Another area we have not done well with in our colleges and universities is in distinguishing between free time and leisure. Leisure in America is only considered to be relaxation. Classically, leisure was time spent reflecting, learning, looking inward. We are the only culture I know of that says it has "free time to kill." We are afraid of free time, but we must teach our students throughout their educations to prepare "time off" and not let annual income become the foremost variable in judging success. In this sense, new presidents should take the opportunity of their fresh starts to focus their institutions on educating their students for life, rather than simply for the moment.

How should presidents in transition address the major technology decisions confronting them?

Presidents have to understand the true impact of technology on learning. Technology is a tool; it is not an end. Also, technology *never* saves a college money. It is not supposed to, and if presidents do not understand this, they will be in big trouble. Technology creates more needs and more expenditures, not less. Technology also adds more factors to presidential decision making than ever before. Generally, technology issues on campus should center on two priorities: the curriculum and student and faculty productivity.

In 1988, you stated, "No amount of money will give a university direction."[5] *What recommendations would you offer to new presidents now undertaking capital campaigns?*

First, all universities must be in the fund-raising business *all the time.* Capital campaigns are episodes in universities' histories. The most important task for presidents in this regard is reconnecting with the alumni. This does not mean simply counting money, but more importantly, assessing their levels of engagement in the life of the college. That is what makes a successful capital campaign. Without engagement, there will be no support, and presidents should not rely on sentimentality and nostalgia to raise funds. Successful fund-raisers rely on the logic that their institutions are serving the nation, the world, and the future and that these are important opportunities for alumni to participate in.

However, some presidents still confuse wealth and security with direction. Presidents emerging from a transition process have a one-time opportunity to decide what the best role of that college or university will be. Then they can be much clearer about finding the specific resources necessary to support those goals. Merely being well endowed will not provide either the security or the direction necessary to accomplish this.

If a presidency fails within its first eighteen months, what would be one of the most likely reasons?

Presidents in transition can lose two years, or more, of momentum simply learning the culture of their college or university. Those presidents who move from public universities to private institutions can face a major crisis if they have never worked at a private university in the past. In public higher education, more effort is usually spent trying to legitimize courses of action. Presidents worry about what the government may think, what the legislature may think, what the alumni may think, and, of course, what the faculty senate may think. This is a culture in which process is as important as its results.

Presidents moving from public institutions to private ones often need to work more on the process of delivering results than on the actual results themselves. Conversely, a president moving from a private to a public college can be handicapped by her or his impatience with the democratic process. Second, over-promising to every sector of the new institution can produce a hasty departure. As a rule, new presidents should refrain from informing faculty senates that they will be increasing their prerogatives while also telling trustees that two early objectives will be to economize and cut the budget.

Finally, presidents must get to know the faculty more than they do, even more than they think they need to. The most important ingredient of stability for a president emerging from a transition is to know the faculty. Thus, serious candidates should read faculty senate proceedings before accepting any position, not just to learn the key issues, but also to learn how they are being settled. Presidents cannot bring the cookie cutter that they have been using in prior positions and expect the same results.

What should today's faculty expect of leaders who are completing transitions and starting their presidencies?

Having chosen the new president, the faculty should give him or her time and support, most importantly. Faculty should also not tie the hands of the president with minutia. The president needs to set priorities. If one loves every cause with equal vehemence and dedication, one loves no cause. Total commitment equals total apathy, and there will be no room for action. In turn, presidents need to develop close understandings with their faculty, as they can easily be ambushed in critical moments. Therefore, it is extremely important that all actions to be taken are announced and prepared for rather than sprung upon the community.

What is the best position for presidents in transition to take regarding athletic programs and priorities?

Athletics are important for at least two reasons; tradition and the opportunity to demonstrate talent and ability. On this issue, I have felt most comfortable with the Ivy League model, in which athletes are perceived as amateurs and attend school, principally, to learn. The message needs to be that one is free to study and not play, but not free to play and not study. However, at major universities and many colleges, such as Indiana, Michigan, and others, athletics bring significant income to the university, and this has to be considered. In the future, I would endow all athletic programs, making them self-sufficient and independent of state pressures, while still keeping in mind that the primary purpose of the college experience is to educate within a context of amateur rather than professional sports. The goals must be to develop a person's intellect, judgment, and discernment. Put another way, athletics should not abuse its athletes.

How have your views about faculty members changed since you began as the President of Brown in 1988?

Whether as provost at Penn, president at Brown, or a professor at Texas, I learned in each instance that my role as an administrator was to serve the faculty. I was there to help the faculty reach its potential and aspirations. The better they are, the better the institution will be, and the better its education will be for its students. With this in mind, I have never had any major conflict with faculty members. This does not mean that I have always agreed with them. I have had countless discussions, even arguments, but I have never lost their support, because there is a difference between genuinely believing this and just publicizing the idea.

Faculties have great radar, and they can distinguish the difference between publicity and belief very easily. Thus, to succeed, new presidents must know and respect academics. If they do not, they are in the wrong business.

What is the most important trend in higher education that presidents should prepare for over the next ten years?

Distance learning and its implications. That, I find, is going to be the biggest challenge for presidents. And within that trend, intellectual property rights will be the most powerful engine. As an example, do the faculty "own" their lectures, or does the college or university own them?

Second, how will we populate our colleges and universities? By absentee professors from a long distance and part-time adjuncts? These are issues no one appears to be talking about as higher education faces new and difficult for-profit competitors. Universities have sustained our culture, in both its profitable and unprofitable aspects. The Sumerian Dictionary at the University of Pennsylvania was worked on for over a century, and it may now only be used by a handful of people each year. Who will take care of this cultural continuity, if not colleges and universities?

For-profit education will survive and remain important for three reasons: training, retraining, and continuing education. However, these "corporate colleges" will not replace colleges or universities and their academic freedom, their athletics and orchestras, their acculturation, and their innumerable models of formal and informal learning.

Regarding the rising interest nationally in the presidential transition process as an experience in itself, how can this process be made more effective and strategic?

It will be very difficult to accomplish this. In the past, a new president was lucky if he or she found an outgoing president who was willing to admit where he or she failed and to share a warning about the reasons. Even then, presidents in transition did not always want to follow this advice, because academicians possess one major flaw: They cannot say, “I don’t know.”

As long as attitudes like this persist, it will be a challenge to make the presidential transition process more strategic. Still, new presidents, and those departing, who can avoid these stereotypes will see the road ahead more clearly and have a head start in leadership.

CHAPTER THREE

Pressures on Presidents and Why They Should Leave

Steven Muller

In the world of American higher education increasing attention is now being paid to presidential leadership of colleges and universities, particularly to presidential selection, performance, and transition. Such attention is of course eminently justified, but it is interesting to note that very little analysis has focused on when and why successful presidents should retire from office. That presidents whose performance in office is deemed insufficient are therefore dismissed is taken for granted, but it seems also to be taken for granted that a successful president should remain in the job as long as possible. Of course, a tempting offer from another institution may lure a president away, and death or illness will terminate a presidency, but otherwise continued success in office leads to continued presidential incumbency. College and university presidents are not usually appointed to fixed terms of office, and it seems not only natural but indeed desirable to maintain an effective leader at the helm as long as possible.

The trouble with this obviously sensible assumption is that successful performance in office inevitably casts an afterglow of continued success, even when the actual performance is beginning to lose vigor and energy due to accumulating fatigue. It is often difficult for an experienced leader to admit any reduction in effectiveness, and also equally difficult for a loyal and admiring community to acknowledge a diminution in the effectiveness of its leadership.

By no means is this analysis intended to argue for fixed terms of office for presidents. On the contrary, the time of decline in successful leadership arrives very differently and unpredictably for different leaders, and thus does not justify arbitrary or formulaic restrictions on the terms of presidential performance. What is needed is an effective mutual recognition, shared among the president, key trustees, and leading members of the faculty of the college or university, that the moment for a change of leadership has dawned.

Indicators of the Need for Change

There is no simple way to arrive at such a conclusion, but there are various indicators which—in concert—reveal that the need for a change of president is in the offing. A couple of these indicators are simple and definitive but frequently become evident only late in the game. The first and most obvious is age, yet the impact of age on any particular person is extremely variable and not always easy to assess. The second is exhaustion, which manifests itself only relatively late, so that it is definitive but much too tardy.

However, the most significant signs that the time has come to retire a successful president do manifest themselves both to the president and the trustees, faculty, and administrators of the institution. For example, a first-rate president will almost certainly innovate within the institution, but after a number of years of achievement the burdens of improvement and innovation may become ever greater and more demanding, and the incumbent president may simply be running out of steam. Such presidential combat fatigue is easily understandable, and it is also visible to trustees and faculty, who also typically note increasing presidential exhaustion.

A different manifestation that the need for change has come, or is coming, may very likely appear in a decline of perceptible extent in the appreciation of presidential leadership on the part of the faculty. Any president will inevitably, over the course of time, respond to any number of faculty and other requests, positively as well as negatively, but it is generally the case that affirmative presidential responses are remembered more as faculty initiatives which obviously deserved support on their merits and therefore accrue little credit to the president. Denied requests, however, tend to be resented and are likely to be remembered indefinitely. As a result, the level of disenchantment with the president within the institutional community rises incrementally each academic year, and as the years pass there is a continuing—even if mild—decline in appreciation of the incumbent president.

Yet, another aspect of needed renewal of the presidency consists of the ever more demanding burden of the president's fund-raising activities. In earlier days presidents of colleges and universities were selected primarily with an eye to their qualifications to lead a community of scholars. The ideal presidential appointee was himself or herself a professor, preferably of well established scholarly achievement of his or her own, including publication. An agreeable personality was certainly also an asset—it was assumed that the president would deal with internal disputes and develop at least tolerable relations with even the most curmudgeonly but brilliant professorial genius. Also, the president was expected to interact positively with trustees or overseers, local—and if appropriate national—dignitaries, and of course institutional benefactors. In all, the president was expected—in appearance, bearing, writing, and deportment—to be an attractive and impressive personification of his or her institution.

Since 1950, however, the president has also become the institution's chief fund-raiser, supported in this role by a whole staff specializing in the solicitation of financial support. Both on campus and on the road, the president is the college's or university's chief almoner, and presidential success is significantly calibrated in effective fund-raising. In purely human terms, this situation represents not only an unavoidable demand on the president's time and energy, but a demand that increases each year. A successful president will continuously identify and solicit new benefactors, but of course also continue to court and honor previous donors as well. This situation is now well established and known, and in principle there is nothing wrong with the president's cultivation of institutional support.

However, after a number of successful years in office, the incumbent president's time and energy are ever more devoted to past, present, and potential future donors, to the point that this obligation invades the time for other crucial presidential tasks and threatens delay or even neglect of other institutional, as well as personal, presidential obligations. If the old slogan for the retail trade was "location, location, location," the counterpart for institutions of higher education is "cultivation, cultivation, cultivation," and the president is unavoidably the institution's chief cultivator. A successor will of course have the same obligation to raise funds, but it will normally take at least several years before his involvement can attain the full level of his predecessor's.

The preceding observations concerning an ever-increasing obligation to ever more demanding presidential tasks also point to a continuing erosion of a successful president's private time. It is not necessary to specify details of the obvious impact of an achieving and demanding presidency on the incumbent's family and private life. However, no matter whatever adjustments characterize the private and family life of the successful college and university president, it can be taken for granted that the longer a successful incumbency lasts, the greater the erosion of private and family time becomes. Success is worth a lot of effort and sacrifice, and brings many benefits; but the longer it runs, the more it demands of personal and family time. A successful president can and should have a personal or family retreat as a brief but cherished breakaway from presidential duties, and should also break away from duties for sheer pleasure, which is a necessary relief from the mountain of obligations. Again, however, the longer the incumbency, the harder it is to find time for the "merely" personal.

There is yet one more aspect of long-enduring presidential service which may suggest that the time has come to move on. This has to do with the team on which every president in office relies. This team, composed of senior colleagues such as provosts or vice presidents, and office staff, is not only indispensable but closely linked to presidential success. There is an unavoidable "political" component in all forms of institutional governance, and no president can function successfully without loyal senior colleagues who provide good judgment, advice, and information. It is equally essential to have loyal, competent, and totally reliable personnel in the president's office.

Assembling such a team is a crucial task for a new president, and if that task is done well the presidential team functions as a powerful source of support. With good luck, this team will effectively function together and serve the president's need for an extended period. Inevitably, however, the passage of time will involve departures and additions to the team, and that is normally likely to erode some of the cohesion and mutual commitment that should have characterized the original group. Such change in the personnel of the team can also lead its more recent members to advocate continued presidential performance, lest the president's departure from office affect their own position. The likely consequence is also that the fresh loyalty of additions or replacements to the team will favor continuation of the incumbent president even in the face of evident presidential fatigue.

Resistance to Change

What is it, then, that leads successful long-term presidents to wish to stay in the job despite signals that the time for a change is at hand? The principal reason—though not the only one—is uncertainty as to what situation will follow the presidency. If there is an enticing offer—often one to head up another college or university—that usually makes an exit from the presidency relatively easy. Offers from foundations or other not-for-profit organizations can also be extremely attractive. However, a president whose long tenure in office provokes the conclusion that the time for a change is at hand may also have reached an age which makes attractive offers of new employment somewhat less likely. If the president's age is sufficiently advanced to consider retirement, however, then the transition from a tremendously hyperactive existence to serenity may be appealing at some point. Nevertheless, the decision that now is the time to do this may be so difficult that it can easily seem best to defer it, at least for the moment.

For someone who has led a single college or university for a long stretch of time, the departure from office is inevitably likely to be complicated by real and deep devotion. Is the job really done? How will the institution function without its long-time and successful president? Is it treason to leave? Would it perhaps be better to delay this decision for at least another year? In this situation the best course to follow is for the president to consult trustees, not formally at a board meeting, but informally in conversation with trustees whom the president has liked and respected, and regards as friends. If these trustees argue against retirement from the presidency now, the decision to delay is apt to be easy; but if they agree that the time for a change is at hand, then leaving the job becomes unavoidable.

In fact, the trustees—as a board or as individuals—have a key role to play in addressing the question of change in the presidency after a long and successful incumbency. Their role is not only to confirm a presidential concern that retirement from the job is indeed appropriate, but also to facilitate such retirement to the best of their ability, and a truly devoted and effective board of trustees can do much while the presidency is in full bloom to lay the groundwork for the best possible presidential departure from office. A variety of considerations may need to be addressed, some of them long before retirement is due.

One easy step, for example, can be trustee participation in a decision, fairly early in a presidency, to treat a portion of the presidential salary as deferred income, to be paid to the president only after retirement, either directly or to his or her heirs. This does not cost the institution anything, but has significant benefits to the president. During a presidential incumbency, presidential expenditures on travel, entertainment, and meals tend to be minimal, because so much of these activities are on institutional business and thus are appropriately treated as legitimate items in the presidential budget. Absent special circumstances or extraordinary acquisitions, it is in fact unlikely that a president drawing a relatively standard presidential salary would find it easy to spend all of his or her annual income. This situation could of course result in substantial savings, but these would be taxed annually upon receipt. The advantages of deferred compensation are that taxes to the recipient are only paid when the funds are actually received, and that the college or university will invest the funds which are deferred annually so that—properly invested—they will also yield additional income, which again is not taxed until received by the individual. A long presidential incumbency would yield substantial post-employment income for a lengthy period, and therefore would at least partially relieve concern that leaving the presidency would necessarily involve financial scarcity.

Another possible situation which may become awkward for a president contemplating retirement arises from the fact that a substantial number of colleges and universities find it appropriate to house the president and his or her family in a presidential mansion, usually on the campus, which is designed to facilitate relatively large-scale entertainment for donors, trustees, and visiting dignitaries, as well as groups of faculty or students. Such president's houses indeed can be extremely useful and attractive, but their use often results in the fact that retirement from the presidency also involves a move to new housing. For a president who does not own a house of his or her own, the need to buy a house may also play a role in reluctance to retire from the presidency.

There are various ways of avoiding or mitigating such a problem. A number of presidents use presidential mansions for entertainment or meetings but actually reside in quarters they own. Presidents who live in a president's house thereby save the cost not only of a mortgage, but also of maintenance and property tax, and therefore are able to receive deferred income which would facilitate the mortgage payments for newly acquired housing of their own. Nevertheless, however, the loss of free and comfortably familiar presidential housing can occasionally be another factor which delays any easy decision to retire from the presidency.

In a more positive vein, steps can also be taken to make retirement attractive even from a successful, long-lived presidency. The most persuasive such step would be not merely to name the retiree president emeritus, but also to assign him or her an official role as well as assign an office on campus for his or her use, and to provide secretarial support. Various ways of doing this have indeed already been taken at a number of institutions. One successful option is to name the president emeritus as chairperson of the college or university foundation—chairperson, not CEO. In that role, the president emeritus can remain in touch with donors both old and new, not to solicit them but rather to make them feel important and respected. Much of this interaction can be done on campus, but another tried and true alternative is for the president emeritus to travel occasionally, to visit donors and also to address meetings of alumni in various cities. Alumni who developed respect and even affection for a president in office respond warmly to renewed occasional contact with the president emeritus.

The risk in making such use of the president emeritus is possible resentment on the part of the successor president in office. The golden rule for a president emeritus is to avoid—at all costs—any interference or negative expression regarding his or her successor. There can only be one president at a time, and any visible friction between the president and his or her predecessor reflects badly not only on the two principals but also on the trustees and indeed the whole institution. Friendship between president and president emeritus is universally desirable; friction between the two is not only unattractive but potentially destructive. Thus it is on the one hand easier and safer if the president emeritus is away from the institution and busy elsewhere; but on the other hand the institution can also benefit if a respected president emeritus visibly and enthusiastically supports and assists his or her successor.

The Need for Trustee Engagement

Having now given consideration to the complications of terminating a lengthy and successful college or university presidency at the peak of achievement and before delay taints long achievement with growing perception that a change in leadership is needed and is on the edge of overdue, what conclusion can be drawn from our observations? The problem of retirement delayed too long is real, although far from universal, but there is no magic formula to address. The only valid conclusion is that in this matter—as with most other matters concerning institutions of higher education—the crucial responsibility lies with the trustees. Charged with the supervision of the institution, the trustees must engineer presidential retirement in timely fashion, with due regard to the needs both of the institution and of a deserving and successful incumbent.

What we have considered is why even the strongest and most innovative of presidents is likely to have some difficulties with the need to retire, and why therefore the trustees must take action to resolve it with deep respect for the deserving incumbent but an equally deep obligation to select a new president. The paradox of course is that an achieving, long-term president will have been the stalwart leader of the board of trustees, but that the trustees themselves may have to take leadership so as to effect a timely succession. It is easier for trustees to plead with an achieving president to stay in office longer than the incumbent wishes than it is to persuade a successful incumbent that the time for a change is now—not tomorrow.

CHAPTER FOUR

Passing the Baton: Leadership Transitions and the Tenure of Presidents

Arthur Padilla

The Arrival of the New President

Leadership transitions in organizations are often evocative of stately political events, with implications for the stability and interruption of regimes, the loss of power and influence, and the creation of clear winners and losers. Therefore, it is not entirely surprising that changes in top management have been among the most studied topics in organizational theory.

The hiring of a new president at a college or university can be a remarkable event for the institution, with the inauguration ceremony and its full pomp and circumstance. This chapter examines the environmental conditions and factors affecting leadership transitions in higher education and presents evidence on increased turnover at its institutions. Among other things, it documents that the tenure of university presidents, particularly those in the public sector, has fallen to historically low levels.

Typically, as soon as the intentions of the departing president are known, the wheels of a common and fairly cumbersome search process begin moving. Fellow trustees and other institutional boosters will call the chairperson to express their opinions and their specific interests about serving on the search committee; some will suggest potential candidates. The chair of the faculty senate will receive calls and e-mails from several concerned colleagues, insisting that the voice of the faculty be heard throughout the process. A few will express a willingness to serve on the committee. A series of broad campus and off-campus meetings will be scheduled to hear comments on the condition of the university and the profile of the new president to be chosen.

If the departing president was well liked and had a generally successful tenure, the local media may run a few stories listing some of the major institutional accomplishments, which typically will have to do with greater endowments, larger enrollments, or noteworthy partnerships with colleges and corporations. Most of the focus will be forward-looking and about new directions, and various factions will emerge with disparate views about the kind of leadership that is needed.

The search will eventually cost a major institution several hundred thousand dollars, counting the fees of the search firm, the travel back and forth of the many candidates and committee members, and the time of the dozens of people directly involved. If there is no viable internal candidate, the process may take a year, or even two, a period during which the departing president will experience the dwindling of his or her power, influence, and perhaps interest in the institution. Preferences of the varied stakeholders are increasingly revealed: a scholar of international repute who will help us with our external image; a businessperson or financier who knows the value of a dollar and who has a proven track record in raising money; someone who understands the importance of athletics; a strong advocate of diversity who will connect effectively with all of the students and staff. Even before the committee is named, several of the stakeholder groups will have clearly expressed their opinions and worries.

The democratically chosen group, numbering up to twenty, will place ads in appropriate publications describing the presidential opening, but only after the wording of the ad itself is carefully studied and discussed by the full committee. Early on, the search firm representatives will describe what they will do and how they will do it, along with suggestions on the committee's objectives and how it should operate. At this juncture, the committee may choose to become more managerial and let the search firm present candidates, or it may choose to adopt a more active role as a true search committee. While up to several hundred applications may be received, the more savvy candidates are likely to be nominated by others. The search firm will also present its own list of candidates based on prior contacts and work with other universities. Most, if not all, the candidates will be outsiders. Finally, after many long meetings and off-campus interviews, the committee will typically settle on three to five finalists. They will be brought to the institution for periods of two or three days, to participate in several dozen meetings and sessions with trustees, faculty, students, staff, alumni, and administrators.

During much of the search process, the retiring president, or the interim one who may have been named for the transition, faces challenging managerial problems. A natural inclination of the organization will be to run on automatic pilot while waiting for the new regime to arrive. This attitude can influence an entire university, and major initiatives and decisions requiring senior management endorsement and approval may be placed on hold.

Traditionally, new presidents have moved slowly and in concert with whatever directions the board and its key members may have indicated. However, increasingly in some specific areas, presidents will rather quickly carry out the wishes or going-in mandates of the board or other key individuals.[1] Particular administrators or major sports coaches, for example, may be replaced rather suddenly and certain initiatives may begin immediately.

A process of familiarization with the organization's "untouchables," individuals with direct linkages to trustees or to influential alumni or groups, is also begun. Media coverage is usually intense during the first few days. Introductory meetings with students, faculty, alumni, and staff draw great interest and anticipation. The honeymoon period has officially begun and will probably last, under normal circumstances, for at least several months. The departing president may be deeply missed or, alternatively, as one former president once said, may be missed for about as long as it takes the space in a glass of water to fill back up after a finger is removed. The institution gradually adjusts to a new mode and style of management, and old initiatives and practices, such as TQM or tenure peer review processes, may be discarded or put on hold in favor of the newest wave of managerial directives. Vice presidents, deans, and the faculty wonder what the new administration will bring, while they ponder their futures. Two, or even three, years may have elapsed from the time the preceding president announced an intention to leave.

What Do Presidential Changes Tell Us about the Institution?

As suggested by the foregoing hypothetical change event, leadership transitions reveal a good deal about how colleges and universities are structured and how their leadership is organized. Research on succession indicates that CEO or presidential changes are important not only to the presidents, as Michael D. Cohen and James G. March irreverently put it almost thirty years ago, but also to the organizations they lead and to the various stakeholders of the organizations.[2] Leadership positions obviously hold symbolic and material value to different interest groups. The departure of a president and the selection and arrival of the new one can help identify coalitions and political inclinations when various groups mobilize to affect the succession event itself. The capacity of the organization to adapt to a changing environment may be both enhanced and diminished by changes at the top. Too much change can create uncertainty and morale problems and may solidify behaviors; too little change may contribute to a static environment where things continue to be done as they have always been done.

Thus, while the primary focus of this chapter is to discuss and quantify the trends in presidential tenure, a review of conceptual aspects of leadership transitions and succession will be helpful in understanding those trends. And at the heart of the conceptual discussion are these questions: So what? What determines the frequency of transitions and successions? What specifically are the results of the transitions? Do transitions help or hurt performance? Is too much change as bad as too little change? Are transitions the result of performance, or is performance the result of transitions? The remaining discussion revolves around four basic topics or sets of questions, loosely adapted from some similar topics proposed by S. Finkelstein and D. C. Hambrick for the study of leadership transitions and successions:[3]

1. Will succession occur, and what are the frequency of turnover and the length of presidential tenures?
2. How and by what process will succession occur?
3. Who will be selected?
4. What will be the consequences?

When Will Succession Occur?

Leadership changes occur within the context of, and are directly affected by, the trends shaping an institution and the environment within which it operates. In recent years a few key trends have emerged to influence the nature of presidential transitions as well as increase the turnover rate among presidents in colleges and universities:

—Changes in the structure and function of governing boards (they serve less as advocates for and defenders of the institution and more as critics and agents for oversight and accountability) and in traditional faculty governance (governance responsibilities have been extended to nonfaculty administrators and faculty have become less involved in service to the institution).

—Increased vocationalism on the part of students (students and parents ask with increasing stridency, "What exactly are we paying for?").

—The privatization of the university (i.e., the substitution of private funding power over individual institutions such as tuition and fees or grants and contracts from industry for public money).

—The emergence of systems as the dominant form of governance among public universities.

—Increased size and complexity of individual campuses, leading to more difficult managerial challenges and to an inclination by search committees and boards of trustees to hire "safer" and more experienced administrators.

—Consequent weakening of the office of the presidency (coupled with sharply higher pay for top campus executives relative to the pay of the most senior faculty).

Each of these factors affects different institutions in different ways. They have also been present to some degree for many decades. Indeed, many former presidents may say the challenges they faced in the 1950s and 1960s were, though different, certainly not less challenging than those of today. However, all of these trends have become stronger influences in the past two decades. It would also appear that large public campuses have been affected more than private colleges and universities by these environmental conditions. As one example, the statewide multicampus system is now the dominant form of governance in the public sector, whereas most private universities continue to be governed individually by presidents and boards.

There are about 120 public systems covering some one thousand campuses, with nearly 80 percent of American college students enrolled in colleges or universities that are part of multicampus systems. Over 3 million are enrolled in the fifteen largest systems alone. These systems have great diversity, ranging from unified structures with significant governing control over budgets and personnel to highly decentralized ones with single-campus boards responsible for the students, faculty, and staff of their specific institution. And in addition to the boards of regents or trustees and the system staffs that operate the programs of the individual constituent institutions, the voices of the respective legislatures and the governors of the states are also clearly heard. The locus of control and power in many areas is now increasingly outside, rather than within, the public institution.

Recent changes in the structure and function of the governing boards have similarly tended to affect the public campuses almost exclusively. The function and manner of selection of private university boards of trustees or directors is essentially unchanged from the way it operated fifty years ago.[4] But there is evidence that there have been significant declines in the terms of office of public university trustees, that their selection has become more politicized, and that boards are increasingly involved in the operation of campuses rather than in their broad policy concerns. Increased size and complexity again have become relevant factors in the management of all institutions, but private universities have managed to keep their enrollments at much lower levels over a longer period of time.

Frequency of Turnover of Presidents

The frequency of leadership transitions is, of course, related inversely to the tenure (or the start-to-end service) of presidents: the shorter the length of service of presidents, the greater the frequency of leadership transition events and successions. The length of the tenure of presidents is, in turn, ultimately a measure of the fit between the organization and its president and their mutual satisfaction. Higher survival rates of presidents would signal greater satisfaction of presidents and institutions with each other, and lower survival the opposite. As the environment surrounding universities changes, making universities more difficult to manage and the presidency a less attractive alternative, one would expect to see shorter and shorter presidential terms of service. In the terminology of the conceptual framework of Finkelstein and Hambrick, not only will successions occur, but they will tend to occur more often.[5]

In particular, based on this discussion of the major trends and factors affecting the presidency, one might expect three main patterns (stated below as hypotheses) regarding the tenure of presidents:

1. that the total tenure (start-to-end service) of all presidents (public and private) would decline over time, a direct consequence of environmental changes making the job more difficult;
2. that the total tenure of public university presidents, whose institutions have undergone greater and more fundamental changes in governance and in other environmental pressures, would be shorter than that of private university presidents; and
3. that, given differences in size and organizational complexity, the total tenure of presidents of the major research universities would be less than that of the presidents of other types of universities and colleges.

Defining *Tenure*

One of the earliest attempts to define and measure *presidential tenure* is found in an American Council on Education special report on campus tensions in the late 1960s, in a paper by Clark Kerr.[6] Concern at the time centered on the survival of college and university presidents and on the impact that their shortened tenures were having on their institutions. Noting that one measure of the mutual satisfaction of a president and those with whom she or he works is survival or length of tenure on the job, Kerr proceeded to analyze the tenures of presidents of some of the most prestigious American universities: he focused on forty-eight public and private universities then belonging to the Association of American Universities (AAU). He found that the mean number of years that sitting or incumbent presidents had been in office was

—10.9 years in 1899

—9.5 in 1929

—7.7 in 1939

—7.4 in 1959

—5.9 in 1969

The median tenure had dropped from 7 years in 1929 to 2 years in 1969.

Two relevant questions emerge from a scrutiny of Kerr's analysis: Why choose the prestigious AAU institutions exclusively, and What exactly does average or median tenure mean? There are several good, solid answers to the first question, many of them discussed by Kerr. One involves expediency: with thousands of institutions and scores of current and former presidents in each over the period of his analysis, data collection problems are formidable. But there are also more substantive reasons: the major research universities are among the most complex, most publicized, and most rapidly changing institutions in the world. They conduct, as a group, some of the most influential and pathbreaking basic research anywhere; they educate one-fourth of all American college students; and they produce nearly all of the Ph.D. graduates. Their presidencies and other high-level posts have in the past been among the most highly sought jobs in any labor market. They are also subject to intense societal and political pressures, and this is particularly true for those in the public sector.

However, as Cohen and March noted, a variety of definitions may be offered for "average tenure."[7] Three possible meanings follow:

Completed tenure. Kerr's measure, as well as those in Marlene Ross and Madeleine F. Green's American Council on Education report and the studies by W. K. Selden and M. R. Ferrari, refers to what may be called completed tenure, or to the distribution of completed tenure for presidents in office on a particular date.[8] This is perhaps the most widely used empirical measure of the tenure of college and university presidents, but it is clearly not a measure of total or start-to-end tenure. It is simply the average number of years served so far by presidents in office as of a certain snapshot date. Hence, average completed tenure for 2003 is the average number of years in office (since the year of initial appointment as president) for all incumbent presidents. The dates of retirement or departure of incumbents will vary, and what is not known is how much longer presidents currently in office will serve. Thus, the meaning of this tenure measure is difficult to comprehend.

Backward cohort tenure. A second measure of tenure may be called the backward cohort tenure, which gives the distribution of total (start-to-end) tenures for presidents completing their term in a given year. Thus, the average backward cohort tenure for 2003 is the average number of years served by presidents retiring or leaving office in 2003. The difficulty with this measure is that one president retiring in 2003 may have started in 1999, while a second one retiring the same year may have been appointed in 1985. Such disparate first-appointment "vintages" make meaningful comparisons very difficult to explain or understand.

Forward cohort or total, start-to-end tenure. A third, and perhaps the most intuitive measure of tenure, may be called the forward cohort (or total, start-to-end) tenure, which gives the distribution of total tenure for the cohort of presidents beginning their presidencies in a particular year. Thus, average forward cohort tenure in 2003 is the average number of years that eventually will be served by presidents initially appointed to office in 2003. This distribution is known at some future point (say, in fifteen years, when all of the presidents appointed in 2003 complete their total tenures), but it may be estimated in 2003 using survival analyses or other methods. This distribution, of course, is known for nearly all presidents whose initial appointments were in the early 1990s or before, because nearly all of them have already left office.

Ross and Green, like Kerr, report on completed tenure (the first measure discussed above) of incumbent presidents in their comprehensive database.[9] They find that completed tenure remained constant in 1995 compared to 1988 at all institutions but that it declined markedly at the doctoral universities. However, note again that this is simply the average number of years that sitting or incumbent presidents have been in office and that it is affected rather significantly by the particular year that is chosen.

In fact, most people who speak about the tenure of presidents probably refer to the forward cohort measure of total (start-to-end) tenure. For presidents already retired, this is absolutely known, since one knows when they started and when they left; for those still in office, total tenure means their completed tenure to date plus what may be called "additional" or remaining tenure. This would measure, for instance, how long a president appointed to office today may be expected to serve in total (total tenure) by the time he or she retires, or how much longer presidents now in office may on average be expected to serve. However, very few studies give these start-to-end tenure numbers.

Cohen and March's 1974 analysis, which uses the forward cohort or start-to-end method in defining tenure, covered a sample of forty-two colleges and universities of all sorts, for the period 1900 to 1971. They concluded, "Presidential tenure is about what it has been throughout most of the twentieth century, except for the 1930–1944 periods. . . . We do not believe there has been a dramatic recent shift in the time presidents are serving or will serve in the future."[10]

They also contended that the trend Kerr found, that the tenures of presidents had declined significantly in the 1960s, which he attributed to the student riots and campus unrest, was in fact due to his selection of institutions and his definition of average tenure. If Kerr had examined a more comprehensive group of institutions, they argued, the reported decline would not have been observed. But this is not a particularly trenchant criticism: as Kerr notes, the universities in the AAU have some of the most carefully chosen presidents and take great pride in the stability of their leadership, which represents some of the most visible symbols of leaders in higher education in the world.[11] He could have added that these universities were, by far, the most affected by the student unrest of the 1960s and 1970s. Kerr thus chose the AAU campuses because they were and are different from the rest of higher education and because one should expect differences in lengths of presidential tenure among the various types of institutions.

The second criticism, Kerr's use of "completed" tenure to gauge trends and averages, is more to the point. The widely used concept of completed tenure is, as discussed above, difficult to interpret or understand. Since presidents do not all start or end on the same dates, and since the total length of their tenures necessarily also varies, any measure of tenure relying on completed tenure depends on the date on which the calculation is based. This chapter now examines presidential tenure using two separate sources of data and alternative definitions of tenure based on the work of Art Padilla and Sujit Ghosh.[12]

Empirical Analyses of Presidential Tenure

The first data set represents detailed presidential total tenure histories for a large sample (nearly half) of the major (Research I) American universities.[13] This data set, which is similar to the one used by Kerr, covers thirty-nine universities, nearly two hundred presidents, and more than two thousand "presidential years" since 1950. Although these data include all presidents at each university, the present analysis is limited to presidential tenures since 1950. The second data set is from a 1998 survey of all types of institutions of higher education in the United States, reporting on the current or incumbent president and also on the immediately previous president. In this survey all Research I and Research II universities were surveyed, along with a random sample of the remaining types of institutions. The overall response rate was 65 percent. The results using the first data set, covering the research universities, are summarized in table 4.1, and those using the second data set, covering all types of institutions, are shown in tables 4.2 and 4.3.

Table 4.1 presents the most intuitive of the three measures of tenure discussed previously and indicates that average total (start-to-end) tenure of the most recent entering class of presidents at the major public universities is 5.7 years. This is significantly below (at the 5 percent level of significance using a two-tailed test) the total tenures of presidents in private universities. The table also underscores three other points:

1. Kerr's conclusion that presidential tenure at the research universities declined markedly during the 1960s was apparently correct.
2. The total tenure of public university presidents has been significantly lower than that of private university presidents for the last decade.
3. There is a downward trend in average total tenure of presidents at both public and private research universities over the last two decades.

Averages are sometimes deceptive, of course, because they may include a small number of presidents with very long service. However, an examination of medians tells the same story: median tenure rates for public presidents are appreciably lower than those of private presidents; there was a decline in median tenures in the 1960s; and there is a downward trend in median tenure for both the public and the private sectors.

Table 4.1. Total Presidential Tenure, by Year of First Appointment (Research I Universities Only)

Pentad of Initial Appointment	Private	(Sigma, *N*)	Public	(Sigma, *N*)	*p*-value (t-test)	Confidence Interval
1950–54	11.7	6.0, 9	7.8	5.8, 11	0.1604	
1955–59	8.0	2.8, 5	9.6	7.4, 19	0.458	
1960–64	8.2	4.3, 6	6.8	3.3, 8	0.5232	
1965–69	6.5	3.9, 11	11.2	8.7, 13	0.098	
1970–74	13.1	7.2, 10	9.7	3.7, 14	0.1959	
1975–79	11.8	5.7, 8	7.3	3.3, 6	0.1037	
1980–84	11.2	1.5, 4	7.1	3.1, 14	0.0037***	1.6–6.6
1985–89	8.8	1.0, 4	5.7	2.6, 14	0.0028***	1.3–4.9

Source: Padilla and Ghosh, "On the Tenure of University Presidents."

Tables 4.2 and 4.3, based on all types of four-year colleges and universities, not just the Research I institutions, in part confirm the findings of Ross and Green, indicating that completed tenure (table 4.3) of incumbent Research I and Research II presidents is notably lower than that of other presidents.[14] However, table 4.2, which uses the more intuitive measure of tenure (the total, start-to-end tenure of the immediately previous president), does not reveal any major differences among the various kinds of higher education institutions, although no distinction is made here between public and private institutions, as was the case with table 4.1. These tables presenting alternate measures of tenure and using two separate data sets lead to the following conclusions:

—The forward cohort or total, start-to-end measure of tenure, the most intuitive of the measures, shows trends that confirm the first two hypotheses posited above: total presidential tenure is declining at both public and private Research I universities, markedly so in the public sector.

—Total tenure of university presidents, for the first time since the 1950s and probably even before that, is now significantly shorter in the public sector than it is for private universities. This finding is confirmed by both data sets.

The third proposition—that the tenure of presidents at doctoral institutions is shorter than that of presidents of other campuses—is confirmed

Table 4.2. Average Total Tenure of Immediately Previous President (1998)

Carnegie Class	Average Total Tenure
Baccalaureate I	3.5
Baccalaureate II	8.6
Community	5.3
Doctorate I	7.8
Doctorate II	5.8
Masters I	8.6
Masters II	9.3
Research I	8.2
Research II	7.8
Total (weighted)	6.5

Source: Padilla and Ghosh, "On the Tenure of University Presidents."

in table 4.3. This panel defines tenure as the completed tenure of sitting presidents, which is a rather misleading way to define presidential tenure in the first place. It is again noted that table 4.2, which presents total tenure (start-to-end) averages, does not show this pattern. Further work is needed to explore whether the larger institutions have shorter presidential tenures than do the smaller campuses. Table 4.2 suggests the opposite, that is, that in fact the smallest institutions have shorter, rather than longer, tenures of presidential service.

Survival Estimates

Analysis of duration, or survival analysis, is a fairly new statistical technique, and few accessible articles using this technique are available in the management literature. In engineering and biostatistics, however, projecting the length of time until failure or end of an event has been a topic of great interest for decades. More recently, survival or hazard function analysis has been applied to disparate phenomena, such as the survival rates of cancer patients and the expected length of labor strikes. The hazard function in the present context is useful in answering a fundamental question: what is the probability that a president's term of office will last an additional length of time, given that she or he has survived until time t?

Table 4.4 presents probabilities of survival for different cohorts of

Table 4.3. Average Completed Tenure of Current President (1998)

Carnegie Class	Average Completed Tenure
Baccalaureate I	9.0
Baccalaureate II	7.6
Community	7.6
Doctorate I	4.3
Doctorate II	6.0
Masters I	7.6
Masters II	12.3
Research I	5.4
Reserach II	4.6
Total (weighted)	8.2

Source: Padilla and Ghosh, "On the Tenure of University Presidents."

presidents. This table gives in numerical form the projected probabilities for five and ten years after initial appointment, for each pentad. Public university presidents hired in the 1985–89 pentad (excluding all "interim" or "acting" presidents) had a 33 percent chance (.333) of serving five or more years, compared to a nearly 100 percent chance (1.000) for private presidents. Again, sharp declines in total tenure for the more recent cohorts of presidents are confirmed here, as are the sharp differences in survival for the most recent cohorts between the public university presidents and those of private institutions. The probability that a public university president appointed since 1980 will serve ten years or more in office is exceptionally low, close to zero. The declines reported by Kerr during the period of campus unrest are apparent using the survival function estimates, with the problems in the public sector temporally leading those in the private sector. Yet another way to look at these trends is to compute the survival probabilities over time for presidents of similar age and hiring status. For example, a president of a major public university hired internally before 1975 at age forty-five had a 79 percent chance of surviving at least five years in office; a similar individual hired after 1975 had a 50 percent chance of serving five years, a drop of nearly 30 percentage points.

The more precise and sophisticated analyses based on the survival function techniques therefore confirm the simpler statistics presented

Table 4.4. Survival Probabilities for Research University Presidents, by Pentad of Initial Appointment, 1950–54 to 1985–89

	Probability that length of tenure exceeds			
	5 years		10 years	
Pentad	Private	Public	Private	Public
1950–54	0.998	0.848	0.802	0.104
1955–59	0.945	0.983	0.055	0.407
1960–64	0.895	0.754	0.153	0.003
1965–69	0.695	0.984	0.002	0.690
1970–74	0.999	1.000	0.913	0.381
1975–79	0.998	0.833	0.814	0.022
1980–84	1.000	0.908	0.945	0
1985–89	1.000	0.333	0.008	0

Source: Padilla and Ghosh, "On the Tenure of University Presidents."

earlier: there is a decline in tenures of university presidents. It is more pronounced for the presidents of the major public campuses, and for presidents hired since the mid-1980s, there is a statistically significant difference in the frequency of turnover and in the tenure averages of public and private presidents.

How Do Presidents Leave Office?

Recent evidence therefore points in the direction of more frequent presidential transition events and shorter tenure. Presidents leave office in one of four ways: death or serious illness, retirement, resignation (either forced or voluntary), and firing. For the purposes of this chapter, death and illness are the least interesting forms of departure, reflecting the choice of no one in the organization and representing less than 5 percent of all separations.[15] Voluntary or mandatory retirements make up most of the separations from office, and these also have not been studied extensively. However, the adoption of mandatory retirement policies may reflect the organization's beliefs about executive entrenchment or the need for turnover at the top and organizational change and adaptation.

In the major public universities, where the age of presidents at initial appointment now hovers close to sixty, one would expect fewer dismissals and more retirements and departures due to health problems. If the average age of university presidents at the time of initial appointment continues to increase, one may also then expect declines in average total tenures (start to end) and more frequent successions and greater turnover.

Dismissals and firings have been the more interesting transition phenomena for researchers, but such separations tend to be more prevalent among private firms than they are among colleges and universities. Dismissed executives in private industry typically leave the organization altogether, often with significant "golden parachutes." Unlike private company CEOs, college and university presidents have typically been tenured professors in academic departments, and going back to those departments, if feasible, may be the most attractive alternative immediately after a firing.

Why, specifically, are presidents and CEOs fired? The most obvious answer might involve the performance of the organization. However, while organizational performance is related to dismissals of CEOs of private, for-profit companies, it is a rather weak causative factor, according to researchers. Furthermore, in the higher education sector, where there are no stock prices or sales and revenue figures to consider, organizational performance can be particularly difficult to measure and quantify. As R. Ehrenberg and co-workers point out in discussing presidential salaries, the relationship between pay and performance, to the extent it actually exists, is not easily determined:

> For example, the highest paid president in 1997–98 was a liberal arts college president who received a hefty retirement package in recognition of twenty years of outstanding service to the college. The chairman of the college's board of trustees credited the president for having built the college's endowment, reduced its debt, and enhanced its academic reputation. Because this reward for performance was a discrete one that came at the end of the president's term, focusing on the relationship between his compensation change and the institution's performance over any period of time that did not include his last year in office, would drastically understate the long-run relationship.
>
> Similarly large compensation increases may be used as a way of "encouraging" a president to voluntarily resign and thus may reflect "non-performance" rather than performance. One long-term comprehensive university president who retired from his position in 1997–1998 was widely blamed for the financial difficulties that his institution had suffered during his last years in office. His large increase in compensation during his last year of office included a retirement package and a severance payment that will be paid out over time.[16]

The firing of university presidents would thus be the result of a short list of situations that may be summarized as follows: (1) firing due to personal misconduct or behavior; (2) firing due to clear institutional failure, such as a major problem with intercollegiate athletics or with the operation of the institution, determined to be the direct result of a failure of actions by the president; and (3) firing due to a significant conflict or disagreement between the president and one or more board members, which may be the result of a series of problems that develop over time rather than the result of one particular episode or event. In all such cases except the most egregious ones, the central role of the board of trustees is evident. The trustees will ultimately have to decide the issue of the failure; and thus the board, its characteristics and internal power relationships, its makeup, and its relationship to the president and to inside and outside stakeholders play a central role in those rare cases in which a university president is dismissed.

How and by What Process Will Succession Occur?

The process of selection has become both more formal and, in the case of the public institutions, more formulaic over time. It becomes significantly more formal as one moves from the smaller colleges to the larger universities and from the private to the public sector. For the large public universities, it now typically involves a rather large and formal search committee or committees with wide trustee, faculty, staff, student, and alumni representation and is carried out with the assistance of a professional search firm. Just a few decades ago, the hiring process was much more informal and private. It was controlled by a few influential board members who could make crucial and final decisions on behalf of the institution without a great deal of consultation or public deliberation. Public university board members were appointed to longer terms of service and thus were more insulated from political pressures and demands. In contrast to the situation on public campuses, the trustees of major private universities are still selected in essentially the same way as they have been for much of the past century, and their proceedings are much more private and not subject to the same laws and regulations that apply to public campuses.

Many public university presidents, as well as the Association of Governing Boards,[17] report an increased involvement of regents and trustees in the daily operations of their campuses. Additionally, search committees are often composed of large numbers of individuals, and their actions are often reported in detail by the press throughout the process of selection. Professional search firms are more likely to be involved in the selection today, adding yet another level of complexity to presidential searches.

These factors have contributed to what one former president has called safer and more "democratic" candidates. In part, the increased concern for "safety" by search committees may also reflect increases in size and complexity of the organizations: research suggests that larger, more bureaucratic and established organizations tend to hire older, more experienced CEOs and presidents. Turnover thus would be higher because of the more advanced age of presidents at initial appointment. Conversely, outright firings are now less likely because (a) candidates are "safer" and (b) larger institutions would receive more media attention than would smaller ones and would want to avoid the negative publicity that would result from a firing.

How Does the External Environment Affect the "Fit" between the New President and the Institution?

While the selection of a new president is of course necessary to replace a departing one, it is increasingly viewed as an important opportunity for the college or university to adapt to a new environment or to address specific issues of importance to the institution. In the corporate sector, research tends to show that there is a relationship between the external conditions facing an organization and the strengths and characteristics of the new CEO.[18] Thus, a financial background may be preferred over an operational one in situations that require knowledge about corporate diversification (such as a merger or an acquisition) or about fund-raising.

The selection of an "insider" or an "outsider" as the new leader has also received much attention in the literature. The selection of a president from outside the organization is rarer in a business context than it is in the university, but in either case it is often seen as evidence that the board wants change and wants to break with the previous administration. Understandably, the choice of an insider is often seen as a vote for continuity and for the preservation of the basic strategy of the organization. The most obvious predictor of whether a CEO will come from the outside is performance in the period before the succession. Of several studies that have considered this topic, most have found that prior performance was lower in cases where an outsider was appointed than when an insider was appointed. This pattern has been observed in baseball teams, semiconductor firms, and in a cross section of large companies in various industries.[19] While the difficulty of measuring a university's performance may make findings from the private sector less applicable, the general tendency of hiring outsiders is nonetheless often viewed as a cleansing ritual, with insistent demonstrations by the board that the past is behind them.[20]

The information from the two surveys discussed earlier also points in two relevant directions regarding the hiring of insiders or outsiders. First, there has been a greater propensity among the major universities to hire outside or external candidates over the past twenty-five years. Also, public institutions have shown a greater inclination to hire externally. Second, the data also show that internal candidates tend to have longer tenures, other things being the same. The proclivity to hire relatively more outsiders is consistent with other trends: the greater use of professional search firms; the tendency to hire individuals with more experience, such as in the presidency of another institution, perhaps a smaller or less complex one; the desire by regents and trustees to adapt to change and innovation; and the failure of universities and their leadership, perhaps because of a lack of continuity and too much change at the top, to consistently develop and nurture their own talented young people to assume roles within the institution. At the same time, hiring an outsider brings an individual with external experiences and organizational cultures, factors that may produce new ideas and styles but that also may clash with the institution's previous behaviors and habits. Insiders presumably know the institution and its personnel better, and they may be in a better position to "hit the ground running" without the learning process that an outsider would have to endure.

The Rise of the Interim Presidency

Interim and acting presidents have come to represent a new form of presidential succession. Traditionally, interim appointees are not candidates for the permanent job and serve for periods of one to two years until a more permanent candidate is found. Cohen and March's 1974 data suggested that the use of interim presidents was much greater in the post–World War II period than previously and that acting presidents were most common in large schools. They estimated the chance that a college or university in the United States would have an acting president on January 1 in a given year to be about 0.02 between 1900 and 1970. For the period 1945–70, they estimated this probability at 0.04 in all U.S. colleges and universities, and at 0.06 in the large universities.

The 1998 survey discussed earlier indicates that this kind of appointment has become even more prevalent among the large universities, and, again, particularly among the public ones. A typical public research university had a 0.11 chance that at least one of its last two presidents was an interim, compared to about 0.06 for the typical private university.

The magnitude of these numbers suggests that the phenomenon of acting presidents (and perhaps the use of acting officials in other senior management jobs as well) requires further study. Interim presidents confound tenure statistics: some interim presidents actually become permanent presidents, but more frequently they serve for only twelve to twenty-four months.

Increased turnover, the growing size and complexity of universities, and the bureaucratization and democratization of the search process, as well as the aging of presidents generally, suggest a continued increase in the number of interim presidents in the future. It should also be clear that if interims were somehow incorporated formally into the calculus of the tenure of presidents, then the differences in the length of tenures noted earlier among the public and private sectors would be even larger.

After the Presidency

There is little information about what happens to university presidents after they leave, other than anecdotal histories. Yet, for those who enter the job at age fifty or younger, it is clear that, on average, they will not complete their careers as president of that institution. The two data sets used in discussing presidential tenures earlier in this chapter also indicate that about 15 percent of "immediately previous" presidents at the research universities retired and that slightly more than that proportion (19 percent) left for other presidencies. Those who went to other presidencies tended to be leaving a smaller institution and moving to a larger, more complex campus and a higher-paying job. The remaining former presidents either returned to the faculty, became consultants, were deceased, or were employed in another capacity elsewhere. Robert F. Carbone, in his presidential "passages" report, estimated similar proportions: 25 percent in retirement or semiretirement, 15 percent in another presidency, 20 percent back in a faculty position, and the remainder in another administrative post or a job outside the academy.[21]

Thus, for many presidents, the presidency is a kind of terminal position, in that they are unlikely to find another one with the same level of prestige and responsibility. As H. W. Stoke noted, university presidency may be a risky occupation in some cases.[22] Clearly, further research specifically on the career paths of former presidents who leave office before retirement would be informative.

What Are the Consequences?

The results or consequences of transitions are among the most studied in the leadership transition literature, but this important "so what" question has not been carefully examined in the context of colleges and universities. Any prediction about consequences of the departure of one president and the arrival of a new one must necessarily involve a thoughtful examination of the factors leading to the transition, the succession process itself, and the personal and professional characteristics and styles of both the predecessor and the successor.

What is known is that it is exceptionally rare for any new chief executive—even one appointed from within the ranks of the institution, whose style is well known by the board and by the staff—to hit the ground at full speed. Many problems and situations will not be familiar, and the capabilities of various middle managers, such as deans and vice presidents, will not be known. There will be a natural tendency to go slowly in many areas while a general learning process proceeds. At the same time, new presidents may also feel pressure to have an immediate impact and to show the board that it made the correct choice. Many new presidents have implicit or explicit "going in" mandates directly connected to how the organization was performing or how key stakeholders expect the institution to change and adapt. The early survival of new presidents, in fact, appears to depend importantly on adherence to "going in" directions and to an understanding of critical dynamics within the stakeholder community. Gordon and Rosen, as quoted by Finkelstein and Hambrick, put it this way: "Newly appointed leaders do not function totally independently of their sponsor and of how those around them expect them to function."[23]

Following a highly successful individual, whether on an athletic team or in university administration, can also be fraught with danger for the survival of the new person. Successors to charismatic and effective predecessors will generally inherit a top-performing organization, but often they will be expected to keep it that way or even to make improvements. The sharp increases in salaries of university presidents over the past twenty years (in absolute terms and also relative to faculty salaries, particularly among the public research universities) may also be contributing to higher expectations that in turn lead to higher turnover: "superstar" salaries creating increasingly impatient performance expectations.

Conclusions

One is left with a broad and fundamentally interesting question as a result of these findings and observations: does leadership in fact matter? Put somewhat differently, if research is perhaps inconclusive about the impact of leadership changes or transitions, does leadership itself affect organizational performance? This way of framing the question suggests that leadership changes do indeed matter, since clearly leadership itself matters, as continuing evidence from the presidencies of Clark Kerr,

William Friday, Bill Bowen, and Father Hesburgh, among others, clearly indicates. But obviously it has been difficult to answer the question of whether a presidential transition helps an organization's performance, because connecting the transition event to the performance of the organization depends on the leadership context, on the characteristics of the new and departing presidents, and on whether the college or university needs turning around via fundamental shifts in its organizational environment.

At the same time, leadership transitions clearly have a significant effect on the top management of the institution. Cohesive groups of vice presidents, deans, and department chairs can be a great aid to a new president, or they can act to weaken and disperse the new individual's authority. Chief executive turnover has strong implications for the continuity of top management teams, as studies have steadily shown that presidential changes can lead to sweeping overhauls of top managers and strategic reorientations.

Turnover at the top is reflective of current conditions, but it is also important to future events. In private industry, one thread of research has found that the higher the rate of senior executive departure in the first two years after a leadership change, the worse the performance of the new enterprise. Thus, too much turnover at the top, whether in corporate or college settings, can have a negative impact on the bottom line.

This chapter has presented an overview of the literature on CEO or presidential transitions and also on recent trends in the tenure of service of college and university presidents. Empirical evidence presented here shows that the length of service of university presidents has been declining; that internal (as opposed to external or outside) presidents tend to serve longer tenures, but that internal candidates are less likely to be hired today; that current university presidents, particularly those at the larger institutions, are older at the time of initial appointment; that the more frequent search processes and the increased turnover at the top has led to the use of more interim or acting presidents, especially in the public universities; that presidential turnover is closely associated with increased turnover in other senior posts, leading in many instances to greater organizational instability rather than to an increased ability for the organization to adapt and change; and that increasing presidential salaries, relative to those paid to the most senior faculty, have contributed to the increased turnover.

A central element in the survival of presidents is the role of the board, a role that is both complex and quite difficult to analyze except perhaps on a case-by-case basis. In this context, among the factors that appear to be most relevant are the changing roles of trustees and their shorter terms in office and the emergence of public systems of governance. Proactive boards of trustees, in noting these trends, will be well served to consider the conditions leading to higher turnover and to study carefully ways to bring more stability and continuity to their institutions.

II

Action

CHAPTER FIVE

The Role of the Board in Presidential Transition

William A. Weary

> The neutral zone is the individual's and the organization's best chance for creativity, renewal, and development. . . . This gap between the old and the new is the time when innovation is most possible and when revitalization begins.

The board is the key to a successful presidential transition. No matter what the kind of institution or the circumstances of the transition, no group but the board has the power and the perspective to manage the overall process right. Moreover, a transition offers the board multiple strategic opportunities to strengthen the entire institution. Smart boards always prepare for transitions to come, and boards that steadily reflect on how best to handle future transitions prove best prepared for them and manage them most effectively. Some would add that they experience fewer of them, as well.

In a transition, much of what happens relates directly to the relationship the board already has with its departing president. In the context of a trusting and open relationship, mutually expressed appreciation, regular and respected reviews of both board and presidential performance, and clear institutional goals, boards are unlikely to be surprised by sudden departures. As a presidency evolves, the president and board leaders will naturally have conversations on the future of their relationship. Of course, under troubled circumstances, such flexibility and grace may be less prevalent, the anxiety greater, and, on any number of fronts, the chances of failure more significant.

Nevertheless, whether in a large research university, a comprehensive urban university, a small liberal arts college, or a community college, a number of key transition factors must be addressed by the board:

—Arranging for the outgoing president's departure

—Setting up and leading the search

—Seizing related opportunities elsewhere in the institution's life

—Bringing in the new president

Wise boards identify a single group—a small transition steering committee—to talk through the multitude of jobs to be completed, think on how best to address them, and bring back recommendations to the full board, as necessary. Whether the steering committee is formally charged with such an assignment or works informally in the background, its work will play a major role in setting a coherent course of action for the years of transition ahead. Such a group often forms unofficially over a president's final years at an institution to encompass discussion of their future together.

Membership varies from one institution to another. In a liberal arts college with a large board and a powerful and regularly meeting executive committee, that group might take on this task; if it is heavily occupied with other institutional business, it might designate another group. Within public institutions, open meeting and open record laws play a determining role in how such a group may be formed and may work. Particularly in institutions with complex governing structures—such as state universities with advisory boards and a system board, or institutions with religious affiliations—careful advance consultation with relevant multiple governing structures is important in assembling the committee. A campus liaison should be designated to assist the committee with its work.

A word of caution: There is an understandable tendency in the midst of a leadership transition to begin to assume that the sitting president no longer is president and to develop "collateral" communication directly with vice presidents and others on campus as if the president did not exist. Anxious groups and individuals can encourage such communication, which multiplies the challenges for the incoming president. Additionally, rather than continuing to question itself about its own parameters, the transition steering committee can sometimes too easily slip into the role of substitute board. The intent should be to coordinate and guide—not supervise—transition activities.

Arranging for the Outgoing President's Departure

Timing

One of the most difficult questions the transition steering committee must address will be the circumstances of the outgoing president's departure. Issues surrounding that departure will require a considerable investment of time, even before the transition is officially announced, and careful advance thought in this area will pay dividends throughout the process and well into the next presidency.

Although different scenarios frequently are encountered, the largest number of candidates for a presidency expect to start work at the close of the academic year, sometime between June 1 and July 1. Alternative departure dates are to be discouraged, unless an acting president is to be hired for the intervening months. Most worrisome can be a president's stated commitment "to continue until my replacement is found." In fact, if the right new president is to be found, he or she will expect a firm starting date—and the search committee will also need deadlines to accomplish this objective. Of course, the president may not be in the position to decide when to depart, and the board will need to assume the final responsibility for this decision and for designing and leading a smooth transition.

Searches typically take about six months to complete (not including summer), and successful candidates—and institutions—need time to make plans for the change. Appointments for July 1 tend to be made late in one calendar year or at the start of the next, and the largest number of potential candidates will be available from late in the previous spring through early autumn. Thus, if the board asks its president sometime in the spring to leave at the close of a given academic year, trustees should be open to the possibility of securing the services of an interim president. The institution will also typically compensate the outgoing president for the next year as well, particularly if that individual did not have time to find other academic employment so late in the year.

In some instances, the president will announce to the board an immediate departure or one not far enough in the future to allow a proper search (see chapter 7). Although some board members might be tempted to respond in an aggressive manner, wise boards bite their tongues, smile, graciously thank the departing president for services rendered, and identify an interim for the year to come. Sometimes that unexpected interim year proves to be one of the institution's most valuable and productive (see chapter 10).[1]

Terms

Working out the conditions of the departure can prove especially challenging, particularly if the president's contract has not articulated them. Retirement bonuses, possible employment and level of compensation as a professor at the same institution, health benefits, and numerous other possibilities may arise. Negotiations with counsel are advisable and often are necessary.

The following guidelines may prove helpful in working out the terms.

Spell things out. If the current contract does not address postpresidential relationship to the institution, make sure the next one does.

Prepare to justify. If they are not legally required to be public from the outset, terms of any agreement nevertheless almost always end up public. Thus, the board must be able to justify, within the context of its president's performance and the institution's financial condition and precedents, whatever arrangements are made.

Resist any attempts to offer fall-back employment. Particularly in the departure of a president who has served long and well, pressures can arise from numerous quarters "to keep the president involved." Sometimes boards will consider creating a position like chancellor and asking the former president to play a role in fund-raising. Sometimes boards will suggest asking for an overlap period of six months or a year to break in the new president. They may even speak of appointment to the board. Each of these possibilities—and particularly appointment to the board—carries serious risks to smooth transition, success of the incoming president, and even attracting strong candidates for the position in the first place. If continued employment simply must occur—the board's transition steering committee can take a very strong stand—the outgoing president's new and annual contract (as "consultant to the president") should be issued by the incoming president, to whom the former president is to report. The new president then may make such use of the predecessor as is appropriate—including no use. But what a set of decisions to thrust on a new and still vulnerable president!

Resolve the residence question. A related issue may be the president's place of residence after retirement. Although boards are not in a position to dictate with respect to housing off institutional property, trustees will need to determine with the outgoing president the date at which her or his house—if it is the institution's property—will be empty and available for renovation. Plans for such normal refurbishment should be made and approved by the board in advance of the new president's arrival.[2]

Announcement, Celebration, and Final Tasks

Three matters remain for the board to resolve with respect to the departing president.

1. *Announce the date.* Careful thought must be given to how best to announce departures planned long in advance. As a rule, the announcement should follow quickly after the final decision and attendant arrangements. Leaked announcements end presidencies sadly and prevent appropriate celebration of one era's close and the inauguration of the next.

2. *Convey gratitude.* The board and the president together should define the best ways to announce the departure and convey gratitude. Typical scripts include capturing the accomplishments of the era coming to an end and educating the institution's constituencies on how much has been accomplished, conveying the confidence the board has in the institution's future, and communicating the importance of the transition to draw the community together and clarify its strategic objectives.

3. *Finish final tasks.* While making clear that the president remains president until his or her term has ended, the board should work out with precision the president's exact remaining responsibilities. Included here would be any special projects the president is uniquely qualified to complete and appropriate engagement in the search process, if any.

Finally, it should be added that some outgoing presidents will experience difficulties in disengaging from the institution. During the search, this problem can manifest itself as a running and public commentary on the search process, attempts to discover the names of candidates, injection of opinions on finalists, and comments on the board's ability to manage the process. After the new president's installation, the outgoing president may make subtle and derogatory comments about the board, the institution, or the successor. Some former presidents may continue to "hold court" with various trustees or attend institutional events uninvited. In these instances, the chair of the board bears the primary responsibility to visit the president and correct the situation. Boards should also discipline any of their own members involved in these situations.

Setting Up and Leading the Search

Without comparison, the most complex and difficult task the board faces within the transition process is setting up and leading the search. Searches are magnets for politics and problems; land mines cover the route and devastate the unwary. Searches are most successful when they follow a thorough, appropriately inclusive process that has been carefully thought through and articulated in advance. Instinct runs counter to experience, however, and the natural tendency of many boards is to appoint the search committee as quickly as possible, to generate candi-

Best Practices

- Appoint a board-led steering committee to think through, guide, and oversee the overall transition.
- Use the transition process to raise institutional awareness and understanding of the board, the presidency, and the institutional agenda.
- Prepare a comprehensive, inclusive leadership statement to guide the president and the institution over the next three to five years.
- Utilize the transition event to update board policies and procedures and improve board performance.
- Make use of large-group interventions to welcome, orient, and educate the new president.

dates, and to make the decision. Unfortunately, while quick actions can briefly assuage the anxieties of various trustees, they also place a low ceiling on the full possibilities of the transition process. An ad hoc search is an opportunity wasted, yet only the board can make this decision, and it will have to stand united against many calls to cut to the chase.

Preparation for the search tends to fall out into four areas. Before moving into them—some of them can be tackled concurrently—the transition steering committee, as well as individual board members, should pause and access many of the resources available on presidential search. The Association of Governing Boards of Universities and Colleges (AGB) in Washington, D.C., offers not only short and long works on the search process but also guidelines for selecting a search consultant.[3] AGB also presents an annual workshop at its National Conference on Trusteeship, as well as a workshop it tailors to individual institutions. The *Chronicle of Higher Education* and its online Career Network carry regular features on presidential search and individual searches.[4]

1. Identification of Constraints and Possibilities

Many boards discover the constraints upon their search work too late. By ferreting out all possible such limitations in advance, the board—through the transition steering committee—can fashion a process that withstands the inevitable questions and anxieties that accompany any search. The research into constraints begins with the bylaws, the charter, applicable code or the state constitution, and regulations of relevant religious bodies. It produces any and all references to

—The president

—Presidential search

—Presidential search committees, their roles, and their membership

—The appointment of standing, ad hoc, and special board committees

—How a presidential appointment is made

—All other institutional governance documents, including bargaining agreements

—How other searches at the institution are conducted

—Applicable rules within a state system for conduct of presidential searches

—Records of how member institutions in the system actually have led their searches

—Guidelines, restrictions, definitions, and search assistance as applied at other and similarly affiliated religious institutions

—State legislation and rulings on open meetings, open records, freedom of information, and their relevance to presidential searches and search committees

—Definitions of *confidentiality* (changes in the rules in the middle of a search often result in a suddenly empty applicant pool)[5]

—Definitions of *public official* and their applicability to public university employees

—Records of the last presidential search

—The possible impact on the search of key politicians, church leaders, alumni, donors, and media

If the board does not perform this research itself and incorporate the results into wise decisions, others may undertake it on their own and perhaps put into question the credibility of the search process.

2. Consideration of the Search's Logistical Implications

Searches are filled with procedural decisions of varying levels of difficulty and ought to be thought through carefully before the official start. Rapid appointment of a search committee and launch of the search not only exposes the institution to dangers; it also prevents making the most of many opportunities.

Informed by the results of their research related to constraints and possibilities, the transition steering committee can address the following issues:

—The search committee: size, membership, method of selection, tasks, recommendations, the chair

—The leadership statement: prepared by search consultant, another consultant, board committee, board, "large group intervention," or some combination of these

—Internal candidates

—Confidentiality

—Expenses, budgeting, and disbursements

—Staff support

—Retention of the services of a search consultant[6]

—Range of presidential compensation

—Final dissolution of the search committee

—Role of the board

3. Preparation of a Charge to the Search Committee

Often overlooked or ignored is the opportunity to put the results of all this preparatory research into a document that prescribes just how the search committee is to go about its work. That board-approved charge to the search committee, written by the transition steering committee, is formally presented to the search committee, along with a code of ethics for its members to sign.[7] Posted on the Web site, the charge and the code serve as witnesses to the board's level of care in this most important of board responsibilities. The charge and the code also guide the search committee every step of the way and help prevent the politically motivated attempts of individuals and groups to shape the process in ways favorable to them and their causes.

4. Preparation of a Comprehensive Leadership Statement

Another of the significant—and, unfortunately, underutilized—board opportunities in a search is insistence on the preparation of a comprehensive leadership statement.

Appropriately prepared only in advance of the search, before the personalities of candidates have shaped constituents' opinions, the very public leadership statement outlines the work the institution must perform during the next presidency and translates that institutional agenda into the characteristics of the individual most likely to succeed in advancing the agenda. The leadership statement is not a job description that specifies what a president of any institution of higher education must do at any moment in its history; it is, rather, a statement of what this institution, at this moment in its history, requires and, accordingly, what kind of person is sought to do that work.[8]

Well-prepared leadership statements serve the following additional purposes:

—Provide a fixed, objective, and reliable grid for decision making.

—Appropriately engage the institution's multiple constituencies in the search. Through interviews and retreat settings, constituents can reflect together on the institution's history, current situation, and future prospects. They then see their perspectives reflected in the statement, and as a result, they pay closer attention to the search and invest trust in the process. Moreover, this work also grounds the entire search in important institutional realities.

—Help create a single vision on campus. Individuals and groups come to understand, in a larger context, where the institution has been, where it is headed, and how their own particular contributions matter. Finalists, as they visit the campus, are met by a unified sense of the work to be done. A basic reason for failed searches is lack of a single, clear vision, resulting in alternative, sometimes conflicting, answers to core questions about the college or university's future priorities.

—Capture the attention of potential candidates. Every institution, from community colleges to research universities, not only has very specific work it must accomplish; it also has capable potential candidates eager to tackle it. If the particularities of a given position do not emerge until the end of the process, those candidates still in the pool may or may not be able and willing to address them. Boards should not rely on candidates' skillful questioning of the search committee to learn the specific challenges the institution faces. Nor should boards "reveal the truth"—almost as a courtesy—only to those candidates who make it to the end of the process. A public and honest leadership statement from the start is essential, and only the board can require it.

—Force candidates, from the outset, to assess—in a letter of interest that responds to the statement—how their skills and experience equip them to meet the institution's challenges.

—Arguably, increase the likelihood of greater diversity in the applicant pool.[9]

—Provide the new president with a coherent list of expectations for those early years in the position. The campus, the board, and the broader community—alumni, parents, institutional partners, and state and local corporate and political leaders—all can look at the president's work and see expectations realized. The grid for presidential and institutional accountability already is in place.

—Become the centerpiece of a comprehensive presidential assessment process several years after appointment. The statement also encourages ongoing board and board member assessment.

Given the multiple benefits of such statements, one might assume that they are a constant in any presidential search. They are not. Recent considerations of presidential transition have made clear that frankness is one of the areas with greatest potential for smooth transition and effectiveness in a new president. In both *Presidential Succession and Transition: Beginning, Ending, and Beginning Again* and *American College President,* recently appointed presidents indicated that undisclosed issues and problems hampered their transitions into office. Ross and Green report that 80 percent of the new presidents they studied discovered at least one significant problem that was not disclosed during the search process. In both studies, financial and budgetary problems were the most common undisclosed issues. Others included personnel problems, accreditation issues, failing fundraising campaigns, pending litigation, technology challenges, problems with facilities, campus conflicts, and trustees with personal "agendas" or who were not supportive of the candidate's appointment. Some of the newly appointed presidents in this study reported that the issues thrust upon them had the potential to make them either a hero or goat early in their tenure. Some of these undisclosed problems had serious political implications for their successful transition into the presidency, but were not of strategic importance for the institution.[10]

One useful recent publication, *The Well-Informed Candidate: A Brief Guide for Candidates for College and University Presidencies,* in an implicit recognition of this sorry state of affairs, even urges candidates to do the necessary institutional research themselves.[11]

What do boards and search committees tend to use, then, as they advertise the presidential opening? Often they collect—through various means, including e-mail—constituent opinions on "what kind of a president we want," hoping that such descriptions suffice, and they end up with a list of clichéd academic virtues ("collegial decision making," "visionary style," "integrity and honesty," "strong communications"). Those virtues—undetectable in any résumé or letter of interest—bear no necessary correlation to the work the institution and president must do.

Generic leadership statements generate generic candidates, fail to attract the right candidates, and facilitate later problems as newly appointed presidents—and, sadly, their boards—discover the truth. Good leadership statements take time to prepare. Two or more days of interviews with a cross section of constituents can reveal answers to three basic questions:

1. What are the key challenges, opportunities, and issues that the next president must address within the next several years?
2. What are the essential professional experiences and skills that will qualify someone to successfully address those challenges, opportunities, and issues?
3. What kind of personality will succeed within this institution's cultural and historical context?

The leadership statement itself moves through the many sectors of the institution's life, telling each one's story, what must be done next, and what kind of person will succeed in making that happen. The document may be drafted either through a special board committee or the search committee, and sometimes it is best to have it assembled for either group by an outside consultant skilled in that work.

The role of the board—working through the transition steering committee—first is to insist that this piece of the search be done and be done right. Abdicating this responsibility wastes a precious opportunity. Too often it also produces some combination of discord, search failure, stymied presidency, and turnover.[12] The role of the board also is to approve the statement once written, since the board holds itself responsible to that statement as it makes its final selection.

Develop a Detailed Communications Plan

It is a truism, unfortunately not always respected, that the chair of the search committee alone speaks for the committee and that all questions posed to members are referred to the chair. Moreover, members of the search committee other than the chair should not even communicate about the search with other members of the board. Assuming that they legally may be kept confidential, names of candidates and details about them also are unknown to the board.

Conversely, searches provide extraordinary opportunities for essential institutional communication and education. Another task force, no doubt staffed by someone from the institution's office of community relations, should consider developing a comprehensive communications plan for the transition. Such a plan, if well prepared, can accomplish the following objectives:

—Remind (and instruct) constituents of all sorts—including those in the legislature, the church, the foundation, and the alumni association—about the institution's governance structures. Helpful reminders of how decisions are made—and in what context—rarely can be made too often.

—Focus the community on the institution's recent accomplishments and story, thereby making the institution feel justifiably good about its work—as well as become aware of it.

—Define "reality" for the years to come.

—Advance the institution's shared vision.

—Keep constituents—and the media—appropriately informed at all stages of the search.

Beyond the courtesy and respect that such communication provides—at a necessarily anxious moment in an institution's life—is the opportunity to develop a constituency far more knowledgeable than it has been in years. Of course, the potential of Web sites for such communication has only begun to be tapped. Those institutions utilizing them successfully are aware of their value.[13]

Address Key Presidential Employment Conditions Early On

Recently appointed presidents complain about having to accept offers without adequately understanding the conditions of employment.[14] The way to prevent such a situation is to start and complete the research early, learn the answers, and share the results with finalists as they come onto campus. Do not allow candidates a long period of time to reflect on an offer, because the others in the pool of finalists can evaporate during that time. Appointment of a task force on compensation guides the board's work here.

Compensation issues arise early in the search process. Interested candidates wish to have some general idea of the range considered, and search consultants can serve the institution better if they, too, have this information. Some of the issues can be thorny: how, for instance, does one compensate a relatively young, first-time president who follows a long-term, beloved president? Addressing such issues up front can retain finalists in the pool up to the end and also prevent potentially long-standing grudges.

Boards display appropriate effectiveness in areas of compensation by addressing these issues specifically:

—Becoming educated in the complexities of presidential compensation. There are some good materials and relatively frequent workshops on the subject.[15]

—Creating a list of peer institutions, sometimes aided by an expert in presidential compensation, and examining the compensation the peer groups' presidents receive.

—Considering conditions of employment offered the last president and possibly available to the next, such as a house on campus.

—Exploring alternative contracts. An attorney with experience in the field of presidential compensation can play an instrumental role.

—Taking time, often through the search consultant and sometimes through the attorney, to ascertain finalists' needs and wants.

The Presidential Contract

As a wise board enters the search process—whether at its own initiative or the president's—a sound presidential contract is already in place. That contract spells out carefully how the institution will reward and relate to the president during and after departure, with respect to deferred compensation, severance pay, health and other benefits, continuing service to the institution as professor, terminal sabbatical, and so forth. Should the departure prove less than happy, the board will thank itself many times over for having taken the time and trouble to work the contract out right. It may well spare itself costly and painful litigation as well. Should the departure mark the close of a long and successful presidency, the board will be thankful that it can focus on the search and on celebrating the outgoing president, rather than having to enter a process of negotiation that may leave individuals on both sides with an unfortunate and sour taste in their mouths.[16]

Of course, not every board will have a good contract in place when the transition begins. If not, then the board's steering transition committee will want to allow sufficient time to work out the details of the departure with the president. Careful probing can reveal the president's real hopes and, often, mutually satisfactory means to achieve them. Remember that the terms of the departure probably will become public—even in a private institution—and that the board must be able to justify its decisions within the context of its own and similar institutions. Sound legal counsel that is experienced in presidential transitions is invaluable. As in negotiation of the contract in the first place, an outside specialist in this field of law keeps the institution's own counsel free of potentially damaging conflict of interest.

With respect to the incoming president, the steering committee already will have given early and careful thought to the contract—long before finalists even appear on campus. Assembling data on peers' compensation, identifying a specialist in presidential contracts to begin thinking through possibilities, and deciding on the range of compensation to be awarded allow impressive and knowledgeable early conversations with both finalists and the newly selected president. If the board has not completed its preparations early on, it may well decide to fall back on a letter of agreement with the new president and secure the contract later. This option is far less desirable than the first and can lead to disagreements and ill feelings as the final contract eventually is put into place. As elsewhere in the search process, the best opportunities for success require advance thought and decision.

Boards also should remember that presidents today expect to work under carefully prepared contracts (and expect to negotiate for them), are impressed with boards that have done their homework, and, through their insistence on negotiating a sound contract from the start, tend to leave boards that have not done their homework feeling both embarrassed and inadequate. No one wants an awkward and uneasy start to a presidency.

Treating the Transition Process as a Strategic Opportunity

Effective transitions provide institutions with numerous opportunities to review and strengthen their current operations. The transition steering committee should consider carefully all of these possibilities and delegate to special task forces or existing committees responsibility for the following matters:

1. The Role of the Outgoing President

The role of the outgoing president not only is an essential early discussion in the transition (as noted above); it is also an exceptional institutional opportunity. Careful identification of projects for the outgoing president to complete does much to overcome the customary "lame duck" status and even confers something of the productivity of an interim upon her or him.

So, if at all possible, the transition steering committee should, with the president, prepare a list of the major institutional events to occur within the coming several years. Included could be accreditation procedures (regional and individual-program reviews), capital campaigns, anniversary celebrations, significant projects, and retirements or expected departures of other key leaders (in the administration and on the board).[17] Which of these can the outgoing president most successfully address, and which should fall to the incoming leader?

2. Compensation Policy

Issues of the range of actual compensation also figure early in a search, while also conferring a substantial institutional opportunity.

As noted, newly appointed presidents increasingly expect carefully written contracts at the start of their terms in office.[18] Since preparation of a well-crafted contract takes considerable time, the period of a presidential search is ideal for such research. The same group examining levels of compensation also addresses policies.

New regulations (in 2001) from the Internal Revenue Service have increased attention to compensation policy and practice. Concerned with the "excessive compensation" some boards offered their chief executive officers in the 1990s, and unwilling to rescind nonprofit status for such a reason alone, the IRS developed a series of "intermediate sanctions" for private nonprofit institutions (501[c][3]) and for public institutions whose officers receive a portion of their compensation from a legally separate university foundation.

The regulations require of these institutions written policies detailing how adjustments to compensation are awarded, evidence of what presidents at comparable institutions are earning, and demonstration of a connection between adjustment to compensation and review of presidential performance.[19] The IRS holds board members individually and personally responsible for enforcement of these regulations.[20]

Again, most boards are well served to retain the services of an expert in the field to assist the task force with this generation of policy and bring back recommendations to the board.

3. Presidential Performance Review

In keeping with its review of compensation policy and treating the transition as a strategic opportunity, boards are advised to use this period also to consider their existing policies on presidential assessment and to update them as necessary. The task force addressing compensation might also assume this responsibility. The process should address these issues, among others:

—Strong presidential candidates today demand sound assessment policies. The board's dedication to this issue in the course of the search reads well.

—Initiating or altering assessment procedures during the course of a presidency necessarily raises questions about the sitting president's status with respect to the board; that is, "What did the president do wrong?" The transition period's neutral status allows for review and policy-writing without political implication and impact.

—Clear assessment policies, linked to strong leadership statements, form a natural, solid foundation for presidential expectations and assessing performance against them.

Many presidential assessments, particularly within private institutions, continue to amount to little more than an annual conversation with the board chair. Policies within state higher education systems still often display unfortunate characteristics of an earlier era, such as anonymous numerical surveys distributed on campus and reported out with "mathematical accuracy"; reliance on generic lists of presidential responsibilities rather than criteria that relate to this president and this institution at this moment in their conjoined history; or the requirement that members of a system board—rather than the system executive only—all rate their presidents' performances, often in multiple areas of presidential responsibility on which members normally are incompetent to pass judgment.

The evidence fortunately also suggests that institutions throughout higher education increasingly are interested in the development of sound policy and procedure. The upside potential for stronger board-president relationships, better performance, and longer effective tenure is significant.

Best practice in presidential assessment is becoming clearer.[21] At its annual National Conference on Trusteeship, AGB offers an all-day workshop on presidential and board assessment. Not only does presidential assessment rest on annual setting of goals with the president and on the president's self-assessment according to them; it also includes a comprehensive "360 degree" review every five years or so, normally best led by an outside consultant. Ideally, presidential assessment also includes board goal-setting and self-assessment at least every several years, considering board performance as part of the comprehensive presidential performance review, and assessing the work of individual board members as well (see section 4 below).

The lessons learned from several decades now of presidential performance reviews are clear. Presidential assessment works best

—When it has as its major purpose improvement of the president's performance.

—When it engages the president in the process.

—When it occurs within the context of ongoing, expressed support for the president's work.

—When it rests upon clearly stated criteria for performance.

—When it makes use of reliable evidence.

—When it ties into the board's assessment of its own performance.

—When it forms one piece of institution-wide goal-setting and accountability.

—When it occurs as part of a comprehensive policy of presidential performance reviews and is linked with the board's.

—When it respects and strengthens the presidency, the board, and governance.

Poorly designed and led presidential performance reviews not only damage the president, the presidency, the institution, and the board; they can also insult the president, warp the president's relationship with the board, and result in unhappy and early departures.

Once again, careful thought throughout the transition period—and preparation of adequate overall assessment policies—offers an invaluable opportunity to build a mutually rewarding relationship of board and president and institutional stability and productivity as well.

4. Governance Audit Process

One final institutional opportunity that the transition steering committee does well to address is the board's own performance. A governance audit could incorporate one or more of these forms:

—A series of board discussions at each board meeting.

—Review of the bylaws and other governance documents.

—Examination of board membership, structure, and committee work.

—Consideration of board meeting formats and agendas.

—Assessment of how well the board is advancing the objectives in its own leadership statement.

—Development of appropriate policies and procedures for regular assessment of its performance. One standard approach combines annual presidential performance reviews based on the president's self-assessment, board self-assessments every several years, and comprehensive, joint board and presidential performance reviews led by an outside facilitator every five years.

—A retreat, led by an outside facilitator, to draw together the pieces outlined above and result in a long-term board agenda, an agenda that can be used to attract, orient, and develop board members; guide committees; focus board discussion; and permit future assessment.[22]

The opportunity presented by this transition again must be stressed: for some years after arrival, new presidents cannot be expected to tackle fundamental, normally difficult, and sometimes time-sensitive governance issues such as term limits, bylaws, moribund advisory boards, dead committees, excessively large or small board size, the lack of assessment of individual board members' performance, report-oriented and stale board meetings, and domineering executive committees. Effective board performance is a hallmark of the successful institution and presidency. The time to begin is now.

Managing Relationships between Outgoing and Newly Appointed Presidents

The impatience that drives some boards to plunge into a search without adequate preparation can also tempt them to turn to the newly selected president for decisions that appropriately belong to the outgoing one. The current president still is president! And the new president no doubt still has a job as well!

The board's transition committee ideally will have talked over with the outgoing president the tasks best handled within her or his final months and year(s), so good guidelines should be in place. But another conversation, this time involving the newly elected president, makes sense in the context of the issues that always arise late in the transition process. Many of the final issues to be addressed, of course, tend to have to do with personnel and appointments. The new president may well have preferences regarding how to proceed, and there may be ways—here and elsewhere—in which the outgoing president can be of special service in smoothing the transition. The new president, for instance, might prefer that the predecessor focus on completing one project rather than another. It is appropriate for the board to initiate this first meeting.

The two presidents ideally will develop a strong and open relationship during the final months of the transition, a relationship that can continue into the months and years ahead. Open statements of confidence in each other and their work, past and future, will pay handsome dividends for years to come.

A well-celebrated departure of the outgoing president not only demonstrates class; it also allows the institution to close the preceding era and move toward the new. The opportunity is to help ghosts from the past relax and depart. Taking the trouble to hold such celebrations even in the face of a less-than-fully-happy departure is worthwhile. A word of caution: Be careful not to invite the new president to the full "roast" of the outgoing. Give the departing president his or her due, undiluted!

Of course, the board will wish to bring the newly appointed president to campus for celebration as well and to indicate its desire that she or he take a week (compensated, as any such work performed in advance of assuming office should be) to meet with as many members of the community—internal and external—as possible. This moment marks the last time the new president can ask questions and listen as an outsider.

Some boards believe that an overlap of outgoing and incoming president will ease the transition process. Not only is an overlap not necessary to build the desired productive relationship between the two presidents; it tends to create unnecessary tensions and confusion and to frustrate the shift from one leader to the next.

Bringing the New President Aboard

Presidents joke, halfheartedly, about being "dropped at the gate" after the enthusiasm of their appointment has passed. Of course, the high-level, focused energy required of the institution in the course of any transition must abate. Too often, though, the decline begins too soon.

The board's transition steering committee will be wise now to begin delegating the innumerable logistic tasks surrounding the entry of a new president to a welcoming committee of members of the board and the broader community. Some very helpful resources can guide the work of such a committee as it sees to issues of housing, schooling, the spouse's employment, and introductions to a wide range of institutional and community leaders.[23]

Some institutions go several steps further. The power of well-constructed retreats is exceptional in building consensus, setting goals, and focusing energies, throughout the institutional community. One institution, a midsize, religiously affiliated comprehensive university, assembled a three-pronged approach to launching its new presidency:

—As the new president arrived, early in July, the board and the president took over a mountain retreat house for several days, with spouses. Reviewing the university's recent turbulent history, its current situation, and its prospects, the board also examined its own function and emerged with work for both the president and itself to accomplish in the year and years to come. An enormous sense of goodwill—some said relief—pervaded the retreat and also raised excitement and expectancy for the years ahead. Moreover, trustees, spouses, and president and spouse all came to know one another, to feel more comfortable together, and to begin to enjoy one another's company. As important, the president left knowing where to focus his energies, and the board left with clear expectations, some new task forces, and a series of assignments for each standing committee.

—Late in September, the president took his cabinet, deans, and other university leaders to a different retreat center for another several-day session. Working through similar exercises and regenerating the university's agenda, the members of the administration came to know one another and their new president better, shared their own individual dreams, and created a shared vision, one that also matched that of the board from two months before. The president left with yet greater clarity about his work and with a deeper, ground-level knowledge of the institution and its challenges.

—In January, the president called a day-long workshop for more than one hundred members of the broader university community, including not only trustees and administrators, but also faculty, staff, students, alumni, local community leaders, and former trustees. Once again, the institutional agenda not only emerged but also lined up almost exactly with the others. Participants were able to watch their new president in action, and he was able to meet and work with large numbers of significant constituents he'd not yet met. The powerful sense of unity that emerged from the day spread forth on campus. Considerable alignment of the university already had occurred.

Later that spring, using the agendas generated in the three retreats, the president appointed a priorities and budget committee to begin assembling a new strategic plan. With basic assent on underlying directions, the process moved forward rapidly and also included creation of

Emerging Trends

- Ignoring the opportunities in a well-planned transition because too many boards are simply too pressed and too exhausted to profit.
- Addressing candidates' demands for career advancement together with personal and family well-being.
- Making greater use of Web sites in the transition and presidential search process.
- Making more extensive use of search consultants, attorneys, and strategic planners.
- Employing more interim presidents.

a process to review and restructure all academic programs. When, years later, the president again was ready to plan, similar procedures were used, and this time they resulted in the launch of an extremely successful capital campaign. The acquired habit of using large-group interventions to secure rapid and deep direction allowed this round of retreats to proceed yet more smoothly and effectively.

Not all institutions bring their president aboard with so much focused attention on process, but in this instance many on campus believed that these events were key to a successful launch for the new chief executive officer.

Conclusion: Transition Is Now

All higher education institutions are always in transition, and effective boards are always consciously preparing for "the institution to come." For them, a change in presidential leadership thus occurs smoothly and within a broader, well-defined context. In preparation for that day when it becomes clear that a transition must take place, the experienced trustees will respond with the following portfolio:

—A simple, often surprisingly brief, institutional agenda as guide.

—Current bylaws and policies that apply to present institutional needs and realities.

—Deep knowledge of the institution in the context of higher education institutions nationally and globally.

—A long-term plan, with clear leadership succession guidelines, for the board.

—Thorough knowledge of the needs and future aspirations of all institutional stakeholders.

—Implemented policies to assess the performance of the board itself, its members, and its president.

In the presence of the above, surprises are likely to be rare; presidents are likely to be more effective and long-lasting; and transitions, when they occur, will be seen as a natural, yet strategic, aspect of the board's responsibilities. Indeed, one of the key benefits of an effectively managed presidential transition often is improved board performance, with accompanying increases in institutional and presidential effectiveness along the way.

CHAPTER SIX

A Proactive Model for Presidential Transition

Patricia Stanley and Lee J. Betts

Collegiate management systems are more complex and sophisticated than many governmental or business management models. The lines of authority frequently are muted and unclear. Because the often-conflicting concerns of faculty, trustees, students, and primary supporting constituencies, such as governmental agencies, alumni, and denominational sponsors, all deeply influence the institution's directions and success, a college or university president must have the intuitive ability, wisdom, and interpersonal skills to manage and lead the institution by co-opting and synthesizing the input of each of these varied constituencies.

When a president serves for ten, fifteen, twenty years with effectiveness, mitigating conflicting expectations of primary constituencies, establishing and achieving consensus goals, and constructively resolving major college problems and challenges, her or his style and modus operandi generally have become imprinted upon that institution. When such a president retires or resigns to accept another position, the various institutional constituencies can become apprehensive and insecure. Changes in leadership can be disturbing to any organization, especially when most of the organization's constituencies are comfortable and pleased with the outgoing leadership.

In contrast, the termination of a presidency that has been controversial, unsuccessful, or tarnished by unwise, incapable, or inappropriate leadership, can result in a feeling of relief, even euphoria, on the part of many persons and constituencies associated with the institution. Nevertheless, these feelings can disappear quickly if the process for transition to new leadership appears to be inappropriate or unwise.

Increasingly, college and university governance bodies are appointing experienced collegiate leaders to serve as interim presidents of their institutions. This is especially common when the time period is short between the decision to end a presidency and the outgoing president's departure. While this strategy will not be a main focus of our discussion, this model can provide valuable time to the governing board to develop and execute a carefully crafted procedure for selecting a new president. Interim presidents can also be appointed to resolve institutional problems and constituency disputes and address other matters that need immediate attention. In this sense, the interim approach can be effective in preparing the institution and its constituency for new leadership.

A New Way to Think about Presidential Transitions

This chapter offers a new way to conceptualize and design presidential transitions. Following a review of the pertinent literature, we present a proactive model, which includes five interrelated phases. The first one occurs before the search process begins, and the second occurs during the search process. The critical third phase takes place after the selection of the incoming president but before the retirement and departure of the outgoing president. A fourth component is the role of the former president after the new presidency begins. The final phase occurs at the new president's inauguration. This symbolic transfer of leadership brings closure to one phase of a college's history and launches another with positive expectations.

On 1 January 1998 Patricia Stanley officially became the new president of Frederick Community College (FCC) in Frederick, Maryland, succeeding Lee John Betts, who retired after serving as the college's president for almost twelve years. The following strategic model was collaboratively developed by Betts and Stanley leading up to and following this 1998 transition.

What the Literature Says

Very little that is specific to a *proactive model* for presidential transition has been found in the literature.

In 1986 the American Council on Education (ACE) in cooperation with the Association of Governing Boards of Universities and Colleges (AGB) produced an excellent document providing comprehensive recommendations for improving the search, selection, and negotiation for a college president.[1] It focuses on aspects of the search that may present problems. The recommendations encompass a great variety of issues but touch on the actual transition lightly. Quoting Clark Kerr's statement that "the responsibility of the board for a new president does not end with a sigh of relief and a crossing of the fingers," the document stresses the importance of the board's role in the presidential transition.[2] ACE and AGB recommend that the chair or another member of the board spearhead transition planning that will include introducing the new president and any family members to the college community and various constituencies and providing information on institutional politics, campus life, and the institution's history.

One of the most practical articles relating to presidential transitions appeared in the November–December 1993 edition of *Case Currents*. Allison Noonan, assistant to the president for college relations at Finger Lakes Community College, New York, provides numerous examples from different institutions of successful transition strategies in an article entitled "Introductions All Around."[3] She emphasizes four phases of a smooth, well-planned transition, focusing on the introduction of a new president. The phases are ushering in the announcement, making the formal presentation, getting to know the community, and continuing to get to know the community. Examples abound.

In 1996 Alan E. Guskin told college and university trustees that plans should be made for a brief presidential transition process lasting a number of months.[4] His article in *Trusteeship* suggests setting up a transition team to pave the way for the new college or university president. He lists briefly six steps to accomplish the team's goals. Guskin states, "No period is more important for creating a successful president than the time span starting from the appointment and continuing through the first six months of service."[5]

In his book *Balancing the Presidential Seesaw*, George Vaughan's chapter on transitions outlines case studies that provide insights on how that critical period can go wrong. "Do not assume things are going well," he comments, "just because you do not hear complaints."[6]

Kevin E. Drumm presents a story of difficulties that perhaps could have been prevented with a proactive transition.[7] His dissertation case study of Dr. James Baker's presidency at Buckingham Community College revealed a president whose leadership style was substantially mismatched with the demands of the college he had come to lead. The president's collegial leadership style clashed with an organizational culture more accustomed to bureaucratic, top-down leadership. Two of this study's conclusions reflect the need for transition planning: (1) followers' expectations for a new leader bear heavily on the transition period, and (2) leadership transitions substantially set the stage for a leader's subsequent success or failure.

Judith Block McLaughlin, chair of the Harvard Seminar for New Presidents, provides some insights into a proactive transition model in her studies. She suggests that new presidents should design and follow a carefully structured plan to learn about the institution that they have been called to serve.[8] McLaughlin also suggests that the board and the institution participate in drafting the transition plan, which becomes the new president's first act of leadership.

Before the Search Process Begins

It is important that the outgoing president and the governing board of the college clarify all aspects of the president's departure and that the board, in cooperation with the president, determine how the president's departure will be announced to the college community, the press, and other key constituencies. Anticipating questions that may come from the press and others, the board, preferably in consultation with the outgoing president, should reach certain conclusions regarding the transition. The board should provide enough information to the college constituencies and the public to provide assurance that the board is planning a comprehensive, well-thought-out process for the selection of a new president and that college faculty, staff, students, and other appropriate constituencies will be afforded opportunity to provide input when appropriate. At the same time, the governing body should emphasize that the appropriate governing board or boards will make the final decision.

The role of the outgoing president in this process must fit the circumstances. Certainly, when the departure of a president is precipitated by the president's death, serious illness, or other unfortunate occurrences, such as illegal or immoral activities, the president will play little or no part in determining the above actions. However, when the president's departure is for positive reasons, such as retirement or acceptance of another position, it is wise for the governing board to seek his or her advice while retaining its right to make all final decisions.

However, although the departing president may have strong feelings about potential candidates, she or he should not recommend, promote, or denigrate potential candidates. But the president should provide accurate information about candidates the president knows when requested unless there are reasons for not doing so. The outgoing president should not interfere with the selection process determined by the board.

Many private colleges follow a more informal procedure, whereby the president and the board collaborate on the decision-making process for the new president. This is especially true in colleges that have strong affiliations with religious denominations or cohorts and small private colleges that are primarily family owned. It is not unusual in such cases for the departing president to become the chief development officer for the college, while an experienced senior manager is elevated to the presidency to provide institutional leadership and management oversight. Whatever the process, it is advisable to encourage as many persons as possible from key college constituencies to have input into the selection process. As a result these people will have ownership in the final selection, and the more that people feel a sense of ownership in the decision, the more they will be likely to enthusiastically support the new presidency.

At Frederick Community College, the most recent presidential transition began with a decision by the outgoing president to retire. As Betts passed his sixty-second birthday and began his eleventh year as president of Frederick Community College (FCC), he remembered an informal comment from a former professor: "You should have a good reason to leave [a major leadership position] before five years or to stay longer than ten." He had explained that a dynamic organization needed a degree of continuity in leadership. Yet, to remain dynamic, both organizations and leaders need to change and grow.

During the summer and fall of 1996, the college's accomplishments over the prior decade were evaluated. The vision Betts had had for the college since his arrival was well on its way to fulfillment. However, he could sense within himself a degree of weariness. A decade of investing scores of weekends and innumerable late evenings in resolving problems, exploring opportunities, and fanning the flames of institutional energy and enthusiasm had taken their toll.

After consulting with his wife and reviewing their potential retirement income, he informed the board of trustees in November 1996 of his plan to retire in December 1997. The announcement of the president's retirement was made by the chair of the college's board of trustees in late November 1996 to the college faculty, staff, and students at a general assembly attended by the press and community leaders.

Designing an Inclusive Search Process

In the FCC model, the college solicited much input from all stakeholders so that the job description used in the search would accurately describe the profile the college constituents wanted to find in a new president. The board of trustees appointed a presidential search and screening committee of approximately twenty persons representing different constituencies. The committee was led by the chair of the board of trustees and had representation from the faculty, the staff, the students, and the broader community. Although less than 10 percent of the county's population consisted of minority persons, five members of the committee were from minority populations, because these populations were expected to grow considerably.

As a key element of the process, the retiring president asked himself, "What role, if any, should I play in the transition from my presidency to another?" He chose to answer this question with another question: "If I were the new president, how best might the outgoing president assist in my transition and affirm my authority?" He reached the following conclusions:

—He would encourage the use of an experienced, outside consulting firm to guide the process and would recommend the involvement of a broad cross section of the college and community in the process. Before Betts became president of Frederick Community College, no one in the college or the community had the opportunity to meet him. This caused needless anxiety and an avalanche of unfounded rumors to precede his arrival. He was pleased that the board followed these recommendations, selecting the Association of Community College Trustees Presidential Search Program to guide the process and inviting everyone within the college to share their perspectives and opinions and meet the final candidates.

—He would respect the authority and responsibility of the board of trustees to select the new president and avoid influencing the board's decision. Ann Abeles, board chair, assumed firm control of the presidential selection process, enthusiastically investing hundreds of hours into guiding and facilitating the selection process.

—The college would provide a comprehensive, carefully planned orientation and transition week for the new president soon after her or his selection.

—He would relocate outside the region immediately upon his retirement.

The role, function, and composition of the search and screening committee are of paramount importance in the search process. During the search process, the following procedures and principles should be considered. A process for reviewing applications should be agreed upon by the entire search committee before the position is advertised. All members of the search committee should pledge to maintain confidentiality regarding the identity of candidates who have submitted applications for the position, including in-house candidates. Criteria for screening applications should also be decided before applications are reviewed. Each member of the committee should have a convenient, secure place to review and evaluate applications. All candidates should have access to relevant information regarding the college and the position. When a decision is made by the committee to no longer consider certain candidates, these persons should be promptly informed.

When the whole committee agrees upon the final candidates, all finalists should be accorded the same opportunities and experiences. The search and screening committee should try to answer all reasonable questions asked by a candidate. Each finalist should depart from the campus after an on-site interview with the confidence that he or she knows the college, its problems and opportunities, and the expectations of the primary stakeholders sufficiently to respond promptly to an invitation to accept the presidency, if it is offered.

The materials sent to candidates before their initial interview were comprehensive and representative of the college's culture, issues, and climate. The interviews and other interactions between the finalists and the college constituencies also provided a good understanding of the college community, the college service area and clientele, the political environment, and the college's relationship with funding agencies.

All finalists experienced a thorough and challenging two-day schedule of interviews that enabled them to meet and talk with groups of students, faculty, staff, administrators, senior managers, campus leaders, and community people. Candidates first met with the eighteen-member search and screening committee, which was representative of all major areas of the college and the communities it served. The committee's questions were thoughtfully prepared and very comprehensive. Returning candidates were interviewed by a dozen other groups, plus local television and newspaper reporters. After those interviews, college faculty, staff, and students were provided opportunities to express their impressions of the candidates to the board by completing brief survey forms.

The finalists also met with the retiring president and the board of trustees. Each finalist had dinner with the board following the formal interview and another dinner with a senior manager and her or his spouse. The spouses of the finalists were invited to attend both dinners so that they also could assess the potential fit between the college and the candidate. Thus, each candidate and the college community had extensive opportunities to measure their comfort with each other's styles, needs, and aspirations.

The FCC board of trustees made the final decision after evaluating all the input. It was unanimous. Upon completion of negotiations with the president-elect, the other candidates were notified by phone and mail and the decision was announced to the college and the public. "Institutions should allow time for the new appointee to notify his or her insti-

Best Practices

- Plan the transition in conjunction with planning the search for the new president.
- Provide closure and recognition for the departing president.
- Invite the departing president to introduce the new president to all important stakeholders, to the degree feasible.
- Utilize the positive symbolism of the inauguration in transition planning.
- Maintain and preserve records from the entire search, transition, and inauguration processes for future teams and committees.

tution and for the search committee to notify other finalists before they hear or read the news in the public media."[9]

After the Selection and before the Retirement

The period between the selection of a new president and the retirement or departure of the outgoing president is frequently short and almost always a busy time for both. The president-elect is generally very busy planning relocation, enjoying farewell events, and wrapping up existing professional responsibilities. The departing president may also be absorbed in similar tasks. Nevertheless, this period of time is ideal for reinforcing the success of the presidential transition.

Many collegiate institutions will appoint a transition team with broad enough representation to work with internal and external audiences. "Public relations professionals should introduce their new 'Star Player' as professionally as any of their corporate counterparts. . . . Your audiences on and off campus will be eager for news of your leader. But remember that your top priority must be to inform internal audiences."[10]

Whenever possible, the president-elect should be invited by the board to participate in an orientation to the college and the community, preferably while the departing president is still on the job. A week or so spent in the community prior to the beginning of the president-elect's official term can be an invaluable component of a proactive transition.

Following is a list of the activities that Frederick Community College prepared for President-elect Stanley for her week of orientation to the college and Frederick County. As often as possible, the outgoing president or the board chair escorted her and introduced her to community leaders.

Orientation Activities

Receptions

—FCC Fund, Inc. (college foundation), member-directors and community leaders, including Fort Detrick officials (Fort Detrick is adjacent to the college campus)

—All college personnel—faculty, staff, administrators

—Frederick County delegation of senators and delegates to the Maryland General Assembly in Annapolis

Dinners

—Retiring president and spouse

—Vice president of academic affairs and her spouse

—Vice president of student development and his spouse

—Vice president of finance and his spouse

—Chair, board of trustees, and her spouse

Luncheons

—Frederick County Commissioners

—Noon Rotary Club

—Administrative assistant and secretaries in the president's office

—Director of human resources

Breakfasts

—Morning Rotary Club

—Frederick Alliance for Creative Education, a consortium consisting of the presidents of private colleges in Frederick County

Appointments and Meetings on Campus

—Senior management team

—Student newspaper staff

—Student government association

—One-on-one with vice president of academic affairs

—One-on-one with vice president of finance

—One-on-one with vice president of student development

—Acting vice president of administration

—Executive director of college foundation (FCC Fund, Inc.)

—President's cabinet

—President's administrative assistant and board secretary

—Director of marketing and public relations

—Board chair and vice chair

—Human resources benefits coordinator

—Final meeting with President Betts

Appointments and Meetings in the Community

—Mayor of Frederick

—Hospital administrators

—Local newspaper and cable TV executives

—President, chamber of commerce

—An informal but regularly meeting group of retired community leaders

A schedule such as the one outlined above is both exhilarating and exhausting, but the contacts made through these special introductions are extremely useful in the first year of a new president's tenure. Each college and university will have stakeholders for the new president to meet. The rule of thumb is to introduce the new president to everyone who will be important to his or her success.

After the New Presidency Begins

It is essential that new presidents be given every opportunity to exercise their authority and responsibilities upon assuming their role. Neither the former president nor the board chair should interfere with their appointed responsibilities. After the new presidency has begun, the former president should refrain from interjecting her or his opinions or influence unless requested to do so by the new president. At the same time, the former president should be available to answer questions or provide further information, if the new president asks. Before leaving the office of the presidency, the former president should discuss with his or her senior assistant and senior managers ways in which they might assist the new president's ongoing orientation to new people and important college issues. If the former president becomes aware of a serious problem emerging in the new presidency, it may be appropriate to inform, without personal comment, either the board chair or the new president.

After stepping down from the presidency, it would be best for the former president not to return to the college frequently, if at all, during the first year of the new presidency, unless invited by the new president. It is often difficult for former presidents to let go, and it is essential that they try to do so.

Letting go of the reins is especially important when the new president is a person who has been promoted from within the college or university and has formerly reported to the former president. Other managers, who were peers of the new president before she or he was promoted, may find it hard to develop a new style of relating to their former peer. When the former president continues to be a frequent presence and influence on campus, his or her presence can weaken the transition, confuse subordinates, and lead to antagonism.

A strong but sensitive board chair can be effective in clarifying roles and dealing positively with these and other related matters. The chair also must respect the authority and responsibilities of the new president and assist this person in dealing constructively with discordant issues that could weaken the new president's long-term effectiveness. Generally, if the departing president is leaving the area or has accepted a new job not associated with the college, the tendency to interfere is not strong, but if the retiring president remains in the community and interacts with college personnel frequently, there may be a strong temptation to interfere.

A few months after becoming president of FCC, Stanley attended a seminar for new presidents at Harvard University. It was there that she first realized that the FCC transition process may have been exceptional.

> The 39 of us attending the seminar swapped stories about our first months as presidents, and my colleagues confirmed that my transition experience was, indeed, a wonderful model compared to the experiences of others. Some of my peers shared stories of the trial-and-error periods they experienced because no assistance had been made available to them. One horror story was of a past president still living on campus, who dispensed advice and criticism of the new president to all who bypassed the new president's office for the unofficial one of the resident sage. I began to understand how fortunate I was that Frederick Community College had allotted time and resources to the transition process.

Emerging Trends

- Presidential tenures have been becoming shorter for more than twenty-five years.
- A significant percentage of college and university presidents will be retiring between 2004 and 2008.
- New presidents are actively seeking more assistance and guidance during their opening months in office.
- Campus inaugural ceremonies are being conceptualized and designed as a symbolic celebration of presidential transition.

The Inauguration Decision

One should never underestimate the importance of what Lee Bolman and Terrence Deal refer to as the symbolic frame of leadership.[11] Judith Block McLaughlin, chair of the Harvard Seminar for New Presidents, told the 1998 seminar class that the inauguration ceremony with all its symbolism was "making a comeback," because it is one of the most important celebrations for the college or university. In the case of FCC, it was a critical part of the transition. In institutional shorthand, the ceremony tells the extended community, "We now have a new leader, and while we celebrate our past successes, we look forward to a promising future." We also believe that this ceremony should authentically reflect the college's culture. At FCC, the ceremony that was implemented was an effective balance of formality and fun, unique while reflecting the values and traditions of the institution.

Lessons Looking Backward

Higher education institutions should be careful to retain all materials, not only on the search process and its procedures, but also regarding the inauguration ceremonies and activities. Knowing who was on the search committee, the transition team, and the inauguration committee becomes important history for the next time a presidential transition occurs. With the average tenure for presidents in some public institutions at about five years, and eight years for those at private institutions, the next inauguration ceremony will come sooner than many anticipate and will be much easier to plan if an archivist has kept previous materials as part of the living history of the college. Having past inauguration materials to use as a starting point will be extremely helpful.

The inaugural address provides the new president with an opportunity to speak to the future and present goals to be achieved. If the transition has been well planned, this will also be a time to recognize those who have preceded the current college leadership team, those who have "given us a legacy of community support and high standards of performance that lead us to believe that we can make our vision for the future our reality."[12]

Some colleges and universities have traditions that call for a week of inaugural activities that may include lectures, performances, lunches, dinners, receptions, an inaugural ball, and more. Other institutions have found that a single day of celebration is appropriate for their college culture. Attendees will often prefer a ceremony that is reflective of the institution's history and climate and is no longer than one and a half hours in length, with a 20 to 25 minute presidential address. However this climax of the presidential transition period is done, it should be well planned and orchestrated, a smoothly flowing event that pays attention to all details. Where guests park, where to dress for the academic procession, appropriate programs, invitations, and assistance from college staff relating to such matters as directions, information, and maintaining a welcoming environment are all important matters to be carefully planned and facilitated.

The more components of the college that are involved, the more inclusive and appropriate the experience will appear. However, the more people or groups that are involved, the greater the complexity and the need to plan and manage these aspects of the celebration. President Stanley assessed the effectiveness of her inaugural ceremony with these comments to her new leadership team: "For me the highlight of the official ceremony was when the past president, who graciously came to assist in the final transition, placed the Presidential Medallion around my neck. The smiles of both of us, displayed on the front page of the local newspaper the next day, reflected the genuine delight we both felt in a transition well done."

The time, energy, and effort put into a carefully planned and executed, proactive presidential transition process greatly benefit the students, faculty, staff, alumni, and extended community of the institution. In helping new presidents to become successful in their positions, in particular, the plan should include these core components:

—A careful analysis, before the search begins, of the position and the type of leader the institution needs.

—A search process that not only allows all stakeholders to have input but also allows both the institution and all candidates to assess the appropriate match required for long-term success.

—A transition plan with schedule and goals to be initiated prior to the time of appointment and carried out several months into the new president's term.

—An inaugural celebration that conveys the symbolic transfer of leadership in a meaningful manner congruent with the particular institution's culture.

CHAPTER SEVEN

When Presidents Leave Suddenly: From Crisis to Continuity

E. K. Fretwell Jr.

What options are open to a college or university when its chief executive officer departs suddenly? The reason may be a better offer, failing health, termination, or death. Such abrupt change situations are far different from a normal retirement, in which the sequence is not so rushed and the emotional overtones are of a different quality. Each category of abrupt departure is different from the others, but this chapter discusses their similarities and how to prepare effectively for each type. Each one provides opportunities to manage the transition, and while all stakeholders in an institution have a role in bringing about recovery, the primary and legal responsibility remains with the board of trustees.

The first admonition is to *be ready* for the unanticipated emergency. While this sounds obvious, some boards—and entire institutional communities, however well-intentioned—may still be caught by surprise. Each campus has certain unique qualities, but the wise board will learn from the experience of others. For all campuses, the goal is to weather the storm and emerge as a stronger, more resilient and nimble learning organization.

Occasionally—but not always—there may be advance signs of a potential sudden departure of the president: increasing health problems, rumored or actual conversations with other employers, or increasingly strained relationships with trustees, the community, or campus people. Sensitive observers may become aware of significant signs, some of them quite subtle, and seek legitimate ways to ameliorate emerging problems. Happily, some situations can be improved. In other cases, remediation may not work.

Each higher education institution, from the smallest community college to the largest metropolitan university or a complex statewide system, has its own characteristics and methods to address problems. As noted, the first imperative is to be ready. Once the immediate crisis is addressed, and the emergency plan activated, major attention can then be focused on middle-range plans and moving confidently toward the future.

How to Be Ready

As has been frequently noted, it is much easier to plan for a leadership change before it happens. The following guidelines blend a commonsense approach with a built-in sense of urgency.

An order of executive succession needs to be in place. Higher education has learned from the tragedies of 11 September 2001 that it makes a critical difference to have proven, backup leadership. On campuses a second-in-command is often designated (typically but not always the provost or chief academic officer) to be in charge when the president is away on business, is on leave, or is briefly ill.

Backup for that officer, and others, is also needed. Business and industry, although different from college and university communities in many ways, have multilevel backups. The order of succession should be formalized and put in writing by the trustees and should be clearly understood by administrators, faculty, staff, and other campus people. Periodically some corporations may review their plan, since successors identified earlier, Thomas N. Gilmore reports, may be found unsuitable for a firm's changing "new style."[1]

Terms of employment for the current president must be clear and in writing. Ideally the terms of employment were agreed upon at the time of hiring. Formal contracts are increasingly becoming the pattern. Initial commitments must be honored, but adjustments along the way may be desirable. Some may think it unusual to be talking about terms of "divorce" at the time of "marriage," but clarity from the beginning of employment does make good sense. Achievement of goals by the president are discussed below in relation to performance evaluation.

Definitions related to medical leave, inability to serve, insurance, institutional housing, and any survivor benefits must be clear. An annual physical exam for the president (paid for by the institution unless covered by health insurance), with results shared with the trustees' personnel committee, is highly recommended. (The second-in-command of a complex national organization died suddenly only a few weeks into his new job. He had not shared knowledge of a known heart condition with his new employer.)

Presidents should be evaluated thoroughly and regularly. Of paramount importance is a regular and well-developed procedure for evaluation of the president, agreed to at the time of appointment. A good arrangement calls for a major evaluation, incorporating significant campus involvement, every five years, with informal evaluations by the board of trustees annually. Attention should be paid to achievement of institutional goals, hurdles overcome, and challenges faced. Thus, the board will have access to regular updates on institutional progress. If problem areas appear to be emerging, they should be identified and discussed. It is difficult to carry out an unannounced, "surprise" evaluation without sending the public message that the president may be viewed as experiencing difficulties. Executive coaching can sometimes improve executive performance.

The responsibilities of the president should not be a secret. The chief officer's attention to priorities, allocation of time for particular activities, and main aspects of administrative style should be familiar to senior colleagues. If some other individual has to take over the chief executive role with little or no advance notice, it would be good for that person to have more knowledge of the real job than even the president's assistant or secretary might informally provide. Hard and quantifiable facts about the state of the institution should be available at once from its chief financial officer, its admissions office, and institutional research staff, in particular.

The board itself must be functioning effectively. In addition, it should have some built-in and consistently used procedures for self-evaluation and constant improvement. While the crisis transition period is not the time to cease all other functions and look only inward, the board should work more consciously than ever at being completely functional. Consider the analogy that a person who is healthy is in the best position to withstand additional stress. A major characteristic of an effective board, Richard F. Chait points out, is its ability to anticipate potential problems and act before issues become crises.[2] Loss of its chief executive can galvanize a board to rethink the way it operates.

The board must ask for and collect regular institutional updates. Regularly, but especially at times of sudden transition, the board needs to have updated reports on what are now called "dashboard indicators." Even in a not-for-profit organization, there is need to have basic knowledge regarding such matters as income and expenditures. Also important are updates on what's happening on the admissions front (especially in tuition-sensitive situations), graduation rates, and faculty and staff salary trends. These can and should be quantified. Other indicators may be harder to measure but are also vitally important. Board leaders should have an understanding of how well second-level officers of the campus are functioning and how well they work with each other. They should be aware of those who show promise of being of even greater service to the institution and those who do not. At the same time, any tendencies toward micromanagement by board members should be avoided.

There must be a widely shared and collaboratively developed sense of institutional mission and purposes. Ideally, through strategic planning and extensive campus consultation, a clear agreement on the direction of the institution's future becomes a framework for all major decisions. This is a major trustee responsibility, as James L. Fisher and others emphasize.[3] The board should regularly review the mission of the institution (every five years, for example) and a long-range plan should be developed and approved.

The institutional community should be shown how good communication builds morale. Many of the suggestions in this chapter relate to sharing information in a timely manner. At a time of sudden change, stakeholders need to know what's going on, although some personnel matters may need to remain confidential. Appropriate accrediting bodies should be notified at once of major leadership changes. The importance of building and maintaining high morale on campus and in the community cannot be overstated. Openness and clarity in communication both formal and informal is absolutely essential throughout the transition period as well as thereafter.

When Crisis Shapes the Campus: Presidential Endings

The Death of the President

Perhaps the most difficult sudden change for an institution is the unanticipated death of its leader. When this occurs, the transition process should focus equally on humane considerations and the continuity of institutional operations.

Where there is a clearly appointed second-in-charge officer, the board chair should talk with this person immediately and instruct him or her to assume leadership authority. As another key priority, the chair should also confer with all other officers of the board. A meeting of the entire board, by electronic means if necessary, should be held to confirm this action for a temporary arrangement. Faculty, staff, and students, especially key leaders, should be alerted at once, most likely by campus e-mail. A single institutional spokesperson should be designated to handle and control all contact with the media.

In public systems, the chief system officer should be notified at once, as should appropriate state officials. State systems often have clearly defined procedures already in place. A timely public announcement should be released to the media and to stakeholders. Suitable praise for the individual's leadership and service should be included together with significant biographical information. Continued commitment to the institution's future is an important message at this time.

An event to recognize the life of the departed president should be held on campus, if appropriate. Such an event should provide opportunity for venting of grief and bonding among individuals and to the institution. The focus should be a strong, inspirational, and confidence-building message. Immediate contact with the family of the deceased should also be made by the board chair. Their opinions with regard to memorial service plans should be sought. Opportunity for campus community members, as well as members of the external community, to recall the life of the deceased should be provided. The family should be advised that a designated member of the administration will be available to help with interpretation of spousal/family needs such as benefits, transitional use of the president's house, if applicable, and other personal concerns. The elected head of the senate and others representing the faculty should be invited to participate in the memorial event. The naming of a building, other public place, or memorial fund, may be considered after ample time is allowed for thoughtful planning.

In cases of critical or terminal illness, trustees will need to decide at some point when the executive becomes too impaired to carry out major duties. In these instances, the president or family members may choose to initiate the discussion with trustee leadership. After personal provisions have been made, what will be necessary for a stable and effective institutional transition will become the key priority.

Two examples illustrate the specific, usually unprecedented, challenge posed by the death of an active chief executive.

A Small Community College

In a community college in a small city, the president was diagnosed as having a terminal illness, but he would not relinquish his responsibilities even though he was in seriously deteriorating health. He suggested that another individual be appointed as "shadow president" and that he remain as the visible chief executive. The trustees became impatient and asked him to resign or retire. An off-campus intermediary, who knew both the college and the sick president, counseled him at length. As a result, a retirement package acceptable to both parties was arranged. An interim president was named. The former president retired and moved out of state.

A Large Research University

After an exhaustive nationwide search was happily concluded at a large research university, a new chief executive officer was installed. He was described as being a dynamic, visionary, and highly visible leader. This university was looking forward to a time of growth and even greater recognition statewide and nationally.

Soon after his appointment, the new chief executive was diagnosed as having a debilitating and probably deadly disease. According to an observer close to the scene, many loyal supporters could not bring themselves to recognize that the condition might be terminal. The leader's symptoms worsened and an interim chief executive was named. This individual, an alumnus, had been a senior officer in the university system office and was well informed about the campus. The leader, however, then received "medical approval" to resume full-scale responsibilities and the interim officer departed. The chief executive's health suddenly worsened again, and he died. The community was shocked for the second time. The interim head returned.

In the months preceding the arrival of the next "permanent" president, campus morale returned slowly because of the uncertainties just passed. A major memorial event, which overflowed a two-thousand-seat hall, was held for the deceased leader. Activities related to a major fund drive already under way moved forward gradually, with renewed and generous backing. A special health-related research fund was named for the former president. As one loyal supporter noted in retrospect, it was important to let the entire community express their grief by making individual, sometimes private, contributions and recognitions over time. An observer noted that student unrest was at its lowest point in seven years.

The Firing or Resignation of the President

Effective campus leadership can utilize the sudden departure of the chief executive to improve the effectiveness of the institution in a number of timely ways. Only the trustees have the legal power and responsibility to discharge the president. They need to determine if and when.

As in other departure situations, fairness and decency must prevail. Trustees must be unusually clearheaded and decisive.

As noted already, the wise governing board is aware at all times of the president's success in working with and leading the various sectors of the institutional community. While no mortal chief executive can satisfy all of the people all of the time, the successful leader must come close.

Motivation to consider firing the president may arise from a collection of problems ("he or she just isn't handling things right and is infuriating everybody") or from a specific act or acts that range from unacceptable to illegal (claiming degrees or qualifications not actually held, violating academic standards such as tempering with course grades to assist failing athletes, illicit sexual activities, improper financial dealings, questionable judgment in personnel matters, or other breaches of trust).

Fortunately, the need for sudden termination does not arise frequently. Although no two situations are alike, a checklist of suggested steps appears as a shadow box within this chapter.

The following three examples include a sudden voluntary departure, a resignation following a campus vote of no confidence, and a spectacular "firing" of a university board of trustees as well as the president. In each of these very different situations, the university or college improved itself strategically as a result of its president's departure.

An Ivy League University

"He just walked out" describes the case of an Ivy League president who had been on the job for only about two years. While this brief relationship did not represent a perfect match, the perceived reason for the departure was a very attractive offer from another independent university. Hindsight is easier to apply than foresight, but it became apparent to some that during his period of service the president did not seem to feel fully accepted by the faculty. Without significant teaching experience in one of the traditional fields and with top executive experience as president only of state universities, he apparently did not feel comfortable in the new context.

What happened after he left? Considerable campus anger was reported but apparently did not last long. A former faculty dean was put in charge immediately on an interim basis. As the campus community planned its steps forward, the new search committee determined to carry out a more effective search for the next "permanent" president. The new president, from a distinguished private college in a neighboring state, has met high internal success. She is reported to be a good listener but is

Suggestions for Trustees Considering Firing the President

First of all, does this president really need to be fired? As one experienced observer has pointed out, the leader may simply be wearing down or wearing out. A timely sabbatical, which could have been utilized effectively somewhat earlier, is probably too late now, although this tired person may welcome intervention by the governing board or, in a public system, by the system head as a rescue, thus an enlightened win-win situation.

If such is not the case, the following trustee steps are pertinent:

- Assess the nature and depth of the problem(s). Listen carefully to faculty and possibly others. Take their comments seriously but make no commitments.
- Meet quietly off campus in executive session—even rigid sunshine laws may allow this—to determine how serious the problem(s) may be.
- Confer—usually the board chair and possibly one or two other trustees—with the president and share the deep concerns. Determine whether there is a "nonterminal solution."
- Meet confidentially with legal counsel and, as needed, with the chief human resources officer to develop a termination package. Review terms of employment established at the time of hiring. The package should address all financial factors.

"forceful in the best way." The university is energized by a new style and believes that it has "traded up."

A Public Technical College

The next example of a positive change centers on a small, five-campus public technical college in the upper Midwest. The prior president's difficulties in management and community-campus relationships led to an overwhelming faculty vote of no confidence. Accepting his prompt resignation, the state system administration wisely saw this as a timely opportunity to consider redefinition of the college within the context of the cooperative regional approach shared with other institutions. The search for a new president was postponed.

Public input is important as a major tradition in that state. More than five hundred participants met to consider the future course of the institution. In over seventeen hours of public forum, citizens sought to identify ways for the college to serve students, businesses, and the public most effectively in its lightly populated part of the state, where declining agriculture posed major ongoing problems. Strategic recommendations called for pertinent technical education, better community connections,

Suggestions for Trustees Considering Firing the President (*cont'd*)

- To avoid the complications of a split-board problem at a later point, trustees should meet at this point to reach an agreement on the final resolution.
- Meet promptly with the president and indicate the feeling of the board. Once the president realizes the situation, seek a mutually acceptable and reasonable settlement, if possible. If the president is stubborn, a board decision to terminate at once may be indicated, and this will most likely implicate attorneys for both the president and the institution. Put the agreed-upon schedule and financial terms in writing and agree on a general public statement regarding the change. This should be the only public statement by any of the involved parties. Act promptly.
- Before making any announcement, be sure that the acting president, by trustee resolution, is ready to begin serving.
- Insist at all times on complete confidentiality on the part of all concerned. It may be difficult to avoid leaks, but it is imperative.
- Plan and carry out a very timely public announcement to campus and media, with private phone calls to key people, including faculty and student leadership. Indicate the termination date and the name of the acting executive. Delay may cause problems.

and closer relations with the institution's decision makers. For the near future, an innovative plan has been designed whereby the five individual campuses are temporarily assigned to other system institutions for administration while the college finishes redefining its long-term goals and structure.

A Middle-Sized Private University

In this final example, resignations were brought about as a result of an indignant and aggressive faculty movement in which the faculty took matters into their own hands. A news article describing this independent institution told of a president and certain board members who were "plundering" the university for personal gain at a time when full-time student enrollment was dropping about 40 percent within a heavily tuition-dependent context. The president's salary and perks were alleged to be more than eight hundred thousand dollars for one year. One trustee likened the faculty to "barbarians" and blamed all of the university's problems on a small handful of faculty described as "power mad." Another viewed the faculty collectively as a "Judas" responsible for the "crucifixion" of the president.[4]

A committee to save the university was established by faculty and former trustees. They took their case to the legally powerful state Board of Regents, who, following a detailed hearing, fired members of the board of trustees. The regents then appointed a new board, which fired the president. Of special concern to faculty and to the regents was the complete contravention by the earlier trustees of the university's Articles of Governance, unanimously approved by the board only a few years earlier. Other steps that infuriated the faculty included plans to eliminate certain professional schools, which, not incidentally, buoyed sagging enrollments in the arts and sciences. The president had also attempted to decertify the faculty union.

Looking back, one can see that the faculty rediscovered and reconfirmed their own responsibilities as stabilizing factors. In various ways, they advised students and alumni on an ongoing basis as well as continuing to help recruit students, sometimes pairing with current students on teams to visit high schools.

By the time the highly experienced interim president started, about two months after the new board began operating, faculty members were productively involved in planning the present and future of the university. A task force of twenty professors worked collaboratively to address key problem areas. This led in part to a gathering of more than 150 faculty members and administrators to hear two nationally recognized experts speak on the financial status of higher education institutions and on the profile of future student consumers.

The interim president completed his work as the search was concluded, resulting in what was hoped to be a "permanent" chief executive. Unfortunately, this individual was lured away only seven months later by a university system chancellorship. Undeterred, the faculty continued to play their role. When the current president, now on the job three years, arrived, he found the faculty, as he described it, "rolling up its sleeves again and helping to recruit students." The faculty felt it was important for the community to know that the campus had survived and was stronger.

Each of the above unusual examples presents some dramatic moments. Together they represent a wide range of transition strategies and possibilities during crisis moments. Faculty members had major roles.

Keys to Managing an Unforeseen Transition

In the majority of presidential transitions, trustees serve as the major players, often in concert with savvy faculty members. The following rec-

Best Practices

- Have a clear and up-to-date order of succession for the four top administrators.
- Make effective use of specialized consultants in advisory capacities.
- Make decisions on the basis of current institutional data, including both numerical and quality considerations.
- Use an ad hoc campus committee on transition to enhance communication.
- Improve the quality of board members' performance by successfully managing a transition.

ommendations address managing the transition process effectively when the reason for it has been sudden, unfortunate, and irreversible.

Support the person in charge. The decisions (if, when, and who) concerning an interim president should not be made in haste, but they cannot be postponed too long. One fast-moving university system chief executive names an interim president immediately without consultation. This can work, but it can also make the chosen person's role more difficult. Campus traditions, including faculty roles, need to be reviewed; they should not dictate any decision completely, however.

Spend conservatively. Sudden transition periods are not times for significant spending. A financial audit by an outside firm may be called for, especially if there has not been one recently or if special problems are contemplated relating to the departed president.

Think and act positively. When a campus president leaves for another job or is terminated, the decision and announcement of who is now the leader of the institution should be made by the trustees immediately. In cases of presidential health concerns or death, an immediate press release should indicate plans for interim leadership. In all announcements, the board chair should reaffirm the board's commitment to the traditions, importance, and future well-being of the institution. A clear "order of succession" policy should be observed.

Recognize achievements where feasible. When the president moves to another position elsewhere, it is appropriate to recognize her or his positive achievements. Honest enthusiasm, even if tempered with regret, should be shown. It may be viewed as an affirmation of the vitality and quality of an institution for its president to move to an attractive post elsewhere. A positive, upbeat transition will clearly be noted by the national higher education community and can provide positive overtones, which will help attract quality candidates to the upcoming search.

Inform and involve university counsel. When there is an unhappy parting of the ways and a forced resignation, a written agreement of understanding needs to be signed by both parties. University counsel must be involved from the beginning of these aspects of the process. While there may be significant compromises involved, fairness should prevail on both sides. Financial considerations must be addressed openly and thoroughly, particularly if certain understandings were not reached in the initial contract.

Develop a single, clear public voice. There must be agreement on the wording of any public statements and a firm understanding that neither the institution nor the individual will make any additional public statements about the reasons for the departure. This discipline, though it may be hard to maintain, will be required for the good of the college. Some institutions have learned the hard way that loose talk by a member of their board or by the departing officer can lead to adversarial but necessary modifications of benefits for the outgoing individual. In other cases, a resignation to concentrate on a professorship that the president may have already held can make the transition easier for all concerned. Sometimes a legitimate assignment to some other campus function is also possible, but in many instances, a "clean break" may be needed for both sides. Sometimes, state systems have been able to offer employment on another campus, and occasionally a board may consider covering the cost of outplacement services by a specialized firm.

Thoroughly address lingering institutional anxieties. No matter how the situation is handled, there will be anxieties on campus. Rumors may abound and old issues—major or minor—may reemerge inopportunely. In these moments it will be critical for the campus community to see the board collectively as dedicated and informed individuals working cohesively, remaining open to questions and suggestions, large and small, and acting firmly behind the interim or new chief executive officer. While crisis-driven change may cause backward-looking and even nostalgia, it is essential to enhance campus momentum without making too many changes at this juncture. Major program and personnel changes and re-

Emerging Trends

- Improving due diligence in searches, including more candid analysis of campus strengths and weaknesses shared with the new president.
- Using longer-than-average periods of interim presidencies to work out major institutional problems.
- Using the search process to stimulate campus momentum on major endeavors, such as research, public service, and major fund-raising campaigns.
- Being able to identify presidential health or behavior problems in their early stages and ameliorating them.
- Increasing networking and strategic alliances with boards and chief administrators of other institutions who are effective problem-solvers.

source commitment are better left until a new chief executive officer is in place and has a major hand in setting new directions.

From Crisis to Continuity

As David Leslie has pointed out in *Wise Moves in Hard Times,* some institutions undergoing change are "distressingly short on good information" about themselves. Strategizing is important, he emphasizes, but it "distracts people from the immediate situation [and] requires that they divide their attention. . . . People feel compelled to make decisions for the sake of making decisions, which is a good way to produce bad decisions."[5] In these moments, a wise board of trustees will achieve the following:

—Encourage stakeholders to get to know and support the interim president and realize that he or she is in charge.

—Hold occasional open meetings on campus with the interim president, to which stakeholders are invited in order to voice their various hopes for the future of the institution and their observations on how the campus is running.

—Secure the services of an outside professional consultant who will carry out an institutional review of strengths and processes of the college or university. The results of such a review can serve as a set of benchmarks during the search for a permanent head.

The transition period between when it is known that a president is departing and the time a new "permanent" president is on the job presents two major choices. One is to move ahead effectively and use the transition process to improve the institution. The other is to falter and lose momentum. If managed skillfully and courageously, transitions can enhance campus communication and build a long-term sense of cohesiveness. The examples discussed in this chapter provide a wide range of effective steps that institutions have taken as they faced the challenges of sudden exits. Sample cases have demonstrated how colleges and universities have upgraded the quality of executive leadership, learned how to run more effective searches, enhanced fund-raising, empowered faculty leadership, and provided time to consider a different future for each institution.

CHAPTER EIGHT

Presidential Turnover and the Institutional Community: Restarting and Moving Forward

Nancy L. Zimpher

"Presidents come. Presidents go. How they come and go can have a profound effect on an institution—and make the difference between a period of continued success and one of disruption."[1] While presidents come and go, institutions adjust. This chapter addresses the impact of a presidential transition on constituents in the college or university's larger community, all stakeholders but many of them often left out of key aspects of the leadership transition process.

Whatever the reason for the president's departure, the community must say goodbye. For some, it is likely that the leaving will be too soon, for others, too late. On many campuses, it will be a bittersweet blend of celebrative congratulations and sad farewells. Ned Sifferlen, in his study on celebrating presidential transitions, confirms the importance of the two bookends—first, honoring the past while looking to the future, and second, eventually celebrating the new beginnings by devising strategies to introduce the college and local community to the new leader and celebrating her or his selection.[2] It often happens, though, that when finally an agreement is reached and president and campus find themselves contractual partners, both are largely unprepared for the changes that lie ahead.

The presidential search committee, by its very nature, is focused solely on getting the two partners together. Little has been written about how to effectively engage the multiple constituencies that compose the larger institutional community in order to solidify this relationship for long-term success. The shared work of leading an institution forward—whether it is public or private, whether college, university, community college, or religiously affiliated school—demands involvement and accountability from both the president and the campus communities. This proposition is axiomatic for the transition period also, and multiple campus constituencies should be engaged in the entire process. As Sifferlen cautions, "The complex and sensitive procedural aspects (national searches, interim leaders), coupled with the symbolic organizational cultural issues (internal power struggles, uncertainty) can lead to widespread dissent and distrust. In addition, internal constituents (faculty, staff) are deeply concerned with the directions a new leader may take the institution, and external constituents (community members, business leaders) wonder how the new leader will relate to and serve the needs of the local area." In short, "the key factor is to not focus solely on the leaders in transition, but to consider all the people who will be touched by the change."[3]

This chapter first provides an overview of the critical activities for constituent groups in the three major phases of a presidential transition: the search period, the passage between leaders, and the early months of the new executive. It then takes a closer look at "those touched by the change," reviewing the specific needs and interests of each significant campus and community interest group: academic leaders, faculty, staff, and students, and, off campus, system leadership, legislators, business and civic leaders, and alumni.

The chapter concludes with the key steps each constituent group can take to enable a successful transition.

During the Search: Assessing Constituent Opportunities

College community members must remain mindful during the transition process of the consequences of inaction and negative action. John W. Moore, coauthor of a report from the American Association of State Colleges and Universities, *Presidential Succession and Transition: Beginning, Ending, and Beginning Again,* advises that changes in strategic direction often are "confusing and distracting to faculty, administrators, and others who are committed to the well-being of an institution."[4] Too often, however, when a presidential search is announced, the campus goes on automatic pilot rather than pausing to reflect. Even worse, relationships with key donors, legislators, and alumni can be allowed to fray: "The web of relationships is part of what is torn when a president leaves, and the time it takes a new president to forge those ties on a campus as well as with donors and political leaders can hinder an institution's progress," notes Julianne Basinger in her report on the sudden departure of a university president.[5]

It is this fabric of the campus community that a well-managed transition can help to keep whole and vibrant. The transition period can be useful to key constituents as a time for reflection and assessment. When we ask students in our writing classes to practice reflection and assessment, in essence we ask them to participate as responsible and active agents in the process of their own learning. This valuable lesson provides a useful parallel for a strategic and well-managed leadership transition. As John M. Connolly, Smith College's provost and dean of faculty, observes with acuity in an article by Jennifer Jacobson, these gaps give the institution a chance to "get over" the departure of the recent president and develop an "appetite" for the new president.[6] Robert H. Atwell, president emeritus of the American Council on Education, agrees: "I often think that when institutions lose their presidents, they need to pause before rushing into a search."[7] Jacobson gives a graphic depiction of how this gap in time affected Smith College in the recent past when Ruth J. Simmons departed from Smith. She was succeeded by Carol T. Christ from University of California, Berkeley, after a full academic year. According to Jacobson, the chair of Smith's search committee, Mary Patterson McPherson, observed, "Little hiatuses like these are healthy for Smith. It just makes people step up and take responsibility. They always thought, 'Ruth's there, she'll do it. [Now] they'll have to do it.'" From the incoming president's perspective, this time for reflection is a real asset. Jacobson further reports Christ as remarking: "It's wonderful to have the time to contemplate, to learn, to think about the institution and about my position as president, and to work carefully with the current leadership team."[8]

However, often overlooked in the focused activity of the search and maintenance of status quo by the campus is the very idea that is crucial to the university at such a time: that is, the search for a new president offers a unique opportunity for the entire campus and the community to reflect on and assess their mutual perspectives on the mission, values, and hopes for the future and to come together around shared goals. Since the success of the new president will, in fact, largely rest on how well his or her vision for the institution fits with that of the campus and the community, it is crucial that the campus community be able to present a reflective and considered image of itself and its expectations. In "Conditions for Effectiveness," Jeannette Wright identifies a critical requirement for a successful presidential transition when she observes, "Presidents cannot lead effectively if they are not committed to the philosophies or mission of the colleges they serve. Presidents have to believe profoundly in the intrinsic value of their colleges. This belief in the institution, intellectually and emotionally, is contagious and will enable successful leadership."[9] But a new president looks largely toward the campus community to learn about the institution's mission and commitments, and an unprepared, disengaged, unreflective campus will fail to do its part in ensuring a successful transition and presidency. Moreover, studies of failed business leadership mirror this dangerous potential. Eric Wahlgren quotes Roland Van der Meer, a partner in ComVentures: "breakups mostly have to do with differences over what to do with the direction of the company. The rest is noise."[10]

Rather than occupying the search and transition periods with "the noise"—interdepartment battles, bids for power, end runs for funding for pet projects—the campus can infuse the time of transition with a spirit that will help "cultivate the habits of heart, mind and action that build community and enable [the university] to work together effectively in the service of a shared mission."[11] The off-campus community can play a significant role in the transition period, too. Instead of putting key campus community partnerships and initiatives on hold while waiting to take stock of the new leader, such groups should forge ahead to reinforce ongoing work and reflect on future plans. Working closely with already established campus contacts, the new president would then be exposed early on to effective partnerships that have weathered the winds of transition, gaining strength and momentum in the process. The transition period thus can be made into a backdrop for the crosscurrents of voices across campus and community, and broad communication and initiative can be encouraged. "While the debate in some institutions seems to be over who has authority, what matters is who has the initiative" and, one might add, whether those with initiative are talking to each other reflectively.[12]

The presidential search committee itself, in the way it conducts its work, should set the precedent and provide the model for this type of campuswide reflective and constructive activity. When the board announces the search process and instructs the campus to form a presidential search committee, the committee's first priority should be to develop a clear picture of both the institution and the kind of leader it seeks. At most institutions, the committee will create institutional and leadership profiles, often with the help of a search consultant. Campuswide forums, already a feature of most presidential searches, can gather ideas, inviting the community to participate, and the results of discussions and regular updates can be posted on campus Web sites. Concurrently with and mirroring the committee's proceedings, the campus at large should also begin its own activities to prepare for the transition to new leadership. Three main areas of reflective activity can smooth the rough edges of a time of transition by preparing ground for new initiative and change and by revisiting and revitalizing the core mission and values of the institution.

Activities of the Campus at Large

First Priority: Reflect on Mission

Since "the formulation and execution of important decisions, especially on a sustained basis, requires the structured involvement of many participants from top to bottom,"[13] the presidential search committee typically establishes mechanisms for faculty, staff, students, alumni, and significant numbers of community members to examine the mission of the institution and the profile of leadership needs. This may include listening and focus sessions and online message boards. The purpose is to assess the state of the institution and, by involving people as broadly as possible, to build united support for change. Questions should include these:

—What has been our historical mission, and is it still valid?

—What are the three key issues the new president must address?

—What are our strengths, and where do we need to change?

—What are the core values of this institution?

—Are we ready for change, and how can we help?

Not surprisingly, alumni will provide important perspectives at this time, based on what they believe the institution's mission should be, uncompromised by faculty or departmental issues. James Fisher and James Koch make a special note of the heartfelt investment that alumni can make in the institution and thus generate invaluable reflections on what is essential to the institution's success.[14]

Moreover, even as the work of the presidential search committee includes a role for the students, the search process is also an opportunity for the students to mirror the faculty process of assessing goals, strengths, and challenges, both of student leadership and relationships with the administration, for long-term planning. On many campuses, student government is tied to annual elections, with little leadership or issue continuity over the long term. The early stages of the transition process, thus, can also be a time for students to assess their organizational strengths and build longer-term plans or personnel.

Second Priority: Build Bridges

As the campus begins to formulate its vision and identify concerns in the light of the transition, campus leaders at all levels of the organization are key to enhancing communication. They are conduits between the presidential search committee and the campus itself, and their goal should be "transparency." They know which groups need more information and can also help faculty and staff determine the impact that the change in leadership will have on them. These channels of communication, developed during the early stages of the transition, can be strengthened and become valuable tools for campus leadership after the succession is complete.

Faculty and staff also provide important input for the presidential search committee during the search process. As drivers of the academic programs, they can be called on to be strong advocates for the campus to help attract promising candidates. By being available to the committee to "wine and dine the candidates with information"[15]—connecting the candidate to current research, innovative teaching programs, creative institutes, and programs or community partnerships—faculty and staff may provide the final "spark" that will confirm a candidate's choice.

Third Priority: Communicate the Change

The channels of communication established by key institutional leaders during the search process can also serve to unite the campus and strengthen it for change. In his study encouraging universities to be more proactive and entrepreneurial, Burton Clark talks about reinforcing the "steering core," of finding ways to encourage leadership that reaches "across old university boundaries to link up more readily than traditional departments."[16] Especially during transition, this kind of cross-disciplinary communication can help to make the institution more flexible and prepared for change. And the institution needs to be prepared not only for the change but also to address concerns of campus personnel. Key scholars among the faculty may be concerned about their future and the future of their programs. Academic leadership central to the campus, deans and department chairs, can use the search process to reassure key people that they are valued and their work will be supported.

Important academic and alumni leaders can utilize the transition period to solidify connections to donors and political and business leaders. Especially in public universities, state funding on biennial cycles does not wait for presidential searches. Administrative leadership could intentionally form task forces across schools and colleges so that important relationships continue to be with the institution, not individual departments. The donor and business communities may also find the search process an opportunity to extend financial support to the university. Increasingly, especially at public institutions, a portion of the president's salary now comes from private sources. To recruit the kind of talent the public institution needs may require additional support from external supporters. As reported by the Association of Governing Boards of Universities and Colleges, in a recent survey, "one-third of all public-university boards reported that their presidents received supplemental compensation from private sources." This income may come from salaries from an endowed chair or a consultancy to the university foundation, performance bonuses, or foundation underwriting of expenses, such as private clubs.[17]

The Passage: Between Selection and Arrival

After the new president has been selected and announced by the board or the system, or both, there will be a period of several months or even a year or more before the new president is officially on board. Claire Gaudiani, former president of Connecticut College, captures both the significance and the uncertainty that characterize this period's contradictory qualities: "A magical and commonly underutilized period occurs between the announcement of the new president's name and the moment the new leader arrives on campus to take the helm. The trajectory toward success or failure is often set during these months."[18] This is a time when the president and the campus have shared responsibility for steering the institution in the right direction. The onus, of course, is on the new president to set the pace and style for the transition and to try to do so with the involvement of the concerned campus constituencies. The new president has three main tasks involving the larger institutional community during the transition period between selection and arrival on campus.

1. Learn All You Can

A new president is more often than not greeted by the challenging concurrence of the "newness" of it all and the charge to action, with the element of surprise acting as the unpredictable but dependable variable. In such a circumstance, "learning" and "knowing" are the best paths, especially to obviating the element of surprise. According to Judith Block McLaughlin, "In a study of second-time presidents, Estela Bensimon reports that experienced presidents were more likely than first-time presidents to get to know their institutions before 'making any pronouncements.' They 'approached learning about their institutions more aggressively and more systematically.'"[19] Moreover, concludes McLaughlin, "those presidents who work with their boards and campuses to make their entry to the presidency a time of active learning for themselves and their institutions find that they have accomplished a great deal in this transition period. In the process, they have adopted a style that allows for learning, one that will serve them well throughout their presidential tenure."[20] This "learning period" helps reduce surprises. "Eighty-three percent of the presidents who responded to the most recent survey on the college presidency by the American Council on Education mentioned that a significant problem had not been disclosed to them before they took office."[21] Knowing this reality, almost an inevitable consequence of the search process when the campus community tries to put its best foot forward, it becomes all the more important that the new president "listen" and "learn" all the time. Such a reality also highlights how important it is for the campus community, the main source of learning for the new president, to be prepared with a coherent and reflective message to present to the new leader in this time of transition.

How can new presidents structure their learning about their multiple campus constituencies? Claire Gaudiani suggests that the "the prehoneymoon, pre-inaugural period is the time to listen and establish the style of a listening leader." The new leader could call upon the expertise of the presidential search committee and the board of trustees, both of whom have a vested interest in the president's success, to build an important connector to all campus stakeholders and to serve as a sounding board to validate what is learned during visits. Setting up a series of on-campus visits to meet with key constituents not only works as a significant learning forum for the new leader but also establishes a certain critical visibility for her or him. Claire Gaudiani announced in the campus newspaper that over the five months of her transition, she would be on campus for a full day every ten days. All individuals on campus were invited to meet with her—from administration to custodial staff—and to bring any reports or materials they felt she needed to know. Her closing questions with each person were: "What values do you think most people share on this campus?" and "What one change would be most powerful for you, your colleagues and the school?" She followed up these informal meetings with structured meetings with major constituent groups, including faculty governance, administration, and students.[22]

Another valuable lesson in community building was demonstrated early in the presidency of Kathryn Mohrman at Colorado College. After accepting the presidency, she made an early decision to convene a set of nationally located "confidential advisors." Mohrman recalls, "My advisors were current and former college presidents from both public and private institutions, association executives, Washington-types—all colleagues with whom I had worked in previous jobs. The common element was smarts." Moreover, Mohrman implemented a series of steps that included annual meetings in Colorado, preceded by background readings sent out in advance, and a series of letters she wrote to the team about issues that would be discussed. These issues included the kinds of questions that are obvious for a new president:

—How do I build an effective leadership team out of a group of senior vice presidents who are devoted to the college but not necessarily connected to me?

—How do I allocate my time when everyone wants a piece of me—and the sum is greater than 100 percent?

—What are the questions I should be asking that are not on the agenda?

—How should Colorado College position itself, and what can I do as a new president to make that happen?

—What if people find out that I really don't know as much as I should about topic X?

While her use of this set of "confidential advisors" for the "new person in a 'buck stops here' position" decreased over time, she still recalls the power of self-reflection that made writing memos and periodic briefing letters to her advisers, on issues that were "on her mind," a useful and constructive form of learning that may in the end have proved more helpful than the actual face-to-face advisory sessions.[23] In short, the new president must establish a sound foundation by "learning all he or she can."

2. Tap into Institutional History

While most presidential candidates tap into the history of the institution to some degree to prepare themselves for the search process, this period between selection and arrival is opportune to learn in depth the ethos of the institution through interaction with multiple, sometimes overlooked, campus constituencies. Institutional change is most successful when it evolves from existing practice or history. Alan Guskin, who has written extensively on change in the academy, cautions that whatever an institution's vision for its future, it must be grounded in the values of its mission or it will have no meaning.[24]

3. Forge Relationships and Build Infrastructure

In addition to being sources of learning about the institution, transitional presidential visits are an opportunity to begin to build relationships on and off campus. As Judith Block McLaughlin says, "relationships are the coin of the realm for college presidents, both on and off campus. . . . Presidents get things done by the power of relationship and persuasion."[25] Forging relationships is, of course, important for becoming familiar with existing institutional structures. It is equally important in helping to lay the foundation for introducing change and new initiatives. During the transition, new presidents should actively seek those members of the institutional community who will actively support new initiatives. At the same time, the new president can be assessing organizational strengths and weaknesses—consulting with academic leaders to learn about potential allies and the "untouchables" on staff. John Nason notes that the findings of the Commission on Strengthening Presidential Leadership identify recalcitrant staff as one of the most difficult problems for new presidents,[26] that is, staffing areas best left to a later time when the president has had the benefit of additional context and collective insight.

Establishing an "official" space on campus goes beyond mere convenience and appearances. A new president will need help in learning the internal business and organization models well before arrival. She or he will also need to be briefed on the budget process and ongoing internal projects, and, as quickly as possible, he or she will need to put in charge the right people to handle them. Moreover, as in political transitions, a "chief of staff" position is critical and should be in place early in the new president's tenure.

If the new president is expected to take the lead in listening to the campus and in building a strong foundation of relationships, the campus community needs to also play an active role in helping to prepare the college or university to "hit the ground running" when the president arrives for good. The more intentional faculty, staff, students, and alumni can be about their meetings with the incoming president, the more the campus will benefit.

Taking a cue from political transitions, academic leadership may consider establishing a transition advisory group made up of various community members to provide relevant and detailed information and access to institutional networks and history. This advisory group would also serve to involve faculty, staff, and students more directly in the transition, providing another group of individuals who are vested in the success of the new leader.

As new presidents make opportunities for individuals and groups across the campus to present their ideas for the future, the presidents will inevitably learn about the institution's "most popular" issues and concerns—from petty grievance to grand vision. While diverse opinions should be welcome and cultivated, key constituencies will find that a clearly articulated agenda—repeated by all members—can have great persuasive power with a new president. It is not out of line to suggest that stakeholders prepare "briefing books" or reports concisely outlining key issues and opportunities. Students, faculty, staff, and alumni who have used the search process to hone a concise and refined list of priorities and strategies for the future will find a more receptive audience. Creating a strategic agenda can be especially useful for student organizations, for which leadership may change before the transition is complete.

While campus and community may be eager for new leadership, they may not be so eager to embrace far-reaching change. Maintaining the status quo is a natural for humans, and the willingness to embrace change may vary considerably across campus. Academic leadership can prepare the campus for change by reassuring faculty and staff that existing governance, infrastructure, and programs will continue and that campus constituencies will have the opportunity to provide input for change initiatives. Campus leadership can help prepare the campus through focus and listening groups and open communication that reassures stakeholders that change is part of a normal process.

The Early Months: Off to a Promising Start

If the campus community and the president have used the transition period to prepare collaboratively for the future, they will "hit the ground running" together, ready to begin the exhilarating first months that mark what is sometimes, ironically, the most productive period of a president's tenure. The purpose of this time, as Frank Rhodes posits in "The Art of the Presidency," is nothing less than for the president to "employ his or her best skills to dream the institution into something new." Rhodes further states, "The role of the academic presidency is one of the most influential, most important, and most powerful of all positions. . . . its power is most effectively exercised not in managerial aggression or the pursuit of quarterly results, but by championing creative ideas, creating new alliances, and supporting simple, but transforming goals. But it is a power that must be exercised. Passive presidents litter the landscape, and their pallid institutions reflect their listless leadership." A tall order indeed, and one that would argue that the president cannot scale these leadership heights without effectively engaging the entire campus community, early and often, in important dialogue that reasserts institutional mission and sets an ongoing vision. And Rhodes confirms that "the task of the college president, reduced to its essentials, is to define and articulate the mission of the institution; develop meaningful goals; and then recruit the talent, build the consensus, create the climate, and provide the resources to achieve them. All else is peripheral." Rhodes also asserts that this is a joint effort of the trustees, the provosts, vice presidents, deans, faculty, staff members, students, alumni, the public, advisers, and consultants. "All have a role and a proportionate voice," while recognizing that ultimately it is the president who carries these ambitions to a fruitful conclusion.[27]

In the early months of the new president's tenure, the foundation is laid for articulating or reasserting vision and mission. Claire Gaudiani insists that presidents should both announce and summon forth a vision of the future, and in order to do so they must engage their various constituencies early on. The early months provoke intense president-watching: "the announcement focuses everyone's attention on every word, smile, raised eyebrow, and head toss of the new president . . . [making this] the time for the president to capture the imagination of the community and to begin to set the vision and the style of the new era."[28]

Combining the advice of experienced presidents reflecting on their early months forms a composition of steps that, if taken successfully by the new president and the campus community in concert, bode well for a positive beginning:

—Make the first public remarks ones that instill confidence that "things are going to get better" and that the new president is a vehicle for introducing a new era of success at the institution.

—Utilize the resources of institutional archivists and historians to become very well steeped in the history of the place, and learn to integrate this "shared past" to build confidence, among the constituents, that the institution's history will be respected, not violated.

—Engage the broader community in shaping the new president's vision.

—Provide multiple opportunities to meet with different people, to hear their "stories, hopes and disappointments, and to review their warnings and suggestions," buying lots of goodwill along the way.

—Engage official governance structures in thinking about the future, through half-day and day-long retreats, allowing the new president to test parts of her or his own sense of the vision while hearing what assembled groups have to say about what the institution "believes, fears and aspires to become."

To lose these multiple opportunities to "listen" is to lose time that can never be recaptured. "These . . . are powerful signs that the president will lead with the community, that the community has had informal and formal shaping effect on the new president, and that fundamentally they will be able to trust the new vision because it is already 'ours,' not an isolated 'hers.'"[29] This kind of institutional goodwill can carry a new president into the postinaugural phase of leadership smoothly, but it will not be accomplished without the involvement and support of the multiple constituencies identified in this chapter.

Those Touched by the Change

In any institutional transition, there is an array of constituents whose needs and contributions must be taken into account. With more than thirty-five hundred higher education institutions across the country, contexts vary considerably. Still, constituent groups have much in common, no matter what the variation in scale or mission. Accordingly, those responsible for a smooth leadership transition must take into account the needs and interests of the following groups: academic leaders who serve in key all-university administrative roles and unit deans and chairs; regular faculty and academic and support service staff; students at all levels, including full-time and part-time enrollees and even students participating in off-campus continuing education; system administrator and regents, if relevant, or locally, the board of trustees; elected officials at the local, state, and in some cases federal levels; business and civic leaders; and alumni and friends. These constituent groups can also make important contributions to the leadership transition process. In addition to this discussion of the needs and interests of the constituent groups, see the list (below) of specific action steps to enable a successful presidential transition for key campus governance groups and the community at large.

Academic Leaders

It is the responsibility of individuals in key leadership positions to continue to run the university or campus, to follow the existing game plan for institutional management, and to communicate with all other parties during this interim period. In all likelihood, one of these central administrators will also be selected to lead the institution during the interim period. It falls to this designated interim, along with the board of trustees, if one exists, to be sensitive to the personal and professional needs of other campus leaders. The interim period typically creates among most academic leaders a sense of concern for the institution's future that is often personal in nature. Together, the trustees and the interim president can do much to assure other selected campus leaders that even though they may be separated from the individual who hired them, supported their tenure on campus, and planned with them for their future, all will be well once new leadership is selected. These key academic leaders also need to assure middle management that the institution's future is secure, that existing academic planning, programming, and budgeting will continue as usual until the new leader is clearly in place. This provides for a transition period filled with security and stability, keeping the institution's mission and vision and the best interests of the campus community at the forefront.

Faculty and Staff Members

At the core of any institution's mission of research, teaching, and service are the faculty, instructors, and research associates; and the administrative staff, clerical and classified staff, and custodial and other labor constituencies. They will likely be most concerned on two fronts:

1. Stability, continuity of leadership, and job security (although that is not the primary issue of regular, tenure-track faculty).
2. Direct access to the presidential transition process. They also can be the best, or the worst, ambassadors to a range of public audiences. If their influence is negative, there is great instability, ill ease, and lack of communication.

But there are numerous positive ways that these important constituent groups can assist in the transition. Information is the critical lever. Academic leaders have to find myriad and creative ways to tap the interests of faculty and staff and provide up-to-date information and assurance that the institution will continue to maintain its strength and that their views are valued in the search and screen and transition processes.

Students

What applies to faculty and staff also applies to students. There is probably not a college or university in the country that does not view itself first and foremost as student-centered. Students have the same needs and curiosities as other key constituents. They need assurances that their programs will continue, that services will be uninterrupted, that the vision and public image of the institution will be maintained, and that new leadership will signal even better status for the institution in the future. Like faculty, they require much communication, even more so since their lines of communication must be very diverse; and they need to know as much as is appropriate about the search and screen process and the transition plans. Institutional leaders must recognize that students are essentially of two types: there are those involved in the academic and extracurricular leadership of the campus, and there is the general student body, which can range from very homogeneous (on small liberal arts, residential campuses) to exceptionally diverse (at large universities, with multiple student constituencies, from commuters to doctoral, resident researchers). While any student survey might reveal that many students don't know, or care, who the president or chancellor is or was, they pick up the perturbations or vibrations from their parents and others with whom they come in contact—that change is in the air.

For student leaders the crucial questions are these: How can the needs and interests of my organization remain stable and attended to during this phase? What is our rightful role in the search and screen and transition processes? How can I be a good communicator to my constituents during this time and assert the interests of my group with the new president? Among the general student body, a student might be asking, What does this transition mean for my program and the continuing availability of required courses? What are the implications for tuition and fees and other institutional costs and for the general direction of the institution during the change in leadership? These are needs and interests that can and should be responded to, whether the response involves those at the highest leadership levels or those serving in decanal, chair, and faculty and staff roles. Treated with a high degree of inclusion, students can be the greatest asset of the entire transition process.

System Leadership and Trustees

Governance formats for schools and colleges vary, and there are many institutional types. But no matter the structural variant, the observation of David H. Auston, past president of Case Western Reserve University, rings true: "The job of university presidents is a very demanding one, even at the best of times. Without the full and active support of a strong and well-functioning board, it becomes intolerable."[30] Knowing and understanding the role and function of the board is crucial to a successful presidential transition. Many institutions of all sizes are governed by appointed or elected boards of trustees, whose legal responsibility is to run the institution in a time of transition and to ensure a successful search and screen process while connecting with the various constituencies noted here. The boards may not have others to answer to; or they may be obliged to governors, the church, other proprietary groups and also need to keep lines of communication open, as they are obliged as well to communicate with the general public on the search process and plans for the university's future and new leadership. Alternatively, the organization model may be a statewide system of campuses with an appointed president of the system, who staffs an appointed or elected board of regents. Typical of large state systems is Wisconsin's organization. Together, the Wisconsin System Board of Regents and the system president oversee twenty-six campuses, 160,000 students, 35,000 faculty and staff, and an alumni base of more than 600,000 system campus graduates. The seventeen-member board of regents is appointed by the governor, save for two seats reserved for the superintendent of public instruction and the chairperson of the board of the technical college system.

If a school, college, or university is part of a larger state system or is under the policy direction of an appointed chancellor, either through the State Higher Education Executive Officers or some other state arrangement, then transitions get managed accordingly. As with large state systems like Wisconsin, Maryland, and North Carolina, the role of the system head is critical. In all likelihood, the system head has precipitated the search, called for the formation of a local campus presidential search committee, and formed a final review committee within the system regents or curators. The culmination of the search and the selection of the candidate in this mode is the primary responsibility of the regents, appointed or elected, and will be handled accordingly. Still, this constituent group relies on local campus leadership to continue campus momentum, communication, and the details of the transition process. As with other arrangements, the campus leadership must keep the system head informed of institutional management issues during the interim period, and the system head must keep in constant communication with the interim leadership about important system issues. Clearly, the most pivotal action is at the level of clear and direct communication.

Local campuses not under some system organizational structure are most likely operating with trustee oversight. In this scenario, the trustees convene the search and screen process, forming a local campus presidential search committee, probably led by a member, often the chair, of the board of trustees. The committee, in turn, produces the position description; decides on whether to involve an executive search firm and, if so, which one to contract with; and manages campus input into the search process, the confidentiality of the search process, and, of course, the outcome of the search.

Elected Officials

With regard to many campuses, and especially state-supported institutions, elected officials have great interest and stake in leadership transitions and should be kept informed in matters related not only to the search, but also to the general transition process. Effective relationships with elected officials require maintaining momentum in any partnership projects in which they may be directly involved. This effort may involve, for example, local alderpersons or city council members who work with the campus on neighborhood issues such as parking, zoning, and housing compliance; mayoral interest in city revitalization initiatives; congressional leadership in funding major research and development efforts and in financial aid and student recruitment initiatives; legislative oversight of budgetary initiatives that require ongoing oversight or of campus-related concerns of parents and student constituents; and gubernatorial interests in campus initiatives funded by the state and/or pivotal to regional and state economic and educational development. The broader concept of elected leaders could also include elected and appointed school boards and K-12 administrators; other higher education constituents from local universities, colleges, and technical schools; and other community boards and elected officials.

Alumni and Friends

This constituent group represents the lifeblood of the university, first because these are people who care a lot about the institution's future and, second, because they are significant funders and serve as ambassadors for the institution's programs and initiatives. Very often, alumni are the first to come forward if a new leader needs help, especially with community issues. They need information and communication about the search process and all transition activities and have a vested interest in contributing to these processes and to the new leadership.

Having the president of the alumni association on board during the transition period will ensure that a system is in place for open and frequent communication between the new leader and alumni and friends. Such an officer should arrange meetings between the new president and the alumni association, its board, and past boards. The president of the alumni association should also help identify those friends and alumni who have been especially active in the past and enlist their support and advice. At the University of Wisconsin—Milwaukee, for example, the president of the alumni association at the time of my arrival on campus set up legislative meetings where alumni invited elected officials into their homes. The alumni association also proposed the idea of a new alumni magazine, an idea I embraced because I realized that it would function as a communication tool benefiting all parties. According to a guideline that many alumni relations professionals have echoed, it is as important to treat graduates as "friend raisers" as it is to consider them fund-raisers.

Business and Civic Leaders

Representatives of the business and civic community could easily be subdivided into numerous sectors. These constituent groups are typi-

Action Steps to Ensure a Smooth Transition

The unique and distinctive role each of these groups can play generally includes staying current with the search and screen and transition developments and passing along key communications to their constituent members. They also can stand ready to serve the interim president and the new president. Beyond these identified needs and interests, each group of community stakeholders can take certain specific action steps during the span of the presidential search and transition periods, including the early months of the new president's tenure.

Academic Leaders

- Form a transition committee to oversee the interim period and the induction of new chief executive.
- Prepare topical briefings and make them available during the search and once the new leader is selected.
- Prepare for multiple action and backup plans for arrival of the new leader and associated inaugural details.
- Conduct internal assessments of mood, plans, issues, and concerns.
- Encourage deans to brief faculty and staff on a regular basis.
- Connect the new leader to the broader higher education community.
- Ask deans to create key constituent itineraries to be followed by the new leader, reflecting key constituencies of each division, department, school, or college.
- Create a media plan and launch of the new regime.

cally local in nature, although for larger public institutions they could include state interests such as business roundtables and other corporate structures. The business sector certainly includes local, regional, and international corporate leaders, both graduates of the institution and those served by the institution. Closely related to the business sector are labor leaders. Most campuses are served by one or more labor unions, whose leaderships connect regularly with community-based labor leaders. Further, labor leaders work hand in glove with major industrial and corporate interests, so it is within the interests of the campus to communicate with these leaders throughout the search and screen process and the leadership transition. Increasingly, venture capitalists have interest in the capitalization of intellectual property and technology transfer, and as such clearly represent a constituency whose interests include transitions in leadership.

Action Steps to Ensure a Smooth Transition (*cont'd*)

- Propose a set of external consultants that might be available to the new leader when he or she arrives.
- Assist the new president in assembling key staff quickly upon arrival.
- Assist in any spousal or family recruiting issues that may be required.

Faculty and Staff

- Organize priority "tours" of key academic areas, which should be ready and available when the new leader arrives on campus as a quick way to help make her or him knowledgeable.
- Create focus groups that can be regularly communicated with throughout the search and screen and ultimate selection and entry process.
- Assist in communication, rumor control, and maintenance of morale during the course of the transition.

Students

- Create student-led ambassador teams to provide broad-based information to other students and to assist in welcoming the new president.
- Create focus groups that can be regularly communicated with throughout the transition process.
- Give briefings to the new leadership on student concerns and key student initiatives.
- Create a student-initiated agenda to help the new president be successful in his or her early and continuing tenure on campus.

A sector of increasing importance to the campus is the nonprofit community. For instance, the greater metropolitan Milwaukee community is served by more than twenty-five hundred nonprofit health and human services agencies, which employ more than fifty thousand individuals. This sector also includes officials from museums, theaters, and other significant arts affiliates; the faith-based communities; and local, regional, state, and national foundations. Nonprofit organizations are critical to an institution's future through their investments in programs, partnership initiatives, internships, and the general viability of communities served by the campus. Moreover, the service agendas of these organizations are very compatible with institutional programs and degrees, so their interest in leadership transitions should be obvious. This is also a constituency populated by various ethnic groups who have their own chamber of commerce organizations and other critical civic leadership

Action Steps to Ensure a Smooth Transition (*cont'd*)

System Leadership and Trustees

- Host events for faculty, staff, students, and other key constituent groups periodically during the transition process.
- Provide regular media briefings to dispel rumors and misinformation.
- Plan an early board retreat to welcome the new president and to assess priorities under the new leadership.
- Brief key system and regents personnel regularly.
- Prepare other chancellors to welcome the new chief executive.
- Provide access to key legislators and other significant elected leaders upon selection of the new leader.
- Get the governor on board early with the new leadership by creating an opportunity for introduction of the new leader.
- Provide access to other elected officials who have a vested interest in the selection of the new leader.
- Provide a list of key contacts statewide that would assist in successful entry to the state.

Elected Officials

- Convene heads of the higher education committees of the state senate and assemble higher education and/or P-16 legislative committees for presidential briefings.
- Provide legislative oversight briefings on key state funding issues.
- Convene local elected officials for early meetings with the new president.

organizations, which can gain from and contribute to the diversity initiatives of the local campus.

Conclusion

The success of the new president will be determined in large measure by how well all community stakeholders and their new leader have been able to form an authentic partnership that will outlast the excitement of mutual infatuation and the honeymoon months. The patterns of collaboration and communication begun, or not begun, during the transition will govern the success of the long-term relationship.

Some aspects of presidential searches are very secretive. While boards of trustees or system regents are quite public regarding the presidential search process relative to committee membership, goals and procedures, and even its timelines, the actual conduct of the committee's business and

Action Steps to Ensure a Smooth Transition (*cont'd*)

- Conduct focus sessions for elected officials at local, state, and national levels to ensure that the institution's mission is understood by these representatives and convey confidence that the new president will reinforce these goals.
- Provide briefing documents on key local and state issues, organizational structures, challenging problems, and perspectives on how the institution can contribute to creative solutions.

Alumni and Friends

- Create event-specific introduction opportunities.
- Assist in communication throughout the transition.
- Create plans for local, state, regional, national, and international alumni tours to introduce the new president.

Business and Civic Leaders

- Prepare briefings for the new president about issues relevant to the larger community.
- Host welcoming events.
- Use house media publications and networks to communicate about the new leader.
- Create a donors' forum to introduce the new leader to the philanthropic community.
- Design specifically targeted ethnic events to highlight the existing diversity of the community and its international connections.

the results of the candidate interview process are very closely guarded. Thus, the various constituencies commented on in this chapter need to be granted multiple opportunities to inform the committee and the board about their aspirations for the institution and its prospective president at key junctures in the decision making. If such an openness can be achieved both in fact and in the constituencies' perception, it will lay the kind of firm foundation that can make a presidential transition successful.

III

Key Issues

CHAPTER NINE

When Colleges Should, and Should Not, Use Executive Search Firms

Jean A. Dowdall

Opportunities and Hazards in a Presidential Search

The search process leading to appointment of a new president raises complex questions for the transition process overall, ranging from the broad conceptual issues of institutional leadership to more concrete operational matters of finding and attracting the best candidates and managing the logistics of the search process. Confronting the uncertainties of a transition period, many boards of trustees in all types of institutions—from small private church-related colleges to large public research universities—now seek the guidance of professional search consultants. This chapter explores the place of presidential search consultants in higher education. It considers the advantages and disadvantages of using a consultant for this process; the hazards that can plague searches in general, apart from their use of consultants; a brief history of the rise of higher education executive search consulting; the costs of retaining this kind of assistance; and some best practices.

Deciding whether to use a search consultant has both practical and symbolic dimensions. For many boards, it resembles the decision whether to buy an insurance policy. Presidential transition is a situation in which the risks are very high: failure to find a president and finding a president who does not succeed in office are major and visible setbacks that can reverberate through the institution and its community for long periods, with costs that are both financial and organizational. Paying an insurance premium today in the form of search consultants can provide some reassurance that tomorrow things will be under control.

Retaining a search consultant can also provide a symbolic stamp of prominence upon an institution whose reputation has been midrange.

Using a "blue-chip" consulting firm will, for some boards, signal institutional quality, just as contracting with a well-respected accounting firm for the institutional audit can convey a particular institutional image.

A board that is alert to campus politics may know that there will be some difficult issues in the upcoming search. For example, there may be one or more internal candidates, current faculty or administrators who are interested in becoming president or who others think should be encouraged to apply. Depending on board preferences, the consultant may encourage such internal candidates to enter the search process. Some of these individuals may have been controversial figures—they may be especially liberal or conservative, especially aligned with certain programs or institutional priorities, and so on—and the consultant can be a sounding board on the implications of this "baggage" for the new president.

In addition to internal candidates, there may be prospective candidates who have been close to the institution in one way or another. For example, there may be legislators or prominent corporate or community leaders who have an interest in the position; if the board finds them attractive candidates, the consultant can cultivate them appropriately, and if the board needs assistance in gently discouraging them or dropping them from the search process, the consultant can do that as well. There may be major donors who feel some sense of entitlement to select or at least to approve the next president; the consultant can help the committee to evaluate the wisdom of considering the donor's past or future financial contribution when deciding whether to give him or her the right to influence presidential selection. All these issues surrounding candidates who are known to the institution can be very thorny, and an outside consultant can help to address them.

The process used by the search committee is important in the culture of higher education.[1] The composition of the committee, how its members are selected, its charge, and its timetable all can easily become matters of considerable dispute before the committee even begins its work. In some public institutions, committee composition is prescribed in institutional governance documents, but in most private colleges, especially those that have not carried out a presidential search in recent institutional memory, there may be no policy or institutional history to provide guidance. Once work begins, controversy can erupt over many aspects of the process: committee procedures and decision-making rules, personality conflicts, breaches of confidentiality (real or imagined, accurately or inaccurately attributed), the role of the consultant, the handling of internal candidates, and many more. Candidates may be few or flawed or both, or they may appear to be stronger than they actually are. The finalist whom all constituencies hope to hire may in the final moments of the search decline the offered position. In institutions of all kinds, the consultant can often assist in resolving these disputes and difficulties and can serve as an adviser and sounding board for the chair. An awareness of these hazards in the search process may be the impetus for considering consultant assistance.

From a practical perspective, the consultant can carry out work that others do not have time to do, such as drafting and sending letters of acknowledgment or nomination, arranging for verification of candidate credentials, and suggesting questions for committee members to ask in interviews. Institutions with especially limited resources and staff support may find it easier to outsource these tasks to a consultant than to stretch existing staff or budgets to the breaking point, with the attendant risks of embarrassing errors.

Advantages and Disadvantages of Using a Search Consultant

An awareness of the hazards inherent in the search process provides a starting point for trustees planning a presidential transition. The process itself can be both complex and contentious, and there are several advantages of using search consultants.

Smoothing the search process. The consultant is an experienced outside observer who can help the institution to see itself clearly and can help to prepare for leadership transition. The consultant can prepare candidates for the reality of a troubled institution so that the new president has a clear understanding of key information and is not surprised by what she or he learns after taking office. The consultant can suggest best practices that smooth the way throughout the search process. A survey of presidents reveals that

> one in five presidents indicated that he or she had not received a full and accurate disclosure of the institution's financial condition. Nineteen percent reported that during the search process, they did not receive a realistic assessment of the institution's status. More than 20 percent of presidents in 2001 indicated that they did not clearly understand their spouse's role upon accepting the job. Presidents also reported not clearly understanding the board's or institution's expectations: Nearly 18 percent of all presidents stated that they did not receive a clear description of these expectations. Presidents of private institutions experienced the most difficulty obtaining information about their institutions prior to accepting the job.[2]

These difficulties should be reduced by the involvement of a consultant.

Recruiting. The consultant can find candidates who do not yet know they want this job, especially successful leaders who are not presently looking for jobs. He or she will also engage in intensive recruiting, draw on existing networks, and make cold calls beyond anything that committee members would have the knowledge or the time to do. If an institution is especially eager to attract a diverse candidate pool, the consultant can be asked to make special efforts in this direction, seeking out and persuading women, people of color, and other underrepresented groups to enter the search.

Screening. The consultant has a professional network and search experience that allow quick screening of "false positives," that is, candidates who appear stellar but have serious flaws, and identification of exceptional candidates who might otherwise be overlooked by the committee.

There can also be disadvantages or risks associated with the use of search consultants.

Poor grasp of institutional character and needs. Some consultants may not take the time or have the skill to develop a complete understanding of the institution and its needs. In some cases, the institution may lack clarity or agreement about its own leadership needs; not all consultants will have the skill to ferret out this problem. Some consultants may portray an institution to a candidate in a more positive manner than is justified by the facts, in order to attract good candidates. This could contribute to the problem noted above, in which presidents are not provided with full and accurate information about the institution and learn key facts only after accepting the position.

A critic of search consultants has argued that "an ad that says 'Wanted: President' and the name of the institution should give enough information to anyone worthy of consideration."[3] Certainly there are some broad characteristics that all institutions seek in the president, such as leadership ability, and a great deal of information is easily available to any interested candidate on the institutional Web site or through search engines. However, for the many institutions whose names are not well known, and for the many prospective candidates who do not know or seek out the full range of institutional information, a consultant can offer a prospective candidate an engaging and "inside" portrayal of the institution to pique initial interest.

Loss of institutional control. There may be uneasiness among search committee members about using a search consultant. Faculty members, in particular, are sometimes fearful of losing control of the search process and especially of candidate selection. Reference calls to presidential search committee members at other institutions can provide information on whether or not the consultant normally takes over the process beyond what the committee prefers.

"Recycled" or preferred candidates. Some committees are especially worried about the consultant who is thought to have a stable of candidates that she or he routinely recycles, bringing them to the attention of one search committee after another. Similarly, some committees are concerned about a conflict of interest in which the consultant has a particular allegiance to a candidate and a commitment to try to place that person in a presidency, rather than a commitment to serve the institution by helping it to find the best candidates. Again, calls to other institutions can provide information about whether the consultant typically favors candidates in spite of their lack of fit with the institution's needs, or disregards candidates who appear to be well suited to the position out of loyalty to other candidates.

Recruitment of predictable candidates. Critics have suggested that the stratification system of higher education makes the pool of candidates very predictable. In institutions of all types, from major research universities to baccalaureate colleges, church-related institutions, and community colleges, there is a tendency for search committees to seek candidates who have experience in similar institutions. "The applicant pool . . . is limited to a small number of existing or potential leaders at similar schools who are at a certain stage of their careers and are likely or widely known to be 'on the market.' . . . Players in the higher education administrative game know what is going on in their leagues and where they are likely to be welcome as candidates."[4] It follows from this claim that a committee can easily, on its own, determine who the likely candidates are and pursue them without expensive assistance. Committees with the knowledge and time to carry out this kind of search can certainly do so on their own. This approach is most likely to be effective in institutions whose institutional peer group is relatively small and well defined (e.g., church-related institutions in which candidates must be members of the church and are likely to be currently working at institutions linked to that church, or major research universities, such as those belonging to the Association of American Universities [AAU], in which preferred candidates must come from AAU institutions). This approach is less likely to be effective in attracting "nontraditional" candidates who come from other types of institutions or who are currently working outside the academy.

Cost. Search consultant costs typically have two elements: a professional fee and expenses (the cost structure of searches is described in greater detail below). While the total amount may seem high, the expenses typically are incurred whether a consultant is used or not. The fee is usually one-third of the first year's compensation. Institutions must decide whether that investment is worth the benefits.

Recent Trends in the Use of Higher Education Search Consultants

The use of professional search consultants has been growing. In her 2002 American Council on Education (ACE) report, Melanie Corrigan asked current presidents whether the searches that brought them to their presidencies had used a search consultant.[5] As table 9.1 shows, the newer the president, the greater the likelihood that a search consultant was involved. The percentage reaches 50.6 percent for presidents in office less than three years, compared to 15.8 for presidents in office for seventeen or more years. There is no evidence that this trend is abating. However, there are some variations among institutional types. Doctorate-granting institutions are most likely to use search consultants (69% of publics, 58% of privates). In public master's-granting institutions, 45 percent of public and 50 percent of private institutions used search consultants. Among baccalaureate-granting institutions, there is the largest public-private difference: 33 percent of public and 53 percent of private institutions used consultants. In two-year institutions, 46 percent of publics and 30 percent of privates used consultants.

In higher education,[6] and in the nonprofit arena more generally,[7] the 1990s seem to have seen a significant expansion of the use of search consultants. The ACE data reflect this, with the largest increase in reported use of presidential search consultants coming from presidents in office since 1990. Even in the Ivy League, half of the institutions conducting presidential searches between 1990 and 2002 used search consultants (Brown, Cornell, Dartmouth, and the University of Pennsylvania). Judith Block McLaughlin and David Riesman observe that if some of the searches they report on in 1990 had "been conducted half a dozen years earlier, the idea of using a search consultant would hardly have occurred to anyone. The chair of the search committee might have consulted informally with retired presidents or other academic eminences within the college's geographic orbit. . . . Today [1990], by contrast, the use of consultants in presidential searches is common. . . . Higher education is a

Table 9.1. Percentage of Presidential Searches Using a Search Consultant, 2001

Year in which Presidency Began	Used a Search Consultant
1968–84	15.8
1985–89	28.6
1990–94	43.0
1995–98	49.5
1999–2001	50.6

Source: Corrigan, *American College President,* 44.

relative latecomer in the use of consultants in . . . recruitment."[8] The trend toward using search consultants in higher education parallels the same trend in the rest of the nonprofit world; using consultants was rare in that sector in the 1970s, but by the 1980s they were becoming more common.[9] In the corporate world, large executive search firms "run the job market for chief executives."[10]

In 1990 McLaughlin and Riesman provided a list of search consultants working with higher education institutions (admittedly incomplete because, as they observe, "As the demand for consultants grows, the supply increases"). They identify four not-for-profit firms, six corporate search firms that also serve education, and six "smaller firms which have spun off from these larger firms."[11] In 2002 the membership list of the American Council on Education Executive Search Roundtable included twenty-five firms working in executive search in higher education.[12] The 2002 *Presidential Search Guidelines and Directory* of the Association of Governing Boards shows that thirteen of these firms assist with presidential searches.[13]

Executive search firms in higher education are experiencing several challenges in the first decade of the twenty-first century; especially noteworthy are the changes driven by technology and the impact of fluctuations in the economy. As Internet use expanded, starting in about 1997, several prominent search firms established Web-based search functions. These Web sites allow candidates to submit their credentials online for consultant review and for matching with the needs of employers. Although some of the Web sites for these firms say that they work with executive positions in corporate settings, the approach seems more focused on midlevel positions. For example, the FutureStep Web site offers employers "instant access to the world's largest database of prescreened middle-management professionals. The candidate pool complements our international presence, assessment tools and comprehensive sourcing strategy to ensure speed, efficiency and quality of service for clients across a range of industries."[14] At LeadersOnLine, candidates are told that "Management Search is an executive search firm—not a 'job board.' . . . After registering, your profile and resume are matched against available positions requirements using proprietary technology. When you 'match' to an available position, you'll be contacted with more information."[15]

Few consultants working with presidential searches in colleges and universities see this kind of approach attracting their current clients, who continue to want the traditional search process—a consultant personally and actively recruiting candidates who are not necessarily looking for a new position, drawing upon a professional network rather than a Web-based search. Like the firms that conduct Web-based searches, search firms using a professional network have become more technologically sophisticated. They expect candidates to submit their materials in electronic form rather than on paper and maintain electronic databases of candidates, board members, and others; strive to provide secure Web-based locations where search committee members can review candidate files; use e-mail to communicate among search committee members; poll committee members using Web-based tools; hold some committee meetings and candidate interviews by audio or video conference; and provide electronic support for various functions such as rating files and contacting candidates. The traditional search process is enhanced in various ways, but not fundamentally transformed, by technology.

The downturn in the economy that began in 2000 has had an indirect impact on presidential search in higher education. Private colleges and universities that rely on their endowment payouts for resources have had less to spend on a presidential search consultant, and some have chosen therefore to carry out the search on their own. Publicly funded institutions in states with significant budget cuts have found their allocations reduced, and some of those too have carried out searches on their own as a result. Impressionistic evidence suggests that reductions in the use of search consultants have generally been felt at the somewhat lower levels of the institutional hierarchy (in searches for vice presidents and deans), with presidential searches continuing to be the most likely to use consultants.

The growth and contraction of search firms is driven to some degree by these same economic cycles. This is seen most clearly in firms that conduct searches on behalf of both corporate clients and nonprofit clients and search firms whose parent companies are businesses of different types. When such large multisector firms find their other businesses impacted by shifts in the economy, there may be an indirect impact on the education search business. Staff and other resources may be reduced because the firm as a whole is contracting, rather than because of downturns in the education search marketplace itself.

Deciding Whether to Use a Consultant

Perhaps partly in response to an awareness of the long-term trend toward using search consultants, boards of trustees facing a presidential vacancy often begin by at least considering the possibility of engaging a consultant. For some boards this is an easy decision—as businesspeople, they instinctively expect to outsource a rarely performed task to a specialist. They are seeking a consultant who has seen it all before, who can help to anticipate challenges and opportunities, and who has a network of prospective candidates to bring to the board for consideration. The logistic complexities of acknowledging applications, managing paperwork, and notifying participants of the outcome of the search all can be completed by someone who has the appropriate professional infrastructure. For other boards, a certain amount of data gathering is required, beginning with getting a clear understanding of what search consultants actually do. In fact, search consultants do a wide variety of things, ranging from the overt and material to the far more subtle. A review of the consultant's role provides a foundation for discussing pros and cons of appointing one, and it can yield ideas about how to select the best consultant for a particular search.

A consultant will bring candidates into the search process who would not otherwise have been there—and institutions can expect these to be better candidates than they would otherwise have. The goal of the search process is to find the best candidate for the job and persuade him or her to consider the position and ultimately to accept the board's offer. The consultant's clearest contribution to this goal is first identifying candidates who bring the qualifications and characteristics that the search committee is seeking and then cultivating their interest in the position. There are certainly searches that, even with a consultant's help, ultimately appoint someone who responded to the advertisement in the *Chronicle of Higher Education* or elsewhere. But far more often, the person selected is someone whom the consultant identified, cultivated, and recruited on the institution's behalf.

Research on searches for corporate CEOs shows that the role of search consultants in that situation is very different from their role in higher education presidential searches. Data gathered in 1995–2000 show that "in most of the successful searches studied, the board of directors, not the consultants, produced the list of primary candidates. Search firms may add one or two names, but knowledge of the industry makes directors better at identifying candidates."[16] In executive searches in higher education, it is the consultant who typically has greater "knowledge of the industry" than the trustees on the search committee, and even faculty and administrators on the search committee rarely have an extensive network among presidents and potential presidents. Those members of the institutional community who do have good contacts are rarely able to devote the time to ferreting out contact information, placing a series of phone calls to cultivate interest, and so on. Suggestions from these individuals can be very useful, but it is rare that they have the resources to do this work on their own.

A search consultant can provide an objective appraisal of the institution. Search committee members often bring unrealistic expectations to the search process. Committee members who have a strong sense of loyalty to and enthusiasm about the institution may believe that the best candidates will share that enthusiasm from the start and be eager for the opportunity to lead Community College X or University Y. Committee members hope that these eager candidates will come forward as candidates, on their own and openly, and make known to the search committee their enthusiasm for the position. The enthusiasm generated by the institutional loyalty of trustees and others, unrealistic to varying degrees, is seen in all types of institutions and appears unchanging over time. Describing a presidential search at Winthrop College, McLaughlin says that many faculty "were bothered by the fact that none of the finalists had produced what they considered serious scholarly work, and they were unimpressed with the institution, all of them small and undistinguished, from which the finalists had come. 'We had hoped to have someone with degrees from prestigious places, someone who had been the academic vice-president at Duke, Chapel Hill, or Virginia.'"[17] Some have called this the "where are the candidates from Harvard" syndrome, and the search consultant can provide a breadth of perspective and some data to bring expectations into line with reality.

A consultant can provide deep insights about candidates. Consultants will do the deep background checks that give a board confidence that a candidate is what she or he appears to be, and they can weed out the candidates who make an excellent first impression and have excellent initial references but do not deliver on the promise of the interview and the initial reports. The network that a consultant has cultivated, often over decades, contributes both to the candidate pool and to the process of checking references. After making hundreds of reference calls, consultants become reasonably skilled at hearing between the lines. Often they can find longtime colleagues who will be candid, off the record, about a candidate's shortcomings, and a person providing a reference who wants to protect his or her reputation with a search consultant is motivated to be particularly candid. This capacity of a consultant to ferret out all essential information is as valuable as the ability to find the candidate in the first place.

A consultant helps to work through the many choices that emerge during the search process. What should the committee do about the strong candidate who is not available on the designated interview dates? Should the full committee read candidate files, or should the consultant prescreen the files? Should reference reports be typed and circulated or provided only orally or in summary form? Not all consultants will agree about how to handle these dilemmas, but most will have thought about the pros and cons of each approach and can provide the committee with enough information to enable it to make a good decision.

A consultant provides an overall approach and framework for the search that is derived from a sense of best practices, having worked on far more searches than any trustee. Most institutions have a general sense of how to run a search but may not have scrutinized their approach in some years. In a public institution, the composition of the presidential search committee may be specified in an institutional statement of policy and procedures. But many institutions have a great deal of flexibility, and a consultant can offer good advice about how to structure the search committee and provide it with a charge. The board may hope for a search that begins in April and appoints a new president who is on the job in July; a consultant can suggest what it would take to accomplish this goal and may suggest alternative timetables. A particularly thorny issue is how to handle the first contact of the final candidate with the campus community. Committees must consider the advantages and disadvantages of bringing several candidates to campus for a day or two of interviews with all interested parties, and they should consider what might happen if the committee brings only the selected candidate to campus, after the board has appointed her or him to be the new president.

How Much Does a Search Consultant Cost?

Some boards are alarmed by what they perceive to be the high cost of a search consultant, while others take the amount in stride. As mentioned above, there are some search-related costs that will be incurred as out-of-pocket expenses regardless of whether a consultant is retained (e.g., candidate travel expenses) and some costs that can be absorbed by the institution if they are not paid to a consultant (e.g., secretarial costs), although these items may still have either a direct or an indirect cost for the institution. While different firms handle these expenses in varying ways, there is always a professional fee associated with retaining a consultant, and that should be seen as the major cost of using a consultant. Virtually all firms structure their fees in the same way, charging one-third of the president's first-year cash compensation; some firms also set a minimum fee that, for searches offering modest salaries, can raise the fee beyond the normal one-third. (The major exception to this fee structure is to charge a flat fee for all presidential searches, regardless of the president's compensation.) Typically the fee is billed at the start of the engagement, even though work on the search usually continues beyond the time when the fee is fully paid. Although there are some search firms that work on "contingency"—that is, their fee depends on their identifying and introducing the institution to the candidate who is ultimately selected—this is not the approach used by firms working in higher education. In higher education, search firms are of the "retained" type, and thus their fee must be paid regardless of who is appointed. For billing purposes, the consultant and the board reach agreement on what the compensation for the new president is likely to be and calculate the fee accordingly; the fee is then adjusted once the appointment is actually made and the compensation set. Some might say that this fee—one-third of the first year's cash compensation—is excessive. Others view it as an investment that will be repaid, if the new president is successful, many times over both in enhanced philanthropic revenues and in general institutional health.

How Do Search Consultants Identify and Recruit Candidates?

Although the nature of the search and the general candidate pool that it attracts is fundamentally a reflection of the institution that is searching, the conclusion of the process ultimately depends on the candidate. Unless a candidate accepts the position, the search does not come to a successful conclusion. The search consultant's role is to identify candidates who can do the particular job the institution needs to have done, focusing on candidates who are willing to take on the job. Within this broad statement are many complex decisions that candidates must make: Are they interested in changing institutions? How do they appraise the fit with the searching institution? Are they willing to have others know of their interest in moving? How do search consultants find candidates and address the issues that are on their minds?

The Process of the Search

How Do Consultants Find the Strong Candidates?

If there is a single most significant contribution that search consultants make to the search process, it is the identification of strong candidates who would not otherwise enter the search. How is this accomplished? Broadly speaking, there are two strategies most commonly used. First, search consultants are in the business of maintaining extensive networks among individuals in their fields. Consultants are only as successful as the people they place, and so they strive to know those people who may be strong candidates, either immediately or after a few years of professional growth. That network of colleagues comes, for some consultants, from years of serving as senior administrators in higher education; it also arises from work as a consultant on many other searches. Second, search consultants are able to call upon a network of "sources"—others in the field who have been watching emerging leaders, supporting the professional growth of colleagues and staff, and generally making an appraisal of who is willing and able to move up in the administrative hierarchy.

Many who wish to be candidates will volunteer themselves and apply directly for the presidency. Consultants often observe that one-half to two-thirds of the candidates who come forward in this fashion are completely unqualified for the position (e.g., lacking education beyond the bachelor's degree, never having shown any prior interest in higher education, lacking any significant administrative experience). Consultants go beyond these unqualified applicants and seek candidates who are more plausible "suspects" for the candidate pool. They are currently in the midst of successful leadership roles; they have current or previous experience at institutions that resemble the searching institution as it is now or as it aspires to become; they have been in their jobs long enough that departure will not be viewed as premature; they are not in the midst of a capital campaign or other multiyear commitment that would make it difficult for them to leave. Search consultants analyze the array of institutions across the country and pursue individuals who are most likely to bring the right experience and other characteristics that make them potentially strong candidates.

Sometimes even individuals who are actively looking for a presidency will wait for the consultant's call, perhaps reflecting a preference not to appear too eager. Others are actively looking for a new position but do not know enough about a particular institution to pursue its presidency, or they may have heard negatives and need to be told about the positives as well. Others are really not considering making a move from their current position, but a well-timed call with the right approach can change their minds.

Some have claimed that these approaches to candidate research (networking, "sourcing," and focusing on comparable institutions) lead to an insidious conservatism in presidential selection, especially when a consultant is involved. They argue that consultants and the trustees they work for prefer to have presidential candidates who have held most of the roles in higher education that would seem to prepare a president for a full understanding of and readiness to lead the institution—having been a faculty member (preferably one who taught, was an active and successful scholar, and was tenured and promoted to full professor), a department chair or a dean, a chief academic officer, and perhaps even a president in a comparable institution. There may be some truth to this claim; the "outside the box" or nontraditional candidate who comes from another sector will not normally be sought out by a consultant; for example, the consultant to a community college is not likely to bring candidates from research universities, the consultant to a research university is not likely to bring candidates from small church-related colleges, and the consultants to most higher education institutions are unlikely to bring candidates from the corporate world. The latter group, candidates from outside higher education, are especially unlikely to be brought forward, and in any case they are difficult to identify. If these are accurate descriptions of search consultants in higher education, should the approach be changed? If committees are open to these various kinds of nontraditional candidates, search consultants can seek them out. There are many examples of candidates who have moved into academic presidencies from nontraditional academic backgrounds and from outside academe entirely. There have been many appointments of a president who had been a senior university officer but had never been a faculty member or an academic affairs administrator, and there have been appointments of lawyers, corporate leaders, and elected officials with little or no college or university background. There are no data to reveal whether these kinds of appointments are more or less likely to be successful than traditional ones.

The more common pattern is for committees to ask their consultants to suggest some nontraditional candidates—but when those candidates are invited to interview, they are seen as "alien." A committee chair recently bemoaned the effort it would take to "teach them what an FTE is" if an outsider to higher education were appointed. Committee members, particularly faculty, routinely worry that a corporate leader will not grasp the culture of higher education. Search committees in public institutions worry that candidates from private institutions will not be able to master legislative relations, and committees in private institutions worry that the candidate from a public institution will bring a bureaucratic frame of mind or a lack of fund-raising experience. When it comes time for the final decision, the candidate who seems most ready to move into the new role smoothly, with the least risk of misstep, is usually preferred. It should also be noted that the ACE report on college presidents shows a substantial increase in the percentage of presidents appointed from outside higher education, from 8 percent in 1998 to almost 15 percent in 2001.[18] Half of these nontraditional candidates came from an "other" background that was not corporate, governmental, or K-12 but may have been some other nonprofit setting.

Analyzing Candidates' Strengths and Weaknesses

Every candidate is of course a mix of strengths and weaknesses, and one of the challenges of the presidential search is to decide which weaknesses are tolerable and which strengths are absolutely essential. For example, the ideal presidential candidate brings fund-raising experience, whether the searching institution is a public community college or a private research university. But in the absence of documented success in fund-raising for their institution, some candidates may bring "proxy" experience—fund-raising for a community arts organization or an alma mater, or cultivation of donors without actually making "the ask." Board members may decide that they can tolerate this limitation, planning to prop up the new president with attendance at fund-raising seminars, a strong vice president for development, or a fund-raising consultant who functions as a coach. An example of a limitation that is not tolerable might be an autocratic tendency, reported by several credible references, suggesting lack of fit with a small private college that has a long tradition of shared governance. There will be other candidates who have some of the technical credentials that suggest they can do the job but lack other key features; for example, some candidates bring extensive administrative experience but none of the scholarly accomplishments that signal deep roots in higher education, or they may bring a strong scholarly record but never have made a decision about hiring or firing or promoting faculty or staff. There will be candidates who seem on paper to have everything that is required but who in person just do not make the grade, and the reverse as well—candidates with apparent flaws in their credentials can convey a professional presence that is so stunning that their limitations can be overlooked. This last point is most definitely not the least; personal presence, or "looking like a president," is often a key factor, spoken or unspoken, in presidential selection.

Many times, however, these strengths and weaknesses are more subtle. There are often candidates with great potential who do not appear to be strong candidates on the surface but who, on further examination, reveal enormous strengths. One of the consultant's responsibilities is to assist a committee in dropping the weak candidates who appear strong and pursuing the strong candidates who appear less strong than they really are—that is, helping the search committee to get beneath the surface. There is an enormously successful president today who was initially passed over by the search committee and only invited to interview because the consultant encouraged the committee to see beneath the surface of the résumé. When some other candidates dropped out and left a vacancy in the interview schedule, the dual impact of chance and persuasion changed the course of the search and the institution. At the same time, there are candidates whose résumés and even references are stellar but who will never be successful presidents. The consultant often knows about these limitations and normally will share them with the search committee, which disregards this advice at its peril.

Assessing Candidates' Interest in Changing Institutions

While some candidates do learn about a presidential opportunity in advertisements, these are normally candidates who have some reason to read the advertisements, usually because they are preparing to make a career move. There are certainly many successful academic administrators who seek to move on in the midst of great professional and institutional success, but there are also many whose readiness to move is driven at least in part by current difficulties. Difficulties are not unusual for academic administrators and are often created by the decisions that administrators must make, none of which can possibly please everyone. At the same time, search committees are well advised to look carefully at candidates who are especially eager to move on, in order to be sure that there is no undue pressure on them to move or, if there is, that its origins are understood and that it brings no discredit to the candidate. Search committees can expect a search consultant to be alert to these possibilities; their professional network will often enable them to gather the kind of background information that answers these questions.

Assessing Candidates' Interest in the Particular Position

How do candidates know that a particular institution is one whose presidency they are well suited for? They must know enough about the institution to make a good appraisal of the fit. As discussed above, enthusiastic search committee members may imagine that their institution is better known than it actually is; in fact, while many administrators have a wide knowledge of institutions around the country, and most have a good familiarity with a certain group of institutions (those in their region, or those of their particular institutional type), few have a strong and accurate insider knowledge of the critical issues, culture, and current challenges that a particular other institution is actually facing. An institution whose visibility is limited because of its resources, scope, or location will probably not be well enough known to many potentially strong candidates. The extent to which a candidate is or is not interested in the presidency of a particular institution is not a good indicator of whether he or she is a good candidate; search committees are often entranced by a candidate's enthusiasm for their presidency, and they may be reluctant to cultivate the interest of a candidate who is initially neutral or even negative toward their institution. Focusing on the candidates who already know the institution could be, for many institutions, to cast a very small net.

Appraising Candidates for Institutional Fit

Although there may not be data to address this issue, one might speculate that candidates normally seek to "marry up"—that is, to move to an institution of greater stature, more substantial resources, stronger student quality and selectivity, and so on. Search committees are often looking for the opposite, seeking candidates who are already at institutions with at least the size and strength that their institution has already attained, and preferably an institution of even greater reputation and health—in other words, seeking a candidate willing to "marry down." The inconsistency between these competing goals can often be seen in the candidates who enter searches on their own; they are typically from institutions that the searching institution perceives to be weaker than their own. The search committee therefore views them as less desirable than candidates from stronger institutions, from whom they can learn the strategies that might lead to success and from whom they can gain the aura of the stronger institution. Although there are many examples of candidates who stepped up to institutions of greater stature and made significant contributions, that is rarely the image that the search committee holds at the start of the search process.

Best Practices

- Design a search process that earns the respect of the institutional community so that the new president begins with this measure of credibility.
- If you use a search consultant, learn about the nature of the firm and check its references as carefully as those for each candidate.
- In selecting a search consultant, test the chemistry of the relationship between the committee, especially the committee chair, and the consultant.
- Take advantage of the unique opportunity the search process provides to bring varied campus constituencies together and increase understanding of the institutional culture.
- Evaluate candidates with both objectivity and intuition, and validate this appraisal via careful conversations with those who have observed the candidate firsthand, including the search consultant.
- Enlist the help of a transition committee, community leaders, the outgoing president, if appropriate, and others (such as a search consultant) who can assist in making key introductions and in helping the new president to avoid fatal mistakes.

Helping Candidates Begin Again

Some search consultants are able to assist significantly with the process of transition, from the president's departure to the establishment of the successor, and their advice should be sought. The departure of a president is a complex event that extends over a potentially lengthy transitional period, and it is an event that both the institution and the president will want to manage. Although departures occur in different contexts, there are some valid general observations about managing transition from the perspectives of the institution and the individual, particularly during the period of the search.

The institution reveals its character and core values in the way it handles the transition, so the plans and events should be handled with care. Public events are of course most visible. There should be an opportunity to recognize the efforts and contributions of the outgoing president and to honor her or him in the presence of key audiences in celebrations that can range from vast to intimate. Internally, planning the transition process is critical as well. A transition committee should be appointed, with functions that can range from communication management to organizational work within the president's office and among the senior staff.

The president has a considerable stake in the transition as well. Most presidents welcome the attention that is focused on them during this period, but the outgoing president's greatest challenge is to let go at the appropriate point. Many long-term and successful presidents have considerable affection for their institutions and their colleagues and want to continue to be part of the institutional community and to help the institution thrive. They make offers of assistance that include continuing to work with major donors with whom they had strong relationships, establishing themselves in an office just down the hall from the new president so that they can be easily available, becoming a tenured professor and seeking an active role in faculty governance, and so on. Although an outside observer might speculate that this is not a healthy relationship for anyone, outgoing presidents seem often to be blinded by their institutional commitment or their anxiety about the departure and propose approaches that can be alarming to the incoming president. The board's role is essential in this process, and it should allow the new president to decide on the arrangements he or she prefers. Some will welcome the active role of their predecessors and some will not. Of those who permit their predecessors to be involved, some will regret it and some will be delighted. Each case is obviously distinctive, but all should be handled with sensitivity to both presidents.

The outgoing president typically has several broad choices: to stay within the same institution, often as a tenured faculty member; to stay within higher education but at another institution; and to leave higher education. Those who remain on campus often are given year-long sabbaticals, which can help to address the uneasiness alluded to in the previous paragraph. Becoming a faculty member can be a very attractive option, offering a lifestyle usually quite different from the relentless demands of the presidency but also quite different in the perquisites and satisfactions that it provides. For those not ready to retire, moving to another institution as a president is probably the most common option; the ACE report on presidents finds that in 1986, 17.3 percent of presidents were coming from a previous presidency, and in 2001 that group had grown to 20.4 percent.[19] Some former presidents seek positions outside of colleges and universities but not far from them. For example, some become consultants (possibly search consultants), some take up other academic or professional interests like international education or the arts, and many hope for (but do not always find) positions in foundations, where they can distribute grants instead of asking for them and shape educational policy and practice at a broader level. Presidents whose terms have concluded under unhappy circumstances face a greater challenge as they move on. Although some take several years to make a transition, others move on to new positions quickly and successfully, particularly those who are flexible in the career moves they consider.

Candidates' Concerns about Confidentiality and Wish for Deniability

Why would a candidate be reluctant to have others know that he or she is applying for a position? There are many reasons, and they can be very compelling. Most obvious, perhaps, is the notion that most people do not want others to know that they tried and were rejected; with no certainty of getting the position, candidates would rather have no one know they were interested in it. If someone must know, a candidate would often prefer to say that she or he was recruited for the position, with a great deal of pressure exerted by an energetic and purposeful search consultant who drew the reluctant candidate into a conversation about the position; the candidate might portray himself or herself as having been polite enough to listen to the story of the institution but never having formally applied for the position and therefore never having been formally turned down.

Other candidates have equally grave concerns about becoming lame ducks in their current positions. This is especially true of candidates who are currently presidents, considering a move to a second or third presidency. These people have an enormous amount to lose in terms of credibility with their board of trustees, effectiveness in working with faculty and other campus constituencies, success in working with major donors whose contributions are premised on continuity of institutional leadership, or with elected officials who make significant budgetary decisions. It is not at all uncommon for presidents seeking additional presidencies to refuse to enter the search until the last minute, to be very reluctant to provide a letter expressing interest or even a résumé because it might reveal them as willing applicants, and to refuse to participate in a public appearance on campus until after being selected for the position. If the search committee wants to move such a candidate to the final stage of the search process, and perhaps even to offer her or him the presidency, it is extremely important for committee members to try to understand the candidate's concerns. The committee should strive to construct a selection process that balances the wish to engage the campus in the search process with the need to protect the candidate's confidentiality.

In the end, the selected candidates are in control. If they decide that the spotlight is too glaring or too damaging, they can withdraw from the search and deny ever having had an interest in the position, potentially leaving the committee empty-handed. The committee, in shaping its search process, must decide whether to risk losing the candidate. Faced with this decision, some committees will say, "We wouldn't want a president who wasn't willing to appear before the full campus community and allow us to invite input from everyone." In fact, there are many fine and inclusive presidents who would be unwilling to do this, and search committees should try to understand the meaning of exposure from the candidate's perspective.

The Impact of "Sunshine Laws"

Because of the preference of strong candidates for confidentiality in the presidential search process, it is no wonder that "sunshine laws" pose major problems. Sunshine laws are those state laws that require public agencies, including public institutions of higher education, to permit public access to their meetings and their records. Although "freedom of information or public records [acts] are in place in all 50 states,"[20] each state takes a slightly different approach, and anyone interested in the laws of a particular state should seek specific information about that state's policy and practice. In addition, "an increasing number of state legislatures are enacting exceptions to their open records laws to exclude candidate names from mandatory disclosure. . . . There appear to be at least twenty-two states in which there appear to be statutory exceptions for the names of applicants or candidates for public employment. Three of these exceptions are limited to candidates for chief executive of a state institution of higher education."[21] Three states offer examples of different points along the continuum.

—In Wisconsin, any candidate for a chancellor's position in a public institution may request to have his or her name kept confidential until the final five or so candidates' names are presented to the president of the University of Wisconsin System for selection. Search committee meetings are public except that when candidate names are to be discussed, the committee may vote to move into closed session, providing significant candidate confidentiality. The work and records of the search consultant are confidential.

—In Nevada, the search consultant's recruiting efforts and preliminary conversations with presidential candidates may be kept confidential, but the approximately ten candidates whose names are brought to the board of regents for review must be made public; candidate interviews and the committee vote must be public, but a report on their references may be made in closed session.

—Florida offers an example at the "sunniest" extreme. Florida stipulates that presidential searches at public institutions must be open at every phase, with public access to even the most preliminary and sensitive work of the search consultant. In searches at Florida's public institutions, committee conversations about candidates may not occur outside of public meetings or, conversely, any conversation among committee members about candidates, no matter how informal, must have prior public notice. Search consultants are often reluctant to assist institutions in states with strong sunshine laws because the quality of their professional work is so seriously impeded by those restrictions, because candidates can be so seriously harmed, and because the outcome can so easily be compromised by the lack of open exchange and candor associated with public meetings.

Rescuing a Failed Search

In spite of following the best advice, and sometimes in spite of using an excellent search consultant, searches fail. A failed search is one that comes to the conclusion of the planned process without an offer extended to and accepted by a candidate. Why do searches fail, and what can an institution do to recover? Searches fail for many reasons. In some cases, the offering was weak: the position was unattractive because of low compensation, undesirable location, a dysfunctional institution or board, inadequate public resources or philanthropic support, a weak or negative institutional reputation, the assumption on the part of potential outside candidates that an insider was certain to be appointed, or other factors. In other cases, timing may have been a problem; a search begun late in the academic recruiting cycle may lose its strongest candidates to other searches that are concluding sooner. Recruiting efforts may have been limited—most likely a problem in searches that have not used consultants. Committee expectations may be unrealistic, with several strong candidates rejected because they did not conform to the aspirations of the search committee, as described above. The candidate selected may decide, in the end, that she or he does not wish to move to a new position, and in the absence of strong alternate candidates, the institution may be left empty-handed.

What can be done when this happens? It is essential to begin with an equally careful and candid analysis of what went wrong. If the offering is weak, it makes little sense to repeat the same search steps without first at least trying to address the problem. While there is not much that can be done about an undesirable location, a search burdened by that problem may decide to focus on prospective candidates who already live in the region or in the same kind of location. There may be other features that can be modified, such as compensation, clarification regarding inside candidates, addressing issues of dysfunctionality, and so on. The new search should be started early in the annual presidential search cycle: for example, there are more advertisements placed in early September than at any other time of year. While some might say that searches occur at all times of year, candidates are often reluctant to decide to move after having made commitments for the upcoming academic year, including commitments by spouses and children enrolled in school; this creates a tendency to search during the fall, make appointments during the spring, and work through the process of transition during the summer.

Having analyzed the failed search and addressed the problems that are identified, the institution has some choices. It may decide to launch a new search and simply try to do a better job—looking harder for strong prospects, being more enthusiastic in recruiting, being more realistic in expectations, being more sensitive to candidate concerns, and so on. Or the institution may decide to take a rest from searching and to appoint an interim president for perhaps two years. This may provide time for addressing the concerns that were identified, and it allows a new pool of potential candidates to emerge (e.g., those who need just a couple of additional years in their current position before being ready to consider a new opportunity). Another possibility is to make an internal appointment of a candidate who might not have initially seemed like the right choice but who, on further reflection, brings a strong understanding of institutional culture and history, is comfortable in the local community, has a network among donors and legislators, and may look better at the end of a long unsuccessful search than he or she did at the start, when expectations were perhaps unrealistically high. In the corporate world, many CEOs are promoted from within, and there is much to recommend this practice for certain institutions of higher education at certain moments in their history.

Making the Decision

Boards must address both objective and subjective considerations in selecting a search consultant. There are three natural starting points.

—Review the materials assembled by the Association of Governing Boards, describing firms that have carried out presidential searches in the preceding several years, or similar information that can be provided by the American Council on Education. Look for firms that have worked with a list of clients that makes sense to you. Church-related colleges may seek consultants who have worked with other church-related institutions. Midwestern research uni-

Emerging Trends

- Costs will increase: As the presidency becomes more difficult and turnover more rapid, retaining the consultant perceived to be the best will become increasingly important to boards, and boards will be willing to pay a premium for that service.
- Financial pressures will increase resistance to using consultants: Institutions caught in a financial crunch will try to carry out presidential searches without the assistance of a consultant.
- Time pressure will increase: Trustees with corporate backgrounds will insist on a rapid search, creating increasing pressure to use a search consultant who can bring the search to a rapid conclusion.
- Sunshine laws will be increasingly contentious: As trustees see the problems created by sunshine laws, they will use their legislative influence to seek modifications that allow protection of candidates, while the media will continue to seek greater access to the search process.

versities may want someone who has worked with other institutions of any type in the Midwest—or may prefer a focus on research universities in any part of the country. Private colleges striving for stronger national reputations may want a consultant who has worked with selective national liberal arts colleges.

—Review the *Chronicle of Higher Education,* including its Web site, to evaluate the advertisements placed by other institutions carrying out presidential searches. In addition to indicating which firms have worked with similarly situated institutions, this source will also show which institutions are currently competing for the same candidates.

—Talk with colleagues at these institutions and on the professional conference and association circuit to learn which firms they have worked with, as well as what their experience with these firms has been.

Once the list of search firms with appropriate experience has been assembled, the list of questions to ask them can be compiled. Public institutions may have a formal process of creating an Request for Proposal (RFP) that can be sent to these firms. Whether through informal conversation or formal RFP, determine which firms seem most likely to be a good fit for your search. Some may not have a strong network of relationships in institutions that resemble yours, some may be too busy with other engagements or be unable to begin work promptly, some may charge fees that exceed your resources, some may take a more flexible or a more structured approach than you are comfortable with, and so on.

After gathering this information about the firms on your list, select a smaller number, perhaps three, and ask them to meet with members of the board or the search committee. Spending one or two hours with the person who would be your consultant can be extremely revealing and should help you to select the firm with which you want to work. The work will be intensive and the consultant will be your representative to candidates, so it is important that you feel personally confident in that individual. Test your impressions by phoning some of the references that the consultant provides, including both client institutions and individuals whom the consultant has placed in their new positions.

The Future of Presidential Searches

Presidential searches will increasingly claim the national higher education spotlight. Because of the multiple constituencies of any college or university presidency, the appointee will be equally visible once she or he begins the position, but the greater visibility of the search process also suggests that candidates may be increasingly reluctant to enter it. Institutions eager to capture the interest of highly successful administrators to become candidates construct processes that protect these candidates from public view until after they are appointed. The new president then must lead powerful constituencies who did not have the opportunity for direct involvement in the search process and who may or may not have full respect for their representatives on the search committee—if indeed they had representatives. This can leave the new president in an even more vulnerable position, with constituents who are mistrustful from the start. The challenge for trustees is to shape a process that maintains the trustee responsibility for selecting the new president while carrying out a search process that earns the respect of the campus community and simultaneously provides sufficient confidentiality to engage the most reluctant candidate. In all institutions—public and private, large and small—the selection of presidents will continue to be a decision that defines the institution and thus must be undertaken with the greatest care, whether with a search consultant or without one.

CHAPTER TEN

The Interim President: An Effective Transitional Leader

Thomas H. Langevin and Allen E. Koenig

There is a need for more effective transitions between outgoing and incoming presidents. An interim president often can prepare a smooth transition from one administration to the next. Additionally, an interim chief executive can play a unique role in helping a college or university to reevaluate its longer-term leadership needs.

The placement of interim presidents involves a different process than that of permanent presidential searches. Simply put, the interim candidate is prequalified to transition quickly and easily into temporary leadership responsibilities. And the process to place an interim leader can be designed to be as user friendly as possible, particularly for institutions under stress or in crisis. One model for the interim president transition process is outlined in the "Handbook for the Placement of Transitional Leadership."[1]

This chapter examines the differences between interim and acting presidents, the purposes and scope of interim leadership, the successful attributes of an interim president, and several case histories of effective interim service. The definitions, the interim scenarios, the proposed transition processes, and the case studies in this chapter come from our eleven years of experience in developing and building the Registry for College and University Presidents (the Registry).

Interim versus Acting

The placement of interim presidents at higher education institutions has become a documented trend over the past twenty years. These appointees serve as high-profile substitutes while the institution conducts a search for a new chief executive officer. Although there are similarities between the positions, there are necessary and important distinctions between acting and interim leaders.

For instance, a person from inside the college or university traditionally has filled an acting position, while an interim president has typically come from outside of the institution. This distinction is a critical one because acting and interim leaders can encounter very different experiences during their temporary terms as presidents. The appointment of an interim president helps to avoid the "baggage" that an internal appointee may have, particularly since an impression associated with the term *acting* generally is that the person is "holding the line" and does not have the full power of a regular president.

An interim president is often more desirable than an acting president for several reasons. First, to achieve the fullest degree of flexibility in a vacancy while the search goes on, it is important that the interim person be already qualified for the post by virtue of having past presidential experience. Often, acting presidents step in from other administrative positions, such as an academic vice presidency, and do not have the experience necessary for immediate presidential responsibilities. Second, it is imperative that the temporary person not be a candidate for the permanent job in order to avoid having the search process become too politicized. Third, the temporary president should serve only for an agreed-upon term limit that clearly notifies the campus community that there is a beginning and an end to the work of this transitional officer. Finally, the person should not have had a prior relationship with the institution that may have caused the accumulation of "baggage" destructive to the full empowerment of the position holder.

An interim president must be experienced enough to know what to push and what not to push during the interim period, recognizing that the goal of the interim service is to keep the institution moving carefully but steadily forward, since no college or university can remain "in neutral." *Ultimately, the goal of interim service is to prepare for new leadership*. Ideally, an outside interim president can be a transitional adviser to the incoming new president, because the person does not have a vested interest in the institution's future. For a new first-time president, the benefit of drawing upon the presidential experience of an interim can help the permanent president avoid many hidden agendas and pitfalls. This is often not possible when an internal person has been the transitional president and will remain at the institution when the new president arrives, particularly if that person has been an unsuccessful candidate for the job.

Best Practices

- Utilize the benefits of having an interim president prepare a smooth transition from one administration to the next.
- Invite interim presidents to assist in the presidential search process for longer-term leadership.
- Allow interim presidents to take the internal politics out of the workplace.
- Value successful presidential experience as the most important variable in leading an institution.
- Advise interim presidents not to appoint permanent senior administrators.

When Interim Leadership Is Appropriate

There are a number of scenarios that call for the placement of an interim president, including the resignation or retirement of a long-term president, the sudden departure of the president, a presidential sabbatical leave, or the need to fill this senior vacancy on a temporary basis.

The departure of a long-term president. This almost always calls for a buffer or cushion between the old and the new. A new person coming immediately after a recently retired and revered president can have significant identity problems, especially if the former president remains, lingering as president emeritus or returning to a tenured faculty position. The interim period provides distance in time and space for both the previous president and the new one. An experienced interim person can demonstrate a new style and prepare the institution to expect and more readily accept a different style of leadership in the future.

The sudden, unforeseen departure of the president. Usually this brings trauma to an institution that may cause serious disruption, especially if the circumstances surrounding the departure are unknown or unfortunate. This can result in severe morale problems and a lack of direction for the institution. An experienced leader in an interim role can serve as a soothing presence while quietly keeping key issues moving forward.

Presidential sabbatical. This does not take place in higher education as much as it should, since many governing boards think either that the sabbatical leave is designed only for faculty or that they can't get along without a president even for a short period of time. When it does take place, an outside interim is imperative, for a few reasons. Such a placement avoids internal fighting and is not threatening to the leadership of the absent president because the outsider has nothing to gain, particularly the president's job. A person with presidential experience elsewhere can move into the office on a temporary basis and follow a prescribed agenda from the president and the board.

Filling a chief academic officer vacancy. In some instances, institutions need to fill temporarily the positions of chief academic officer and provost, and in such cases, a former president from another institution is an excellent interim choice. Since many presidents rose to their positions from serving as chief academic officers, whether by coming in temporarily to pick up the pieces after a failed search or serving after the former CAO departed suddenly for a new position, the use of a president as interim CAO is reasonable to provide an institution the time to search for a permanent successor in this area. And, if the president is also considering departure options, employing an interim vice president ensures that the next president can pick the chief academic officer's successor.

Characteristics of Successful Interim Presidents

The successful interim president possesses many of the following characteristics.

1. Previous presidential experience
2. Integrity
3. Honesty
4. Self-confidence
5. Fair and even-handed treatment of colleagues
6. Tough decision making within a consultative style
7. Broad and authentic communication skills
8. The ability to work cooperatively yet forcefully with the board of trustees, particularly the board's chair and its executive committee members

Potential Benefits and Drawbacks

For effective interim leadership, a variety of initiatives and responses should be pursued to maintain and increase institutional momentum during the interim period. In situations of low morale, an interim leader can be a calming, stabilizing presence. As CEO, the individual should be candid, open, and caring, thereby providing the institution with a positive frame of reference to help it persevere through the real uncertainties of a leadership turnover.

An interim may also be a significant agent of change in preparing the college, sometimes still in a wounded, vulnerable condition, to accomplish the search for the permanent successor. There may be situations to resolve, not only out of necessity, but also because change will enhance the school's chances of procuring the best candidates for the new presidency. For example, if one or more senior administrators need to be terminated, the interim president can act and separate the individual(s) from the school. Also, an interim can take advantage of the temporary position to get widespread cooperation and involvement in matters such as curricular reform. Such initiatives relieve the new president of immediately expending "capital" on these types of activities.

An interim should use the temporary leadership position to evaluate thoroughly the affairs of the school, monitoring and controlling expenses as necessary. He or she can also bring about an objective review of enrollment management and admissions policies or practices, or keep an ongoing capital campaign focused and on track.

Finally, the interim president can serve as a valuable resource to the search committee in the designation of the permanent president. Having experience, yet not harboring aspirations to stay on or move up in a career, the interim can be a credible and key adviser to the search committee, to the campus community overall, and even to the finalist candidates when they arrive on campus to be interviewed. Interim presidents can answer candidates' questions candidly and are able to prevent the "skeletons in the closet" syndrome that still surprises a fair number of incoming presidents.

There are also potential drawbacks to the interim approach. If interim service is too prolonged, the interim leader can become entangled in the campus's long-standing traditions and cultural patterns, and these actions can disrupt more immediate and pressing matters. As a general rule, interim chief executive officers should not appoint new senior administrators. New presidents should be provided the opportunity to make and "own" these appointments.

Interim Presidents in Action: Pertinent Case Histories

The following case histories come from reports to the Registry from our interim placements. Wherever possible the reports are quoted directly, but without attribution or identification.

A Catholic College

In 1995 the college here described[2] decided to hire an interim president after having appointed three presidents over a period of seven years. These short presidential tenures had prompted the board of trustees to take a fresh look at the governance of the institution. In fact, dissatisfaction with the inability to sustain presidential leadership went beyond the board and concerned the regional ownership body. A two-tiered board governance system and the religious sponsoring body was not working well, and the campus was characterized by low morale among faculty and staff members. There was distrust of the board by the faculty and distrust between the board and the sponsoring body. In the midst of the presidential "merry-go-round," the faculty was also divided and dispirited.

Although institutional concerns related to enrollment and curriculum were manageable, in general, the college's internal constituencies were not working well together, and many felt that there were no significant strategic planning efforts to remedy the situation. The issues facing the institution were so serious that some board members believed that the college might have to close.

A small Interim Presidential Committee was appointed to secure an interim chief executive. The committee included representation from the board, including its chair, the president of the sponsoring body, the chair of the faculty senate, and one representative each from the staff and the student body. After interviewing three finalists, all of whom were retired presidents, the Interim Presidential Committee recommended one, who had been president of a college in the South, to serve as interim president. A two-year interim period was arranged with the board's executive committee, in part because of concerns about past instability in the office of the president.

By the end of the first year, it was evident to the board and the sponsoring body that they did not want to search for a president during the interim's second year, and they requested that the interim president be retained for an additional year. This would allow for various governance issues at the college to be resolved before beginning the search for the permanent president. The faculty and staff increasingly accepted this objective as the interim president's leadership gained widespread credibility on campus and within college constituencies.

One key to a successful presidential transition at the college was the intentional restoration of trust between the chairman of the board and the president of the Dallas chapter of the sponsoring body. This sense of trust grew throughout and across the constituencies as they recognized the integrity, leadership style, and substance of the interim president. In the local and regional communities, this restoration was instrumental in gaining support for a capital campaign nearing its launch.

When the school embarked on the presidential search, it was known that by the time the new president arrived, the board would be reorganized, simplified structurally, and aligned with the faculty governance committees. During the interim president's leadership, lines of communication and arrangements for joint procedures between the board and the sponsoring body were developed. Clear relationships were also established and self-assessments were undertaken by both groups, and the institution began to move forward as a team. As the chairman of the board noted at the end of the interim president's term, "The interim president was just what the doctor ordered. . . . The College now has a Strategic Plan, we concluded a successful Capital Campaign, and all the members of the organization are on the same page of the hymnal. In addition, with the help of the interim president we now have a president who can lead us into the future."[3] When the new permanent president was appointed, it was apparent that the campus was effectively employing the new governance structure and that many institutional processes were working well. With more than five years in leadership at the college, the permanent president has been accepted into a strong campus community, whose strength had been temporarily constrained because of significant flaws in governance and leadership. The board now operates more effectively and with a clearer sense of its roles and responsibilities relative to the campus and the sponsoring body.

A Major Public University

As in the situation previously described, there was an abrupt change in presidential leadership at the university presented in this case study from the early 1990s.[4] The president resigned suddenly, and for the next six months, a well-known president emeritus of a midwestern public university served as an interim president. This was a critical time for both the campus and the larger university system. The interim president was a key figure in working with the state legislature to improve internal morale and to keep the university's strategic plan moving forward.

As the most complex professional institution within the state university system, this institution incorporates a medical school, several allied health schools, and a law school. The sine qua non for improving the overall campus situation was to recognize the needs of the medical school and to restore its faculty's sense that they were held in high regard. Because this professional school was the "flagship" of the university, these concerns became the interim president's first priority. In order to address the lowered morale in the medical school, he attended numerous student forums, alumni gatherings, and recognition ceremonies, as well as various other venues, where it became possible, after repeated appearances, to foster a feeling of continuity and normalcy.

As cooperation and morale on campus improved, various constituencies stepped forward to help the interim president present the financial "case" to the governor and the legislature. The interim president also presented the university's needs to the system chancellor and the other presidents in the system. The legislature and the governor responded positively to the efforts of the interim president, the chancellor, and others. Each wanted to help restore the fiscal soundness of the university and took action to do so. Subsequently, a number of key capital needs were met.

During the interim president's relatively short term of office, he overcame a set of typical yet still thorny challenges: strategic planning, budgeting, managing a complex daily operation, advising the new search committee, and making the external case for improved support for the campus and university system. A permanent president was appointed as his interim period drew to a conclusion, and the community welcomed this individual to a rejuvenated institution marked by new senses of momentum and collaboration.

An Independent College

When this college decided to retain an interim chief executive officer, it was suffering from broad-based identity and financial problems as well as several more specific human relations and academic policy dilemmas.[5] To start, the trustees created a committee of themselves to search for an interim president following the resignation of a president who had served for five years. Her highly successful predecessor had led the college for twenty years. During the years preceding the presidential resignation, there were large, virtually wasted, investments in ineffective programs; enrollment went into a decline; the endowment lost principal; and the budget accumulated a deficit. The board, in selecting an interim president, set balancing the budget as that individual's first priority. In addition, several campus constituencies wanted the leadership to face the issue of the long-term viability of the school as a women's college.

The interim president, a veteran of three interim presidencies, was appointed and was asked, while working to unify the campus, to address immediately the college's finance and enrollment problems as well as helping the board as it considered its future role in the governance of the school. The interim president carefully established a rapport with both the board and the faculty; and although he could not generate enough funds to balance the budget, in light of an enrollment shortfall that had

Emerging Trends

- The use of an interim president has become more common over the past fifteen to twenty years.
- Many interim presidents pledge, as a condition of appointment, not to be candidates for the permanent presidency.
- More public college and universities are beginning to use interim presidents.
- Firms such as the Registry for College and University Presidents are likely to expand their service of placing interim presidents in the future.
- More institutions now believe that there should be a transition interim president between outgoing and new presidents.

existed for a number of years, he was able to reduce the operating budget significantly and refocus institutional and board attention on the school's most pressing problems.

As an interim president, he was able to deal candidly with the issues of low morale and instability resulting from leadership turnover. He achieved a degree of stability in the day-to-day life of the college, opened many communication channels that had been closed for years, and convinced a cohort of constituents to reconsider their differences and explore possibilities in collaboration.

The newly elected permanent president discovered upon arrival that the college needed a new academic vice president. Not wanting to rush such a crucial appointment, and needing to learn the culture of the institution to a greater degree first, the new president took advantage of the interim president's popularity with the faculty and persuaded him to accept the role of interim chief academic officer.

A Community College

The interim president of this community college began his assignment on a dysfunctional campus.[6] The faculty had taken a vote of no confidence in the previous president, labor negotiations were at an impasse, student enrollment was declining, fund balances had eroded, and the institution was composed of "armed camps" of employees who did not speak to one another.

The previous president had left the institution following a series of disagreements with the board. Written policies and procedures were not in place. Every unit of the institution claimed to have detailed procedures, but they were not written. The college was administered on a model of decentralized decision making, and decisions were made on the basis of an administrator's interpretation of the procedures. As a result, several administrators on campus were making decisions that were clearly the responsibility of the president or the governing board.

Over a two-year period, these circumstances were steadily turned around by an interim leader dedicated to taking politics out of the presidency and reordering the college's policy manuals and administrative handbooks for the permanent president.

Special Cases: Interims Who Follow "Legends"

Unlike the foregoing case histories, the following two cases address the environment and issues surrounding an interim who succeeds a long-serving president.[7] In these examples, the interim leader was brought in following lengthy and successful tenures of previous presidents. In neither case did the interim president face a deficit, an enrollment problem, or the other typical challenges of an institution moving toward crisis.

In both instances, the interim's most critical tasks were social and psychological ones, rather than rectifying budget imbalances or resolving internal political battles. For example, one interim had to speak daily with the retired president, answer her e-mails, and "run interference" between her and the college's employees. For the purpose of comparison, one college is referred to as *A* and the other as *B*.

College A had a long and distinguished history, with many established traditions. Since World War II, however, the institution had changed its mission and its student constituency. College B was a much younger institution. College A's president had served for nearly fifteen years, while College B's president had served for over thirty. Each president was a charismatic leader, ubiquitous in the affairs of the institution and always looked to for vision and direction. Both led with consensus, but the force of their personalities made things go their way. Both presidents left abruptly, and their senior staffs had to deal with the psychologically daunting prospect of steering their institutions forward without anyone at the helm.

The senior staff at College A was sophisticated and experienced. Senior staffers at College B, while well qualified, were either new to higher education or new to their positions. Both groups found themselves in the discomfort of sudden change after long periods of administrative stability and direction. Additionally, both colleges were engaged in long-range planning efforts and considering revisions to their institutional missions. Senior administrators at both institutions could not move beyond collective fears about their next leaders, as characterized by statements like "They won't find anyone like her" and "There isn't anyone else who can play that role in this college."

The interim presidents placed on these campuses faced the task of affirming that the institution did not have to find someone "like her" and that others could indeed play "that role." Both interim presidents were challenged to demonstrate how different people, playing different roles, could provide creative leadership to their colleges. A second lesson to be learned at each school was that a different style of leadership did not signal the abandonment of that institution's traditions, history, and ethos. Further, the interims had to instill in the vice presidents the confidence that having served successfully under one president, they were up to serving successfully with another. Knowing that these key administrators were competent and effective, the interim presidents became coaches, disarming fears that the next presidents would never fit in. A key ingredient in each interim president's success was the decision to provide these same vice presidents with considerable independence and freedom to define their changing responsibilities. This investment was met with correspondingly innovative administrative decision making.

The two interim presidents' creative approaches to leadership also influenced the work of the search firms retained to hire the permanent presidents. The climates of trust on both campuses set the stage for new leadership and helped to prevent the collisions of style and personality that could have occurred if new and dynamic executives had been hired after the departures of long-standing "legends." Sometimes long-term successful presidents can make their successors into inadvertent victims, and the placement of a professionally trained interim president between the two administrations can provide an institution with added stability at this critical juncture as well as raising the likelihood of a smooth transition.

The Future of the Interim Presidency

There is gathering evidence of the value, in selected situations, of using an interim president for the shift between old and new leadership. As the presidential transition process becomes viewed more as a strategic opportunity for an institution to review its mission, programs, budget, advancement, and long-term goals, an interim president who is experienced enough to know what to do and not to do during the vulnerable period of transition can play a decisive role in helping that institution to reevaluate itself and set appropriate expectations for its next leader.

CHAPTER ELEVEN

Leaks Kill: Communication and Presidential Transition

John Ross

Higher education and the fourth estate—the news media—squabble vociferously over the release of names of candidates. Media often contend that it is an abuse of power to withhold the names of the women and men who might be selected to lead a college or university, particularly if the institution is directly supported by public moneys. As Nick Estes points out in *State University Presidential Searches: Law and Practice,* searching in sunshine limits the potential effects of cronyism, nepotism, and discrimination and opens the prospect of greater public involvement in the process.[1] Yet few, if any, aspects of a presidential transition carry greater potential jeopardy than the untimely disclosure of a candidacy.

The media's thirst for news and higher education's real and continuing need for search confidentiality will always collide. Throughout the 1990s, the absence of reasonable assurances of confidentiality and the news media's aggressive quest for lists of candidates under freedom of information statutes kept many sitting presidents from agreeing to pursue their nominations for CEO vacancies at larger and more prestigious universities. For example, Margarita Bauzá, writing in the *Detroit News,* took the University of Michigan to task in 2002 for spending twenty thousand dollars to charter a private plane to facilitate final interviews with candidates for the UM presidency. Hers was the lead story on a front page that also contained articles about reducing the workloads of Michigan doctors, first reports of shootings at the ticket counter of Los Angeles International Airport, and the initial announcement of President George W. Bush's plans for Wall Street reform. In that context, the story about the cost of the private plane seems unimportant.

Yet the reason the *Detroit News* decided to highlight Bauzá's story was revealed after the story had jumped from the front page to page 6:

"It was the first time," she wrote, that "one of Michigan's largest colleges sought a chief executive since a 1999 state Supreme Court ruling said such searches aren't subject to the Open Meetings Act." Further, she reported that attorneys for UM had advised members of the search committee to "keep e-mails and documents to a minimum because they might become public and advised them against contact with the media during the process."[2] Nothing so fires the energies of the media than scorning their desire for information. Presidential searchers, take note: in every controversy, the press will have the last, and loudest, word.

Another hot-button issue over the past decade has been the cost of presidential searches. One search for a University of Michigan president cost taxpayers $503,186. That individual stayed at UM for four years before accepting the presidency of an Ivy League institution in 2001. Taxpaying voters might have noted that that single search cost about half of what a high school graduate makes in a lifetime. The cost of presidential searches now runs from $100,000 upward, depending on the size and reputation of the institution. The cost increases, of course, with any difficulties in finding suitable finalists. In turn, the size of these expenditures—which for tax-supported institutions is generally part of the public record—whets the appetite of the press.

Unfortunately, few institutions bother to create contexts for the costs of searches. What is the economic impact of the institution on the state? What are the names of private corporations in the state that enjoy the same reputation for quality and service as the university and have similar economic significance? How do the compensation packages for their CEOs compare? Can a case be made that, including the price of the search, the cost of securing and maintaining the university's CEO is less than that for a CEO in the corporate sector? The press and the public need to be assured that such costs of presidential searches are worth it.

As one example, for much of the 1990s, Michigan was a hotbed of dissent over how much information about a presidential search process should be released to the public. Media successfully sued Michigan's Board of Regents for access to lists of candidates. After a decade of wrangling, the state's legislature specifically exempted presidential searches from open meetings law. In this Michigan is an exemplar of a developing trend. All fifty states have freedom of information or public records acts. Exceptions to such acts are provided by statute in approximately twenty states for candidates for public employment. Estes identifies three states—Michigan, New Mexico, and Texas—as explicitly excepting candidates for presidents or CEOs of state colleges and universities.

Press victories in freedom of information suits have caused some universities to seek and obtain relief through state legislatures. Normally state statutes require public institutions to release the names of "finalists" in the search; however, specifically what constitutes a finalist continues to be grounds for controversy in a number of states. Typically, institutions make public a short list of three to five candidates who participate in on-campus interviews—a fairly pro forma last lap in the recruitment process. The names of candidates who fail to make it to this point are generally kept confidential, except in a few states like Arkansas, Florida, and Nevada. In these states, if media so demand, the entire lists of candidates is released.

Revised legislation can protect candidates in searches at public universities and add foundation to the decision taken by most private institutions to withhold information on candidates in searches until the very end. This brings a very important measure of security for the candidates themselves. The premature release of the names of candidates always causes the personal and professional lives of men and women to be disrupted such that the consequences can be painful and even career-altering. Such consequences, of course, are inherent in presidential transitions.

The media assert that candidates accept these risks in order to better themselves. Incumbents, no matter the circumstances of their departures, understand that at the points of transition one of their primary currencies—their personal and professional reputations—can be exposed to specious as well as justified assault. While the law can only go so far, it must be understood that the news media will always seek out with utmost aggressiveness that which has been denied them, and it is their right to do so. As one indicator, Jerrold Footlick, former *Newsweek* editor and a College of Wooster trustee, believes that the media's willingness to listen to and abide by reasons for an institutional request for confidentiality depends on the relationship that institution has built with the media previously.

Good press relations begin, not with news releases, but with the willingness of the president and the trustees to meet regularly with the publisher and key editors of a journal for frank and open discussions of issues facing the university and the community that both serve. Savvy colleges and universities recognize that the real role of the media is not simply as a vehicle for good news in good times, but rather as a mirror of the values of the larger community, which may not always be in harmony with those of the institution. Even if a relationship has been contentious, it is not too late to begin to build it again from the first moment of a presidential transition.

Early Priorities: Consensus and Engagement

While issues relating to premature release of search information by news media dominate conversations concerning public relations and presidential transition, they are merely the tail of the communications dog. Far more important are the communications among the institution's constituencies—faculty and staff, students, alumni, and trustees—that build consensus regarding the future of the college or university and the capacities of the next president to head it, according to Theodore Marchese, of Academic Search Consultation in Washington, D.C. The goal of a search is not to pick a president but to secure for the long term a prosperous future for the institution.

Communications surrounding presidential transition begin the moment a sitting president expresses to someone beyond her or his significant other the desire to work elsewhere. They conclude with the shaking of the last hand at the postinaugural reception. In between lies a highly unpredictable path, which is influenced by three key factors:

—The open-disclosure laws of the state in which the institution is located and how those laws pertain to presidential searches and release of information regarding an incumbent president.

—Institutional status: Private institutions have greater latitude in the design of searches, but issues of confidentiality are just as critical.

—The culture of the institution: "A good search and the communication that goes with it has to fit the core culture of the institution," says Marchese. "It's probably not going to be the same in an art institute as it would be in an engineering school."[3]

Inherent conflict between imperatives of confidentiality and participatory decision making may cause the notion of a university as a collegial association where freedom of inquiry (and implicitly, of shared information) to crumble. Institutions, public and private, tend to consider searches and the terms of appointment or severance as confidential personnel matters. Yet, for all of the members of a college or university's internal community, there is no issue more important than the character and capabilities of the new president.

Before all else, a new president implies change, something most higher education institutions do not abide well. As endowments of budget constrict even at top-tier institutions, faculty and staff become increasingly concerned for their own welfare and for that of their departments. Higher education encourages participatory governance, which begets a sense of ownership, and to varying degrees, this sense of proprietorship is threatened during presidential transitions.

From the perspective of communications planning during the transition process, a college or university should think and act strategically at all stages:

—Reinforce the belief that the institution is benefiting from good leadership during transition.

—Engage the entire community in establishing vision for the future and in developing the list of qualifications for the new president.

—Keep the entire community well informed regarding the progress of the search process.

—Invite extensive involvement by all stakeholders during visits to campus by finalists.

—Confirm that contributions by those groups and individuals were given serious consideration in the final choice of the new president.

The structure of the search process will drive its communications. Many institutions take the opportunity of presidential transition to rearticulate a strategic vision for the university, and in that context they engage faculty and staff, alumni, students, and trustees in creating a statement of the desirable characteristics of the new president. If the goal of a search is as much to ensure the long-term future for an institution as it is to hire a new chief executive officer, then the role of the communications plan will be to facilitate the achievement of a transition process that leads to stable leadership with a long-range outlook.

With a broader communications plan, the role of formal statements—the myriad minutia of press releases, publications, postings on the Web, open letters to constituencies, and special events that convey official statements and releases of information—is to provide internal and external constituencies with facts and background that reinforce their engagement in the process. This helps assure that the newly appointed president will take office in as supportive an environment as possible. At the same time, communications must preserve appropriate security so that the search team can conduct its work with candor and confidentiality and so that the rights of candidates to personal privacy are not abused. In almost all instances, the college or university should designate a single spokesperson to handle all public statements; typically this person is the chair of the search committee, aided, in the background, by a senior staff public relations officer.

But what if the approaching transition is not a typical one? What if the sitting president has been asked to resign or forced to retire or has been fired? Or what if unanticipated illness or death truncates a presidency? Each scenario will demand a different communications plan, but the following guidelines should underlie each one.

The Key Components of a Transition Communications Plan

From the moment a president announces the intention to seek another job, through the inauguration of his or her successor, all information must be as accurate as possible. It must be disseminated in strict adherence to applicable state law and any institutional policy. Constituencies should be informed in a timely manner, and information should always be sensitive to the human needs of those involved.

Effective institutions will draft a communications plan for presidential transition, just as they prepare crisis communications plans, and place them in policy manuals and handbooks well in advance of any foreseen change.

If no such plan exists, the time to prepare it is immediately after the decision initiating the transition is made and before any public announcement occurs. The skeleton of such a plan can be developed in a single meeting of the president, the chief academic officer, the board chair, and the senior public relations officer. Details can be added later.

The plan must address the following issues:

1. Circumstances of the transition
2. Timing
3. Interim leadership
4. Structure of the search process
5. Spokesperson for the search

Assuming that the move comes at the president's instigation, the chair of the board of regents or trustees should be the first to know of an impending change in leadership. In university systems, a sitting president communicates first with the chancellor. An effective president develops solid professional and personal relationships with the chair of the board or the chancellor. The board chair holds the strongest position to set the tone for the transition, to amplify the good work that the exiting president has accomplished, and to help align other trustees in the president's behalf. Working in concert, the board chair and the president can inform major donors and other influential persons who are backing institutional initiatives that the presidential transition is not expected to have any negative impact on major unfinished projects.

Often, presidents are approached by search firms seeking expressions of interest in a soon-to-open position elsewhere. Typically, only when the interest of both parties reaches a significant level does a sitting president alert the board chair. Sometimes, however, without such an outreach, a president will decide for the sake of her or his welfare and that of the institution that the time is right to seek a new presidency. What then? Tell the board chair and risk subsequent termination? Randolph-Macon president Roger H. Martin reported in *Trusteeship* that after ten successful years as president of Moravian College, he wanted a new professional challenge. He discussed this with the chair of his board. They agreed on the strategy that Martin would personally announce his plans early in the fall and before the board's October meeting, so that there would be no appearance that his resignation was the result of board action. The board chair also offered Martin additional protections. Language in Moravian's advertisement in the *Chronicle of Higher Education* praised Martin's successes, thus making it clear he was leaving under no cloud, and the chairman provided Martin with a glowing endorsement.

In a different scenario, the board may decide that it is time for the president to retire or resign. In this case, if the president is not a participant in the decision, it will be the board chair's task, or the chancellor's in the case of a public system, to inform the president. Once that is done, transition communications should follow the same processes as in a retirement or a move to another institution.

Preparing the Plan

It is tempting to think of "communications" as simply the steady stream of printed and published materials, letters, news releases, and Web pages created by most higher education institutions; however, those are only substitutes for personal statements. During a presidential transition process, everyone associated with the college or university will be asked for information. Staff from the most senior vice president to the part-time groundskeeper will talk about "what's happening at the college" to friends at the grocery store, the cocktail party, or over the back fence. Such word-of-mouth communication is the most difficult to control.

Thus, from the very beginning of the transition, a set of key statements—talking points—should be developed by the president, the senior vice president, the board chair, and the senior public relations officer.

These individuals will typically function as an unofficial transition communications team, no matter who else is assigned the responsibility. The talking points should frame and define the substance of all initial communications. They should contain not only the initial facts of the transition but also, and of equal if not greater importance, statements that reinforce (1) the ongoing vitality of the institution, (2) stable leadership during the period of transition, and (3) the next steps in the process. An agreed upon statement of "why" may also be strategically helpful.

Designed to address the uncertainty that constituencies will feel during the period of transition, talking points may also include hypothetical questions and answers.

Q: Will we have an interim president, and if so how will he or she be chosen?

A: The senior staff and the board are considering that option and will make a decision as soon as the timing of the transition is determined.

Q: When will a search begin for a new president?

A: A search committee is being formed that will include representatives of faculty, students, staff, alumni, and trustees.

Q: When will the new president be in place?

A: It is imperative that we find an individual with vision and energy who can build on the strengths and initiatives of the institution.

Q: What about the capital campaign?

A: The campaign will go forward without interruption, thanks to the fine leadership of trustees, alumni, and our excellent staff.

Most importantly, the plan should identify a *single* public spokesperson for the period of transition. Usually that person is the chair of the trustee search committee or the chair of the board and is assisted by the institution's senior public relations or communications officer. All official statements should come from the spokesperson or her or his designee. There is no other way to effectively control communications surrounding a presidential transition.

Announcing the Change in Leadership

The crafting of this announcement is extremely important. It will be the first official communication to a broad public that a change in presidential leadership is in the offing. Its tone should be personal and reassuring that, no matter the outcome, the institution is strong and benefits from excellent leadership at many levels. It should also prepare the community for the timeline of activities to follow.

Timely distribution of this announcement is crucial. The president should meet with his cabinet and should call leaders of the faculty, of key boards, and, if appropriate, of controlling government entities. At the same time a letter of announcement should be distributed by e-mail to faculty, staff, and students on campus and to members of volunteer boards off campus. Those who cannot be reached via e-mail should receive the letter by fax. A release should be prepared for the media, to be issued after the campus community has been notified. It will be critical to make all reasonable attempts to notify internal constituencies first. Nothing sparks uncertainty or the feeling of abandonment more than for faculty and staff members to learn first from news media that their president is leaving.

How the news of an impending change of president is communicated to the press depends on the relationship of the institution's chief public relations or communications officer with the newspapers and radio and television stations that regularly cover the university. Either the president or the board chair should be available to talk with the press when they call, as they surely will. A news conference may or may not be appropriate, depending on the size of the media market, the culture of existing relationships with the press, and the level of detail that the institution wishes to provide.

Once these issues are resolved, the chief public relations officer should call his or her contacts, tell them about the decision, fax or e-mail a copy of the release, and inform them of the president's and the board chair's availability for comment. *No more than one hour* should elapse between the notification of internal and external leaders and the time when the press is alerted, because of the possibility of leaks to the media. An institution has a better chance of ensuring that its key messages are included in the story if the press hears first from the college's senior communications officer rather than from a disgruntled faculty or staff member with a personal agenda.

How the media react will depend on the circumstances under which the transition occurs. If the transition is "clean," and no allegations of impropriety are attached, news coverage should be relatively straightforward. Journalists will want to speak with the president and the board chair and will benefit from the public relations officer's help in providing historical background. During these fluid moments, the institution's public relations office should furnish all the interested media with a brief biography of the president, a list of achievements during her or his

Best Practices

- Use the Internet to keep internal constituencies apprised of the search process and its progress.
- Use the presidential transition to create a new agenda for the future of the college.
- Match the process of selecting a new president to the culture of the college.

tenure, and perhaps a chronological list of past presidents. If the president's spouse has been active in the public life of the institution and its community, he or she should be alerted to the inevitability of calls from the media. Reporters will want the spouse's reaction to the news, and he or she should be briefed on the talking points and encouraged to be honest and open.

If controversy is attached to the announcement, and particularly if there are allegations of wrongdoing that may be actionable in a court of law, the institution's attorney should be centrally involved in preparing materials, including talking points that the spokesperson will follow in communicating with the media and other constituencies. However, only in the most severe of situations, when trustees as well as the president may be objects of legal investigations, is it appropriate to use the university attorney as the spokesperson. To do so in other circumstances is to run the risk of drawing an unnecessary kind of attention to the process.

In the event of alleged irregularities, the announcement should open with a short statement that the president has chosen to resign in light of allegations raised in a particular meeting (the date should be supplied) of the board of trustees or other venue. The allegations should be described succinctly and in language approved by the board's legal counsel. The next steps for the investigation of the allegations should be briefly articulated. The announcement should identify the name and affiliation of the interim president and contain an expression of confidence in her or his ability to lead the institution at this time. The announcement should conclude by stating that the board of trustees is creating a search committee and that the campus will be involved in the search progress.

Internal communication channels are also vitally important in an effective transition. The World Wide Web; alumni magazines; newsletters that serve student, admissions, and departmental constituencies;

and the student newspaper should be considered in all announcement-planning discussions and briefings.

Communication during the Search

During the transition process, the institution will be in an unusual stage of flux. Rumors will abound, and speculation will be rampant about who the new president will be. Yet, what the campus community will want most—names of candidates—it cannot have. In their place, the public relations office can and should provide regular, accurate information about the search. Posting timely minutes of search committee meetings is one proven way to keep all members of a university community up to date.

During the search, leaders of the communications process will be faced with striking a very delicate balance. Some on campus will experience an almost overwhelming need to express appreciation and celebrate the achievements of the outgoing president, especially if he or she is long-tenured and much beloved. Yet, going too far with this kind of initiative can create a difficult environment for the new president. The potentially negative impact can be mitigated if the following three themes are interwoven through all communications:

—*Share the credit:* the success that the college or university now enjoys has been the product of the dedicated efforts of faculty, staff, trustees, and other constituencies with which the sitting president has been fortunate to serve.

—*Reinforce the search process,* particularly the qualities desired in the new president and the university community's role in developing them.

—*Encourage the community to extend the same high degree of hospitality to the new president that launched the sitting president on such a successful tenure.*

If the transition is occurring under less-than-pleasant circumstances, appropriate themes would be the following:

—*Support the interim president unconditionally.*

—*Reinforce the search process,* particularly the involvement of various constituencies in the development of the criteria for selecting the new president.

—*Celebrate successful achievements by faculty, students, and staff during the past administration and during the interim.*

Statements about the departed president will be required from time to time in response to questions from the media and other constituencies. They must be scrupulously accurate, charitable, and succinct, and they must comply with any appropriate legal position taken by the university.

The penultimate act of the search process is the slate of on-campus interviews for finalists. A communication plan should also be created expressly for this stage. The search committee and the finalists—through the search service that is assisting the institution—must be fully aware of, and agree to, the plan. Typically, this final stage is largely open to the public, but often sensitive issues are discussed in executive session with the board. The plan should address the following issues.

—Announcing the names of the finalists and schedule for on-campus interviews. Prepare a short statement that

1. contains the names and titles of the candidates,
2. describes the on-campus interview process,
3. stresses that the selection is the result of the search process, which benefited from constituency input, and
4. articulates the process that will be followed after the on-campus interviews are completed. The statement should be attributed to the spokesperson for the search.

Attached to the statement should be short bios, presented in identical format, of the candidates. This material should be released to the college or university community an hour or two before it is released to media. At the same time it is released to the campus community, the information should be sent to the public relations office of each candidate's current institution. The candidates should also receive copies.

—Engaging the largest number of constituencies in meaningful dialogue with each candidate, given the short time that the candidates are on campus, and deciding what communications are necessary to support the interview process.

—Responding to the news media: The moment the names are released, media will call seeking comments. Administrators, trustees, and volunteer leaders of associated boards, institutes, or foundations should be advised to defer comment to the one designated spokesperson. To offer such advice to faculty, however, almost guarantees a flood of inappropriate comment to media.

Announcing the New President

Within three days of the last on-campus interview, the name of the new president should be announced. Whether the new president should be on campus when the announcement is made depends on institutional culture. On one side, the availability of the new president can set the stage early for building relationships. It is a time of celebration—for the institution and for the finalist. Yet, one institution's gain is another's loss, and some new presidents will feel compelled to remain on their current campuses at the time of the announcement, since that campus will most likely be entering the period of transition uncertainty. Ironically, at that moment, the one person who knows most about that institution's immediate future is the woman or man who has just been announced as the president of another college or university.

As with all other phases of the search, a plan should be prepared in advance for announcing the new president. To the degree feasible, this plan should mirror the one created to announce the departure of the former president. If the institution is a member of a public state system, the chancellor's office or the board of regents may take the lead in making the announcement. Whatever the circumstance, the announcement plan should include the following five elements.

1. *A statement giving the finalist's name and title and indicating how he or she particularly meets the selection criteria.*

2. *A timeline for the completion of the transition process.*

3. *The list of constituencies to be notified.* Include not only constituencies that are important to your university; also ask the incoming president to provide a list of persons and organizations she or he would like the university to contact.

Every institution has a short list of influential friends, including large donors, key legislators, and leaders of corporations and foundations. Typically, these individuals should be telephoned, by the chair of the search committee, the sitting or interim president, or the vice president for academic affairs or institutional advancement, whoever is most appropriate. Even if one or more of these influential friends cannot be reached in person, making the effort to do so at this stage of the transition is an important gesture.

For trustees, leaders of volunteer boards and councils, leaders of the local community, and presidents of nearby colleges or universities with which the institution has a consortial relationship, a short e-mail announcement is an important initial step. As with those mentioned above, this contact should be followed by a letter from the board chair.

E-mail and Web site postings are the most effective tools for disseminating the information within the campus community. These, too, should be followed by a letter either from the board chair or the sitting president expressing support for the new president's selection, praising the work of the search committee and the campus community during the period of transition, outlining the schedule for the transition, and celebrating the future of the institution under its new leadership.

The media should also receive a press kit that contains the following components:

—The release

—A statement from the new president and information about the most efficient ways to contact him or her (phone and e-mail);

—The list of criteria used to select the new president;

—A biographical statement for the new president;

—A list of persons who should be contacted for comments about the new president, for example, the president of the faculty senate, the president of the student government, the heads of any unions, and the chair of the alumni association;

—A fact sheet about the college or university, providing accurate figures for enrollment, endowments, and the annual budget and a description of major initiatives;

—A fact sheet about the institution or organization from which the new president comes; and

—Contact information for the chief PR person at the new president's former organization.

This material should be provided to the chief public relations person at the president's former institution before it is sent to the press. Much of this information can be posted on the World Wide Web for easy access by the media; however, to be safe it should also be provided in conventional printed form. The institution's chief public relations officer should also maintain a special list of individuals whom she or he will contact personally at this point. For example, the publisher of the local newspaper and the chief executives or operating officers of the local television and radio stations are important connections and should receive the short e-mail and follow-up letter from the board chair.

Emerging Trends

- Candidates will strengthen demands for confidentiality in searches.
- Public institutions increasingly will conduct searches out of the sunshine.
- Presidential search firms will play an increasingly large role in recruiting candidates.
- Students, faculty, staff, trustees, and other volunteer boards will begin to receive most of their information about presidential searches via the Internet.
- Campus communicators will learn that keeping internal constituencies informed is a significantly more important task than focusing on the needs of news media.

4. The schedule for dissemination. Initial telephone calls and e-mails should be followed within an hour or two by the delivery of information to the media. Most major newspapers are published in the morning. Local news is most often telecast in the evening. Scheduling the announcement for midday gives staff members the opportunity to complete their lists of personal notifications in the morning. The midday delivery of information to media also allows television news operations the time to conduct interviews and prepare a story for their evening newscasts. Major dailies will have time to prepare the story for the next day. The only exception to this plan involves local evening papers, which typically have deadlines at 9 or 10 A.M. If there are no other competing media serving the region, an institution might want to consider advancing its dissemination plan to begin with midday notification of key contacts and an afternoon release of the information to media. If, as is frequently the case, an institution is served by a morning daily from a nearby metropolitan center as well as a local evening paper, the midday announcement should be preferred, because the larger metropolitan daily is the one more likely to be read by opinion leaders. To address disappointments at the local paper, arrangements can be made for its editor and reporter to have the first extended interview with the new president.

5. Optimum use of institutional publications. Many colleges and universities produce a wide range of informational communications, including an alumni magazine and a series of newsletters serving employee, student, admissions, development, and departmental constituencies. Before finalists arrive on campus, the chief public relations officer should convene these editors and create a plan to announce the new president's appointment in each. The editor of the student newspaper should play an integral role in this group.

Presidential Overlap: The New and the Outgoing

The varying circumstances of presidential transition—retirements, resignations, terminations—dictate the level of interaction between incoming and outgoing presidents and how public their communication should be. When Wilson College in Pennsylvania named Lorna Duphiney Edmundson to succeed retiring president Gwendolyn Evans Jensen in January 2001, there began a distinctively public and collegial transition event. As soon as possible after she was named, Edmundson traveled to the campus, where she and president Evans were feted at numerous events. At a special convocation, they celebrated the future of the college and expressed genuine praise for each other's accomplishments. Edmundson said she would like to visit the campus monthly before taking office, so Jensen and her staff made sure that her visits coincided with high-visibility public events, including meetings of the board, faculty meetings, and the annual reunion of alumnae. In a similar vein, the transfer of the presidency of Truman State University in Missouri from Jack Magruder to Barbara Dixon involved many coordinated meetings and a high public profile. One example was a banquet for six hundred state and campus leaders, at which Magruder expressed his full confidence in Dixon, and she her deep appreciation for all that he had done in stewardship for Truman State and the cause of public liberal arts colleges.[4]

Many presidential transitions occur not because a sitting president retires but because he or she has accepted a new position at a larger or more prestigious institution. Opportunities for the new and departing presidents to attend public events together may be surprisingly limited in number, as the new president will be winding up her or his previous position and the outgoing president will be spending almost every spare moment preparing for new responsibilities. Still, a joint appearance at a board meeting or commencement can be a very effective vehicle to reinforce the smooth and orderly transfer of presidential leadership.

But what if a president leaves under a cloud? It depends on the thickness of the overcast. Unless a president has been officially charged with high crimes and misdemeanors, even a president who has been ousted by the board should spend a day or two with the incomer. Says Ted Marchese, "There are things—about the board, about legislators, about faculty and staff—that only presidents can tell presidents."[5] True enough, and the value of such briefings lies strictly in the mind of the recipient.

From a public relations perspective, though the circumstances of the transition may be troubled, changes in leadership are about the future of an institution, not its past. While it may not be appropriate in these circumstances for new and outgoing presidents to appear in the same forum, members of the university community deserve to know that meetings between incoming and outgoing presidents have occurred, but not necessarily what was discussed.

The Media and the End of the Transition

The transition process does not stop with the announcement of the new president. Rather, it extends through and beyond the reception following the president's inauguration. A main priority for the new chief executive officer during this span of months will be to establish personal relationships with institutional constituencies and those leaders whose support is essential for the institution to achieve its expected future. Sometimes, surprisingly, the news media are relegated to insignificant status. This is a mistake. If representatives of the media start to believe that they have been given short shrift, or if they see that an institution is arrogant in its communications, they will be much less willing to give that college or university the benefit of the doubt when unpleasant circumstances arise, as they often do.

On the president's first visit to campus after being named its new leader, he or she should make it a point to schedule a meeting with the publisher and the editor of the most significant newspaper and the chief executives or chief operating officers of major broadcast media covering the school. While the goal of these meetings is to generate expanded and improved coverage for the institution, the new president should simply begin by asking about their perceptions of the college or university. What are its main strengths, weaknesses, and opportunities? What are the regional issues that could benefit from the college's engagement? The meetings should be held at a site of the media executive's choosing, and on-campus meetings should be scheduled as follow-ups.

Often, one or more trustees, alumni, or senior administrators will be connected to a media executive. Such persons should be consulted before scheduling the meetings and perhaps should attend the first one for an introductory period.

As the transition comes to a close, the senior public relations officer should schedule meetings on campus for editors and writers who frequently cover the college or university. In addition to education writers, reporters from the paper's business, style, and sports sections—as well as the editor of the editorial page—should be reoriented. Although in these preliminary meetings it is appropriate to mix representatives from various sections of a newspaper, it would be inappropriate to host representatives from more than one medium. Doing so can turn a discussion into a press opportunity, which it is not intended to be. The purpose of these meetings is to build relationships with the women and men whose words in the future will shape key perceptions of the institution, and while college personnel should not expect a story to result from these meetings, it will be important for all to keep in mind a clear axiom of media relations: *Everything is always on the record.*

Coming some months after the new president has been in office, the inauguration will signal the end of many transition activities, as this ceremony provides an effective vehicle to celebrate the successful completion of an uncertain period between the end of one administration and the beginning of another. In this sense, it is an appropriate time to express appreciation for the engagement of the community's stakeholders during the process of transition and, while articulating new initiatives, to reinforce the values and characteristics that distinguish this college from its competitors.

Some institutions spend $100,000, or even $200,000, on their inaugurations. Others, like Mississippi Delta, spend as little as $2,000. At Utah State, one new president chose to channel the $50,000 inaugural estimate into student scholarships. Activities incorporated into an inauguration set the style and tone of a new administration and should be viewed not as the end of the presidential transition, but rather as the beginning of the campaign to influence those constituencies whose support will be needed in order for the institution to achieve critical goals under its new president.

CHAPTER TWELVE

Weathering the Storm: Institutional Advancement during a Presidential Transition

Charles Brown

How is higher education fund-raising influenced by presidential departures and arrivals? How can an institution avoid having its alumni feel they are watching a leadership transition from the sidelines as their mailboxes steadily fill with letters pleading for annual contributions, special contributions, and critically important resources during a period of institutional change?

Under the best of circumstances, a presidential leadership transition is an intense experience, both for the institution and for its new leader.[1] Numerous environmental factors surrounding the transition will present special challenges to the office of institutional advancement. Whether an institution has embarked on the private phase of a fund-raising campaign, launched the public phase of a campaign, or is merely in the planning stages will affect what the transition issues are and how they should be addressed. These additional factors will impact the fund-raising process during a presidential transition:

—Whether the president is the principal holder of relationships, as in a small private college or a community college, or if others share the stewarding of key relationships, as in a major research university.

—Whether the new president comes from within the institution (with a knowledge of the culture and with solid faculty relationships) or from the outside.

—Whether the incoming president has prior experience at the decanal level or higher or is new to administration.

Advancement Checklist for Presidential Transitions

This checklist has been developed to aid advancement teams when a transition has been announced.

- Upon learning of the upcoming transition, identify the key constituents and determine who will notify them about the departure.
- Establish an advancement transition team.
- Debrief the president on her or his gift relationships.
- Consider a celebratory fund-raising initiative.
- Prepare a transition binder with briefings from administrative departments.
- Undertake a celebratory farewell tour for the outgoing president to provide closure and a sense of orderliness.
- Consider a two-year rolling contract model for the chief advancement officer and other key staff members.
- Consult with alumni leaders.
- Draft a letter from the board chair inviting alumni comment and nominations for the next president.
- When the next leader has been appointed, coordinate an opening tour to meet alumni.

—Whether the incoming president seeks to build on his or her predecessor's programs or institute swift change.

—Whether the relations between the outgoing and incoming presidents are warm or cool.

—Whether the transition is anticipated, and thus can be staged, or is precipitous.

—Whether the advancement function at the institution is a mature or a developing operation.

This chapter identifies several successful strategies for advancement operations during the transition period and examines why they work in those specific situations.

First Principles: Advancement during the Transition Process

Define advancement at the institution. While many still operate with the standard 1980s definition for the field that incorporates public relations and alumni relations along with development, new professionals often blur these distinctions: "Advancement, development and fund raising are often used interchangeably by those who seek resources on behalf of their institutions."[2] Similarly, fund-raising typically now includes the cultivation and informational activities that support a successful resource-generating enterprise.

Protect key relationships. People still give to people, as almost any fund-raising veteran will confirm, and most serious philanthropic commitments come about as a result of interest sustained over time, with the largest benefactions often tied to a specific individual.[3] As one example, in April of 2002 the Walton Family Foundation gave $300 million to the University of Arkansas, the largest gift ever made to a public university. During discussions about the gift, representatives of the foundation sought guarantees that president John A. White would stay at the university for at least five years beyond the gift.[4]

Seek opportunities among challenges. Experience continues to demonstrate that people give to opportunities rather than to needs. Thus, the most effective development programs seek opportunities among their challenges. It was noted as hardly coincidental that Princeton University's first female president, a scientist, worked strenuously to cultivate the largest gift to the university from a Princeton alumna, as well as a major gift from a trustee for a new science building.

Actively involve the board in supporting the new president. The responsibility of the board goes beyond hiring and firing the CEO. As ambassadors, they play, and must play, a unique role in opening doors for the institution and introducing the new president to their circle of associates.

Develop a plan B. After the search committee has done its homework and accounted for all of the institution's major needs, including a candidate with strong experience in advancement, the incoming president should be encouraged to take up the development portfolio immediately and actively pursue it. Despite everyone's best intentions, however, and no matter what the literature says about what the president's fund-raising role should be, the reality is that not all new chief executives will be able to embody that ideal. Furthermore, no matter what the senior development officer may believe her or his role should be, he or she will need to adjust, and quickly, to the new president's own strengths, weakness, and preferences.[5] This reality may mean relying on the provost, deans, trustees, and key volunteers to fulfill part or most of the president's role in advancement.

The Key Elements of an Advancement Transition Plan

Regardless of the type of institution or its circumstances, "the president has a large role as symbol and spokesperson, looked to by external and internal constituencies."[6] The chief executive officer remains the key holder of relationships for the institution, particularly at smaller colleges, and the circumstances of a transition, no matter how sudden, do not change this. In fact, transitions *heighten* the need to keep *both* outgoing and incoming presidents thoroughly briefed on advancement priorities as well as the need for the following components of the transition plan for this area of operations.

Written guidelines. A written plan for a leadership transition is more and more common on campuses; however, very few institutions have developed a comprehensive set of strategic guidelines to manage an advancement campaign during presidential turnover. In its most basic form, this document should convey a sense of time urgency, focus almost exclusively on the financial bottom line, and articulate at least three institutional priorities for advancement during the uncertainties of a transition.

Careful timing. In a smooth transition, the president's decision to step down is known far enough in advance to allow for the scheduling of fund-raising campaigns well ahead of and soon after the major announcement, to reduce development pressure. Harold Shapiro announced that he was leaving Princeton more than a year ahead of his departure, allowing the search committee to design an effective transition plan and the advancement office to work within that plan in the accomplishment of its goals.[7]

Referring to the smoothness of Princeton's presidential transitions, Donald Kennedy, president emeritus of Stanford, speaks of Princeton as the paradigm for a well-managed institution.[8] At the same time, Princeton's smooth transitions have resulted from relatively little turnover in the institution's history: it has had only nineteen presidents in 255 years. Outside of rarefied worlds such as this, transitions may not run as smoothly when a president leaves office involuntarily, for instance. If the departure of an outgoing chief executive officer is not characterized by constructive activities and attitudes, it may be necessary to rethink and start fresh with some campaign strategies.

Parallel staging. If the executive departure is voluntary and allows staging, much can be made of wrapping up relationships with the former leader, structuring the transition hand-off, and anointing the new

Best Practices

- The transition team should prepare a briefing book for the incoming president on the status of all advancement projects, focusing on achievements, challenges, immediate potential, and long-term expectations.
- The incoming president should hold several conversations with the departing president regarding advancement strategies and prospects, if feasible.
- Large events can be viewed negatively during periods of financial constraint; thus, the new president's inauguration ceremony should be planned carefully and wisely.
- Trustees with advancement portfolios should be included on the presidential search committee.

president. If the campaign is ongoing, the tactics should be similar, although there may be a slightly greater sense of urgency with some donors who are actively involved in gift-giving transactions.

Preserved relationships. Given that positive relationships unfailingly form the basis of fund-raising success, the preservation—indeed, the enhancement—of relationships with key stakeholders is a critical step to take as the transition unfolds. From the perspective of a successful advancement agenda, key stakeholders will include trustees, alumni leaders, major donors, key prospects, political leaders, religious leaders, and community leaders. Whatever their affiliation, these individuals must be identified and cultivated during the transition.

Appropriately, one of the first thoughts the chief advancement officer should have after hearing of a presidential departure is the need to assess and monitor the principal gift relationships the president now maintains and how those donors will learn about the departure. The chief academic officer and the president should review this list of names, add other key insiders, and determine who will call each one to discuss the implications of leadership change at the institution. Additionally, the development office should identify the top fifty donors and key prospects who should be stewarded through the transition and should move rapidly to schedule individual, often time-intensive, meetings with all of them during the course of the transition period.

Protecting the institutional memory is also an important component of a successful transition, and the chief academic officer should seek permission to go through the president's files—or to ask the president's staff to do so—to copy information that will be useful for future development initiatives.[9] After the president's announced departure, it will be useful for the chief academic officer to ask the president to assess the present strengths and weaknesses of the advancement program, to ask who the president would have liked to develop a relationship with but was unable to, and to ask if the outgoing president would be willing to talk with her or his successor about advancement priorities.[10]

Commitment to closure. If the tenure of the outgoing president is sufficiently long, or if it follows the completion of a successful campaign, it can be helpful to stage a celebratory farewell tour managed by the development and alumni offices, in which the president visits cities with large concentrations of alumni to thank them for their support and to convey a sense of orderliness about the transition.[11] Coincident with such events, there can also be focused sidebar meetings between the president and selected donors from the list of fifty key prospects mentioned above.

Finally, it will be wise for the advancement operation to seize the occasion of the transition to close on gifts from those with whom the president has had a fruitful relationship. The trustees might also consider mounting a celebratory fund-raising initiative for a capital project or an endowed fund to honor the outgoing president. By making it a targeted objective, the institution can skillfully bring both focus and closure to expressions of support for the departing chief executive.

Maintaining Fund-Raising Momentum

Ensure Stability and Manage Morale

Donors are not the only ones who need attention during a transition. Often, the president has been the inspiration for trustees and others who are charged with obtaining needed resources. The environment for volunteers is increasingly competitive, and maintaining relationships with existing volunteers remains a critical activity during the transition.[12]

Moreover, it is important to pay attention to the staff morale in development during the transition period.[13] After the president, the chief advancement officer will often be the most important holder of key relationships for the institution, and with a new supervisor about to arrive, this individual may well wonder whether his or her job is secure. Richard Seaman suggests a rolling two-year appointment, which could be bought out after the new president has had an opportunity to assess firsthand the employee's performance.[14] Having a contract in force will allow the senior advancement officer to focus on the transition in a broader, less personalized manner, and if the chemistry is positive, he or she could choose to stay on. Or the president could exercise the option to buy out the contract; a two-year rolling agreement can provide stability without tying the president's hands. It is increasingly common for the chief advancement officer to have a contract.[15]

On the subject of chemistry between the president and the chief advancement officer, James Fisher has suggested it is more important than experience,[16] but some disagree. Seaman observes that it is not surprising for a new president to want to shape her or his own administration, but he counsels caution when it comes to development. The importance of the senior advancement officer as a keeper of institutional relationships is key because while the chemistry between this individual and the president may not be ideal, it may be excellent between the advancement officer and the college's leading supporters.[17] Whatever the individual circumstance, the value of chemistry can be overstated; it is more important that the president and the senior advancement officer share values and a sense of priorities and agree on how the job should be done.[18]

Shape Presidential Priorities

One of the first challenges confronting a president who comes to the position from outside the institution will be to learn the institutional environment. Much preparation can take place in advance of arrival, which will ameliorate the steepness of the learning curve. For example, Gerhard Casper spent the summer before he came to Stanford as president studying the history of the university, and when he arrived he was better informed about its past than many of its senior staff and faculty.[19] In some colleges, there will be a greater need to build a basic understanding of advancement, in both its traditional and newer forms, and toward this end, new presidents should be sure to review in detail all institutional development files along with pertinent institutional policy manuals, personnel procedures, budgets, and state codes.[20]

Although it does not always happen, even when transitions run smoothly and relations are cordial, a conversation between the incoming and outgoing presidents can be particularly helpful to the advancement office's short- and medium-range priorities. Obviously, someone coming from within will be expected to have an easier time getting away from the campus, but it is important for *every* new president, whether from the community or not, and whether in collaboration with the departing president or not, to "get out the door," as advancement veterans describe it. Although the new chief executive officer may feel the need to focus immediately on local campus constituencies, because of the rising emphasis on advancement in higher education presidencies, leaders must become more externally focused.[21]

As the new leader, the president will experience a "golden moment" on campus, which he or she must seize, and not just for advancement

Emerging Trends

- Vice presidents for advancement increasingly work under contract.
- Presidential tenure is more closely aligned with the conclusion of development campaigns.
- Advancement plays a steadily larger role in higher education presidential transitions.

purposes. As Roger Williams explains, "People will talk with you more straightforwardly early on. They will be more candid because they know you did not have anything to do with what has gone before, and they will enjoy having their opinions sought." During this honeymoon, it will be critical for new presidents at institutions with meager endowments and limited resources especially, to meet with every institutional constituency as quickly as possible—the same constituencies to which the outgoing president recently said goodbye. The message to be delivered during these first sessions should focus on *continuity.* Meeting with many groups early creates the impression that the new president has hit the ground running and there will be no periods of confusion or turmoil. In addition to meeting with key donors and volunteers, it will be important for the new president to meet regularly with representatives of the news media and, in the case of public colleges and universities, to cultivate key political figures from the outset.[22]

The tradition of the new president taking to the road to visit alumni is a time-honored one that still can reap benefits. Following almost in the footsteps of Woodrow Wilson's "grand tour" as president of Princeton at the start of the last century, Harold Shapiro made a similar tour when he became Princeton's chief executive. Fourteen years later he capped his tenure with a celebratory "farewell tour," which was viewed by many as his victory lap following the successful conclusion of a $900 million fund-raising campaign. Whenever it can be undertaken, what is now called the initial "listening tour" for the new president will carry with it the key question: "What is your vision for our institution?" Effective presidents will be well prepared to answer.[23]

With respect to reserving adequate time for development, the tradition of the "listening tour" is also an early strategic method to claim a commitment of the new president's time. After the tour has ended, savvy advancement vice presidents will replace those recent travel and meeting slots with visits to board members and major donors. Claiming this time as a placeholder early on is an effective way to maintain the development commitment prominently among the president's priorities.

Conclusion: Timing, Transitions, and Campaigns

A presidential transition need not adversely affect the institution's advancement operation, even if it occurs in the middle of a campaign. It has been noted that presidential departures increasingly appear to coincide with the end of a fund-raising effort and that campaigns of size are now undertaken with a president's tenure in mind.[24] However, the thing to keep in mind, according to Robert R. Lindgren, Johns Hopkins's vice president for development and alumni relations, is that an institution is "larger than any one person, and while the president is a very important figure in terms of providing direction and leadership and vision, if you're on the right course, the important thing is to stay that course until you have a new person filling that role."[25] In this context, four months after Johns Hopkins announced a $900 million fund-raising initiative several years ago, then president William Richardson resigned. However, with an innovative transition plan for the advancement area under new president William R. Brody, the university exceeded its original goal, increased the target, exceeded that higher target, and finished the campaign in June 2000 at $1.52 billion.

This level of success comes with a high price tag for transitioning presidents, however. As Converse College president Nancy Gray admits, "I was unprepared for the relentless demands on my time and the extent to which one is a public figure. Despite how prepared I thought I was, I was not prepared for being committed 4 nights a week for the past three years and working 42 days straight at a time."[26] Stanford's president emeritus Donald Kennedy adds: "It is extremely important to project enjoyment in the job, and you can't do that if you're fried."[27]

Robert Birnbaum refers to the current college and university presidency as "the impossible job."[28] And yet, a good percentage of new leaders now subscribe to this longtime observer's view: "One of the discoveries many presidents appreciate is that raising money, far from being an unhappy burden and distraction, is one of the most pleasant parts of the task."[29] Wherever the campus's new chief executive officer starts on the spectrum of advancement experience, however, it is clear that a proactive and precise transition plan for this operational area can make critical differences to the success of both this individual and the institution experiencing a leadership change.

CHAPTER THIRTEEN

Shaky Ground in Troubled Times: The Legal Framework of Presidential Transitions

James E. Samels and James Martin

Through much of the last century, presidential transitions occurred as the result of a collegial selection process that typically elevated chief academic officers—*First among Equals*[1]—to the position of chief executive officer. Looking back, it was a rare occasion when college or university counsel was called by a new president's attorney to negotiate the terms and conditions of a new executive contract, particularly with regard to housing allowances, spousal stipends, entertainment expenses, dependent tuition remission, and the varied perks associated with deferred compensation and tax sheltered annuities.

In the past, college and university presidents were more sanguine about the presidential appointment and transition process. After all, the typical term of office for a college or university president might have been a decade or more. But the average length of service for higher education chief executives has shortened dramatically; by the 1990s, the average presidential term had been reduced in some institutional categories to little more than five years. Additionally, various sources project that between one-fourth and one-third of the accredited colleges and universities in the United States are either preparing for or are actively engaged in the presidential search process each year.[2]

Experienced higher education attorneys agree that the contemporary presidential transition environment presents both challenges and opportunities for accomplishing major institutional change and transformation. In fact, from the perspective of legal counsel, the long-range needs of the institution should be assessed before the search process is even started.

Although it is taken for granted that a fairly standard job description will be formulated, the board should also develop a companion set of criteria to serve as key drivers in the leadership profiling process. This collaborative process should identify the professional skills and experience necessary to be an effective higher education CEO in core areas such as the following.

—Academic leadership

—Evaluation and planning

—Resource acquisition

—Community relations[3]

To Incoming Presidents: Ask Why Your Predecessor Left

The 2000 edition of the American Council on Education's *American College President* confirms what many new presidents learn the hard way—presidents do not know enough about many key campus issues upon assuming the job.[4] As one way to overcome this, candidates should find out the real reason for the departure of the incumbent. They should also candidly ask whether the interim CEO is eligible for the permanent appointment and, thus, a competitor. Copies of the most recent independent audits and financial statements should be discreetly obtained, as well as copies of the most recent accreditation and academic licensing team reports and any other pertinent peer reviews. Candidates should also be certain to review current tuition discounting, conversion yield, retention, transfer, graduation, and graduate school acceptance and default rates. Finally, inquiries should be made regarding hidden liability exposure in the form of pending claims and demands, indirect collective bargaining costs, unresolved lawsuits, or criminal investigations.

Means and methods for gathering a broad spectrum of information should include an unrestricted visit to campus, copies of institutional rankings, press clippings, and market competition research. Candidates should also seek to uncover ahead of time which individuals may be "untouchables" on the administrative staff. It came as no surprise to those serving on the Commission on Strengthening Presidential Leadership several years ago to find the high number of "sacred cows" on an administrative staff to be one of the most difficult problems facing new presidents. "Change becomes not only difficult . . . but for all practical purposes impossible unless the board is prepared to support the president's judgment on who should stay and who should go. Where trustees have established friendships or close working relationships with administrators of long tenure, this issue can become especially delicate."[5]

Disclosure and Sunshine: Check Open Meeting and Public Records Laws

Before becoming an active candidate, one must weigh the risks of "getting tagged off first base" when one's name floats back to the home board as having entered a search. Disclosure of a candidate's status becomes a key issue because it can jeopardize relationships with the candidate's current board and have a potentially adverse impact on leadership effectiveness. For example, an applicant's role in a fund-raising campaign may be badly compromised if donors learn of his employment search. Similarly, a president's lobbying efforts lose credibility if legislators know that the individual might be leaving.[6]

Thus, it behooves the prospective candidate to ascertain the legal and regulatory environment of the hiring institution, including the rules of engagement governing disclosure of a candidate's application, nomination, and vitae, along with the open meeting rules and public documents standards pertaining to interviews and the winnowing process. By learning the rules of engagement ahead of time, candidates will have a better picture of their potential exposure, particularly in the court of public opinion, where such career aspirations can be met with pettiness and professional jealousy.

Most states maintain an open meeting law mandating that meetings of governmental bodies be open to the public. Open meeting laws do allow for the governmental body to exclude members of the public from certain portions of the meeting by allowing the body to convene in executive session for one or more purposes set forth in a statutory exemption. In the case of a public institution, the names of presidential candidates may be subject to disclosure under state freedom of information or public records laws. Although all fifty states have such laws, at least twenty-two states have statutory exceptions that protect the names of applicants or candidates for public employment, with three of these exceptions being limited to chief executive officer of a state institution of public higher education.[7] In general, the further along in the process, the less likely it is that an applicant's confidentiality can be protected. See, for example, *Attorney General v. Northampton,* 375 N.E.2d 1188, 1190 (1978), in which the Massachusetts Supreme Judicial Court stated that an applicant who reached that level of consideration (the semifinalist stage) would expect open and public discussion of his professional competence and that the reasons for protecting the identity of such candidates were less substantial than the reasons for protecting the identity of applicants who had not reached that level of consideration.

As a practical matter, in most recent presidential searches, disclosure of candidates' names is the exception and not the rule. A 1998 survey of presidential search in all fifty states revealed that very few major universities revealed the names of candidates, except for a small number of finalists (three to five). In about 30 percent of the searches, only the name of the winning candidate was revealed. The identity of candidates who did not become finalists was disclosed in only four states—Arkansas, Florida, Nevada, and North Dakota.[8]

Under public records law, the presidential search process is subject to public scrutiny. Public disclosure may encompass everything from the identity of candidates to presidential compensation. From the college or university's point of view, disclosure has the potential to chill the search process. Prominent candidates may be reluctant to apply if their candidacy will be disclosed, because it may weaken their position or bargaining leverage with current board and faculty members, and it may affect their ability to campaign for funds.

The public and the media take the position that an open and public search process helps to guard against nepotism and the perpetuation of the "old-boy network." Colleges and universities have had mixed success in sheltering the search process. Nick Estes cites cases in which universities in Arizona, Georgia, and Texas were required by courts to release names of presidential candidates.[9]

Steer Clear of Defamation

This new area of presidential transition law presents some interesting nuances. Beyond the application, nomination, and winnowing process, candidates should be aware of the obligations of their employers not to defame or materially interfere with their prospective contractual relations. Some would argue that "interference" is often in the eye of the beholder and cannot be independently identified and validated. Still, for purposes of the law, defamation occurs only when the representation is knowingly false and made in order to injure the reputation of the candidate.

Given the potential liability exposure, albeit facing a mountainous burden of proof, institutional employers often err on the side of brevity, supplying only a general acknowledgment confirming the candidate's date, title, and period of employment. Frustrated by such practices and policies, interviewing institutions often engage search firms to conduct extensive background reference checks, including one-to-one interviews with supervisors, peers, and subordinates.

Link Job Specifications, Candidate Skills, and Institutional Needs

From a legal perspective, it is important to link specifically the job description and a candidate's skills in the context of an institutional analysis.[10] This means addressing questions in many substantive areas such as the following.

—*Mission:* Are the institution's mission and the implementation of that mission in a state of flux? Does the institution hold a shared vision for future growth and development?

—*Fiscal management:* Is the college or university's financial house in order, or will this be a task for the new president?

—*Resource acquisition:* What fund-raising or other resource acquisition skills will the new president be expected to have?

—*Educational expansion:* What are the institution's plans for expansion, and what role will the new president be expected to play in such plans?

—*Academic reorganization:* What academic or other reorganization is the institution contemplating, if any, and what is the president's expected role?

—*Educational quality:* Is the new president expected to raise the caliber of education at the institution?

—*Facilities:* What are the institution's plans for acquisition, renovation, and/or modernization of its physical facilities, and where does the president fit into this plan?

—*Collective bargaining:* What are the candidate's history and skills vis-à-vis collective bargaining? Do these match the institution's needs and expectations?

—*Student life and activities:* What key issues need to be focused on in the student life arena? If there have been lawsuits, what actions can be taken to minimize their recurrence? Does this match up with the candidate's history of dealing with student conflict?

—*Self-image:* Is the institution satisfied with its self-image, and what will the new president be asked to do to improve it?

Beyond the horizon of benefits, perks, and privileges, many presidential candidates will seek assurances of job security, asking for multiyear appointments and the right to move to a faculty appointment with tenure. At the same time, presidential candidates and their boards will want to provide reasonable advance notice for negotiating the terms and conditions of successor contracts. Thus, it is typically in the candidate's best interests to stipulate specific annual evaluation provisions and memorialize the interrelationship between evaluation outcomes and continued employment.

Off the record, presidential candidates may sometimes expect the board to provide for the engagement of their spouse or significant other. The informal contacts and associations of trustees and other friends and benefactors of the college or university can play a critical part here in connecting the presidential candidate and members of his or her family with key personal and professional opportunities.

Presidential Appointment and the Employment Contract: Signing on the Dotted Line

Once the successful presidential candidate is selected and ready to receive an offer of employment, the clock begins ticking on building the overall employment package. This should occur within the framework of applicable compensation policies and procedures governing executive employment, compensation, and benefits.

The Adelphi University case demonstrates dramatically why governing boards must closely and independently scrutinize executive compensation policies and practices. First and foremost, "excessive compensation" paid to the president was a critical factor in the 1977 ousting of the board of Adelphi University by the New York Board of Regents. Second, in 1996 Congress passed tax legislation that empowers the Internal Revenue Service to impose "intermediate sanctions" (1) on managers of tax-exempt organizations judged to be paying their top executives "excessive compensation" and (2) on the recipients of the excessive compensation.[11]

A typical president's contract will include a job description containing the following responsibilities:

—executive leadership

—fund-raising

—development

—public relations

—educational programming

—budgeting

—long-range strategic planning

—student services

—recruiting personnel

—recommending the appointment, promotion, and dismissal of all staff members

—formulating the budget

—controlling and supervising all buildings, grounds, and equipment

—directing and assigning all employees

—organizing and administering the affairs of the institution as best serves the institution, consistent with board policy

—recommending regulations, rules, and procedures deemed necessary for the orderly conduct of the institution

—administering the institution under policies of the board

In addition, it is recommended that "catch-all phrases" be included so that a president cannot claim that responsibilities that were not listed are outside of her or his scope of employment. A sentence starting with "The president shall perform" should conclude in several ways:

—such duties as may be required by law and the provisions of this Agreement.

—all duties incident to the office of President of the College.

—all duties customarily performed by a college president.

—such other duties as may be prescribed by the Board.

Presidential Employment Contract Negotiations

Historically, formal contract negotiations were not a part of the presidential hiring process. Presidents either served at the pleasure of the board or accepted a standard form employment contract. These days it is becoming more difficult to find a presidential finalist candidate not accompanied by his or her lawyer or other agent. From the perspective of the board, trustees want to offer a favorable package to attract and retain quality candidates. Yet they also want to conserve financial resources for educational programming and other campus resource needs. From the president's standpoint, large sums for compensation and other benefits are justified, because the scale of responsibilities and unlimited work hours would command a similar or higher figure in the for-profit sector.

Beyond a steadily rising compensation level, presidents now typically expect a presidential residence or a housing allowance; expense accounts;

business automobiles; tuition remission and tuition assistance for spouse and dependents; payment of professional dues for conventions, courses, seminars, conferences, and other professional development activities; reimbursement for travel, including hotel, air mileage, and automobile rentals; paid membership in civic organizations; tenured faculty appointments; health and life insurance; workers' compensation coverage; participation in retirement plans; and even disability insurance and deferred compensation plans.

In addition to these benefits and perks, presidents are also often able to negotiate payment for spousal travel, domestic as well as international, particularly when the spouse accompanies the president in connection with official institutional events.

Performance Reviews: Avoiding Legal Pitfalls

Many presidential compensation plans may contain financial incentives for performance-based outcomes including enrollment, retention, graduation, graduate and professional school placement, national rankings, endowment, and external funding. Yet, for all these relatively objective standards, in our experience, those presidents who are involuntarily terminated are seldom squeezed out by the numbers. Higher education institutions have shown a remarkable ability to sustain momentum as long as the president retains popular favor.

Most performance reviews begin with a presidential self-assessment, which is followed by an evaluation by appropriately involved board members in consultation with various constituents. Sometimes faculty, students, and staff members fracture into polarized factions regarding the president's performance, and then it is imperative for trustees to keep the evaluation process from becoming a popularity contest. For this reason also, performance reviews should be carried out confidentially with due regard to protecting individual privacy. To do otherwise is to open up the process to sometimes fierce political crosscurrents on and beyond the campus. Board members should also remember that satisfactory annual performance reviews do not carry with them by implication any grant of tenure, only the expectation of continuing employment under the terms and conditions of the contract.

Increasingly sensitive to their own profile within the performance evaluation process, many governing boards have adopted self-evaluation mechanisms in order to provide a more informed perspective on their own institution-wide policymaking and presidential evaluation. College or university corporation counsel should take careful note that in matters of appointment and disappointment, counsel represents the board of trustees and not the president. The president must rely on a pri-

Table 13.1 Presidential Salaries, 2000–2001

Top Presidents in Total Compensation	
Claire L. Gaudiani,[a,b] Connecticut College	$898,410
Judith Rodin, University of Pennsylvania	808,021
Harold T. Shapiro,[c] Princeton University	705,683
William R. Brody, Johns Hopkins University	677,564
L. Jay Oliva,[a] New York University	651,000
Constantine N. Papadakis, Drexel University	637,839
Richard C. Levin, Yale University	612,453
Steven B. Sample, University of Southern California	605,086
H. Patrick Swygert, Howard University	603,031
Jon Westling, Boston University	591,017
Doctoral/Research Universities	
Judith Rodin, University of Pennsylvania	808,021
Harold T. Shapiro,[c] Princeton University	705,683
William R. Brody, Johns Hopkins University	677,564
L. Jay Oliva,[a] New York University	651,000
Constantine N. Papadakis, Drexel University	637,839
Richard C. Levin, Yale University	612,453
Steven B. Sample, University of Southern California	605,086
H. Patrick Swygert, Howard University	603,031
Jon Westling, Boston University	591,017
Benjamin Ladner, American University	589,243
Masters Institutions	
I. King Jordan, Gallaudet University	513,368
Donald E. Ross, Lynn University	500,255
Jerry C. Lee, National University (Calif.)	479,375
Ronald K. Machtley, Bryant College	473,014
Joseph Morone, Bentley College	441,634
John R. Brazil, Trinity University (Tex.)	435,890
John L. Lahey, Quinnipiac University	430,000
Rebacca VanHazel Stafford, Monmouth University (N.J.)	429,591
David J. Steinberg, Long Island University	400,081
John A. Yena, Johnson and Wales University	381,720
Liberal Arts Colleges	
Claire L. Gaudiani,[a,b] Connecticut College	$898,410
Robert H. Edwards,[a,d] Bowdoin College	591,006

Ruth J. Simmons,[a,e] Smith College	539,169
Russell K. Osgood, Grinnell College	481,255
Gordon A. Haaland, Gettysburg College	395,551
Frederico J. Talley,[a] Olivet College	392,313
Morton Owen Schapiro, Williams College	354,891
Frances D. Fergusson, Vassar College	353,795
Neal R. Berte, Birmingham-Southern College	351,613
Tom Gerety, Amherst College	340,650

[a]No longer at institution.

[b]Gaudiani left in December 2000. Her compensation includes $551,550 in severance pay, which she received in the 2002 fiscal year and the current fiscal year.

[c]Shapiro's pay includes an unspecified amount of deferred compensation.

[d]Edwards left in June 2001. His compensation includes $217,250 in severance pay.

[e]Simmons left in June 2001. her compensation includes an unspecified amount of deferred compensation.

Source: Basinger, "The Growing $500,000 Club."

vate legal representative, although in some cases the board may pay for the costs associated with such separate representation. Finally, counsel must pay scrupulous attention to the issues of disclosure, recusal, and recordation of minutes, since others will read the memorialization of discontinued employment in the minutes of the trustees.

Presidential Compensation: How High Is Too High?

In the late 1980s, a low six-figure salary with health and retirement benefits, vacation, and personal days was considered a robust package. Now the presidents of major research universities, multicampus proprietary institutions, and leaders in science and technology education command anywhere from five hundred thousand to a million dollars per year. A recent *Chronicle of Higher Education* article reported on "the growing $500,000 club." What is really noteworthy is that master's-level and liberal arts institutions commonly pay their presidents packages approaching five hundred thousand dollars.[12]

For much of the twentieth century, presidential compensation was established by the board of trustees after an informal negotiation or performance evaluation conducted behind closed doors. Today, presidents have higher and higher expectations for compensation, given the shorter shelf life of their college and university presidencies.

With increasing frequency, presidential compensation packages also include a broad range of deferred compensation and annuity variations. These alternative forms of compensation are most often keyed to performance indicators, such as enrollment, ranking, private philanthropic and governmental fund-raising, endowment management, retention, graduation, and financial aid discounting rates.

Often a corporate metaphor was cited as the touchstone for benchmarking compensation. In recent years, trustees have considered more sophisticated and relevant factors, identifying institutional peers and then settling recruitment compensation packages based on labor market demand for presidential leadership at a specific institutional level.

Table 13.1 provides a list of the highest-paid presidents for 2000–2001, broken into institutional categories as reported by the *Chronicle of Higher Education* in November 2002.

From the board's perspective, recruiting presidential talent lends itself to competitive compensation packages. Yet this intense competition for experienced presidential leadership can be constrained by subsisting compensation rates. It is difficult to justify larger than 20 percent increments when moving on to the new institution when a president has been held back or depressed in compensation for an extended period.

For rank-and-file faculty and classified staff members, there is often a skewed perception, particularly given a succession of 2–3 percent raises over recent years despite private higher education's 5–6 percent tuition growth. That said, tuition-dependent colleges and universities continue to struggle to maintain workforce scale, programmatic array, and financial stability while at the same time attracting and retaining the most talented presidents. This, in part, explains why institutions must be both frugal and creative in establishing benefits plans that will attract competitive candidates.

Presidential Perquisites: A Fresh Look

Presidential perks in higher education were once limited to the official residence, a private vehicle, and some support services. Today, the range of benefits on many campuses rivals that of corporate CEOs.

Having recognized the need to expand presidential perks, many trustees are still resistant to adopting a model from business and industry, given the lessons learned from presidential excesses at corporations such as Enron and Tyco. A sample list of recent high-profile perks includes the following items:

—Presidential mansion

—Country club membership

—Private maid service

—Luxury automobile

—Entertainment budget

Although such luxury-tinged benefits may be common in private non-profits, public institutions may be unable to compete at this level because of issues of public perception and accountability for tax dollars. At the same time, in this competitive, less-forgiving environment, presidential perks can sometimes spell the difference between a successful search and a botched one. It may be something as small as the real estate broker's last conversation with the presidential spouse that drives up expectations regarding support services, entertainment expenses, and other aspects of the "package."

To fully understand the spectrum of perquisites deployed by college and university trustees, the following list is illustrative:

—Health insurance, including major medical coverage

—Disability insurance

—Life insurance

—Professional liability (i.e., officers and directors coverage)

—Workers' compensation coverage

—Participation in the institution's retirement plan consistent with coverage offered to other full-time professional staff

—Deferred compensation

—Sick leave (same number of days and basis as for other full-time professional staff)

—Vacation, with a cap on time that may be accumulated from year to year

—Six months' salary if terminated by the board because of disability

—Housing or housing allowance

—Automobile for business use

—Tuition assistance

—Payment of professional dues and fees for conventions, courses, seminars, and other professional development activities

—Reimbursement for reasonable travel expenses (hotel, airfare, mileage, etc.)

—Membership in service organizations and civic groups

—Preservation/nonwaiver of right to tenure

In addition to the foregoing presidential perks, higher education executives also consider the prospects for superannuating, early retirement options, and other vested retirement rights. In negotiating presidential contracts, attention needs to be paid to tax consequences, particularly in the area of presidential housing.[13]

Employer Provided Housing

Under federal tax laws, a president who is required to live in a residence provided by the institution may have the value of the housing excluded from his income provided the following conditions are met.

—The president is required to accept the lodging as a condition of employment.

—The lodging is located on the institution's campus (business premises).

—The lodging is provided for the convenience of the institution.[14]

Utilities such as heat, electricity, gas, water, and sewage are also excluded in the exemption for housing that meets the above conditions.

The "condition of employment" test is met by showing either (1) that the residence is necessary to the performance of the president's duties or (2) that the residence is necessary to allow the president to be available for college business at all times. Whether the lodging is required depends on the actual requirements of the job, not on the employer's characterization of the situation. For example, a residence used extensively for official entertainment and for meetings outside of normal business hours has been held to meet this standard. The "condition of employment" test can also be met by showing that lodging is furnished in order to enable the employee to be continuously available for duty at all times. Although this exclusion has been permitted for a governor occupying a state mansion, a farm manager living on the employing farm, and a hotel manager living in the employing hotel, it has been rejected in a case involving a college president on the grounds that the president was not continuously

Best Practices

- Keep your eye on the ball: Address search and evaluative criteria early in the interview process and be consistent, timely, and effective in communicating expectations, outcomes, and evaluative results.
- Respect and protect privacy: Be aggressive early on with candidates by encouraging them to give the boards of their current institutions a heads-up about their candidacies once they reach the serious, semifinalist stage.
- "Hold your powder until you see the whites of their eyes":[15] Protect the board by giving it "two bites at the apple" in the selection process, first, by trustee representation on the presidential search committee, and second, by exercising its collective will in the final selection of the successful candidate.
- Exercise due diligence: Investigate serious candidates and be certain about matters of personal integrity, professionalism, experience, and credentials.
- Clarify the responsibility of counsel: Remind the board that in matters of presidential appointment and termination, legal counsel represents the board and that the incumbent and serious finalists should retain their own counsel.
- Disclose personal conflicts, recuse, and record in minutes: Encourage the board to be forthcoming about personal and business interests, and ensure that the bright line between policymaking and administration is not breached.
- Do the necessary homework on best practices and comparative models: Be certain there is precedent and/or justification for all benefits and perks.

available, in that most of his duties were performed during his normal working hours and few after-hours "emergencies" actually occurred.[16]

Private Residence

As a general rule, a president living in his or her own private residence may not deduct the cost of the home. Under the following exceptions, deductions may be taken for depreciation, maintenance, and insurance for portions of a residence that are used exclusively and on a regular basis

—as the principal place of business,

—as a place of business used by patients, clients, or customers dealing with the presidency in the normal course of business, or

—in connection with a trade or business (in the case of a separate structure not attached to the dwelling unit).

The first exception is unlikely to apply to a college president. The second exception may be available for a home containing an office that the president regularly uses exclusively for college business such as meeting students and faculty members and others on matters related to official duties. The possibility of leasing space in a private residence to a college was brought to an end by the Tax Reform Act of 1986.

Housing and Other Cash Allowances

In general, cash allowances for housing and utilities cannot be excluded from income for tax purposes.[17]

Severance Packages: New Options, New Expectations

As the issue of presidential job security becomes a higher-profile aspect of many transitions, trustees should consider enhancing their presidential recruitment process through various alternatives for liquidating the relationship, should it take an unexpected turn. In anticipation of the marital equivalent of divorce, some presidential candidates incorporate the equivalent of a prenuptial agreement in their original employment contract via the following elements.

—Length of notice required by the president and/or governing board

—Due process requirements

—Position of responsibility if president stays with the institution, including

—Salary or method of determining salary

—Office, secretary, expense allowance, and other benefits

—Outplacement services

—Relocation expense

—Separation package, agreement, or allowance:

—Lump sum or periodic payment of the salary equivalent of a specified time period (for example, the cash equivalent of six months' salary)

—Mitigation provision (i.e., if the president gets an equivalent job, the earnings are counted against the monetary payments)

—Agreement regarding unemployment claims

—Retraining opportunities

—References

—Designated individual to handle reference requests and press inquiries

—Nondisparagement clause (parties agree not to make negative statements about each other)

Experienced presidents who move on to new presidencies carry specialized technical expertise and knowledge, essential ingredients in effective institutional leadership. In many cases, they are asked to leave a multiyear contract environment for a limited term contract or for service at the pleasure of the board. In such circumstances, it may be in the best interest of the institution to put in place a legal mechanism that can liquidate the institution's exposure, should the president be asked to leave with or without cause.

Naturally, trustees who remove presidents for cause must steer clear of mixed messages. To do otherwise can be perceived as a presidential payoff that is beyond the realm of ethicality and good form. For the same reason, boards may be inclined to address job security and financial concerns by lengthening the notice required for termination.

Under a severance agreement, a president is typically given a cash settlement of from six months to one year of salary. This protects the individual from a major drop in finances, since the moneys available from unemployment will be nowhere near a presidential salary level. And a mitigation provision prevents the president from getting the windfall of a double salary if it turns out that she or he has no significant gap in employment and obtains substantially the same salary elsewhere.

Rights to unemployment compensation are a legal entitlement, which cannot be bargained away as a matter of law, although the parties may agree to a clause that says the institution will not contest the president's unemployment claim. Whatever the circumstances, avoiding a contested claim will save institutional resources that would have been used for litigation fees and can prevent unnecessary unfavorable publicity and the creation of ill will.

Parting Words for Presidents and Boards: Twelve Legal Guidelines

While one of the primary, and hoped-for, reasons for a president's departure may be to accept a more attractive offer elsewhere, more precipitous chief executive endings frequently reflect a deterioration of the relationship between the board and the president that was caused by some form of inattention, lethargy, mismanagement, or misconduct. Among "for cause" scenarios typically encountered in presidential separation agreements are poor relationships with faculty, lack of administrative-level team spirit, ineffectiveness in managing human resource issues, fiscal crisis, personal problems, lack of campus presence, troubled "town-gown" relationships, nepotism, abuse of authority, and inappropriate sexual conduct.[18]

Short of these "for cause" traumas, the following guidelines are offered in closing as summary legal advice for board members and presidents.

Clarify legal counsel loyalties. With respect to presidential transitions, the board should remember that college or university legal counsel represents the president in almost all instances. There are two exceptions, the appointment and disappointment (hiring and firing) of the chief executive officer. At all other times, when the interests of the president and the board diverge, it is the responsibility of legal counsel to represent and advocate for the board's position. When conflicts arise, an outside attorney can be retained to represent either the president or the board.

Remember that legal counsel is not the board's insurer. The board should satisfy itself that it has acted properly in the search process, both with respect to conflicts of interest, if any, and with respect to presidential compensation. Legal counsel is not the board's insurer in the event that problems arise in this area.

If there are problems, the board may be covered by the institution's officers and directors insurance. However, it is likely that such protection will not apply if it is found that the misconduct at issue is intentional or if wanton or reckless misconduct can be proved.

Avoid conflicts of interest. Trustees should work diligently to avoid conflicts of interest. This does not always mean stepping down from the board at critical junctures, but it does imply the following actions by the board member.

1. Disclose conflicts of interest to the board.
2. Recuse and absent yourself from any discussions involving the conflict.
3. Refrain from otherwise influencing the process.
4. Make sure such recusals are recorded in board minutes.

Maintain search process integrity. The board should keep in mind its successorship and fiduciary duties, which are nondelegable, and that

Emerging Trends

- Placing all employment understandings in writing: If there are collateral deal points, such as faculty tenure, be certain that they are explicitly provided for in the employment contract.
- Treating the contract as a prenuptial agreement; i.e., hope for the best and plan for the worst: To ensure fidelity to the institution, include a primary employment provision that guarantees that the president's consulting and speechmaking schedule will not interfere with institutional business.
- Adding noncompete clauses: Protect the institution from unfair competition with a clause that prohibits an outgoing president from working for local or regional competitors; such a clause may be limited as to time and geography.

the search committee is only empowered to make a *recommendation* to the board. Ultimately, the board is responsible for protecting the integrity of the presidential search process and the final hiring decision. Therefore, the trustees should conduct their own investigation, including verification of credentials, following up with references, and conducting a background and criminal record check.

Avoid golden parachutes. The board will be faced with the challenge of offering a sufficiently attractive compensation and benefits package without offering so much that the final result is construed as running afoul of IRS tax laws prohibiting excessive compensation or as a breach of the public trust.

Private institutions are increasingly held to standards of accountability previously associated with tax-supported, public institutions. As a consequence, boards and chief executives should review their policies and practices to ensure that they are consistent with a very broad definition of "the public trust"—particularly with regard to setting and adjusting presidential compensation.[19]

Address affirmative action concerns. Boards also need to take account of affirmative action cases, which present the rights and remedies for protected classes, including age, handicap, race, religion, sex, and sexual orientation. In this context, trustees, acting by and through the search committee, should attempt to recruit a diverse pool of candidates. Boards should act affirmatively but avoid quotas.

If all finalists are substantially equal, the search committee may choose the minority candidate in order to fulfill its diversity goals. If they are not equal, the committee should not choose a less-qualified candidate just because of the candidate's race or sex. Exceptions to this would obtain at a single-sex school or at a school composed primarily of a particular ethnic minority.

Competitively price search firms. The board should make a thoughtful, well-researched choice of search firm, if appropriate. In selecting a search firm, the following steps are recommended.

1. The board may wish to put out an RFP (request for proposals).
2. The board should gather price quotations from several search firms and interview their principal members.
3. The board should secure and review references very carefully.

Avoid personal prejudices. Boards must remain vigilant to avoid decisions that could give the appearance of animus at any point in the search and transition process. Boards should be insulated through a multi-tiered search process; they should not have too many board members on any single search-related committee.

Do not burn bridges. To the degree feasible, collaborate with the incumbent by preparing a joint press release and public statement demonstrating that the parties are on the same page. In general, and absent any major scandal or misconduct, take steps to maximize goodwill between the institution and the outgoing candidate, as there could be considerable future benefits from a positive relationship with the outgoing president.

The institution should endeavor to make the departure of the past president as graceful as possible. It is typically recommended that the college or university take the high road and issue a gracious statement wishing the president well in future endeavors. This can help maximize the remaining goodwill between the parties and, importantly, lessen the chances of a defamation suit.

Offer outplacement support. Since employment prospects are better for employed individuals than unemployed ones, it is often recommended that the outgoing president be granted outplacement services as part of any separation agreement.

If practical, outplacement services can include the use of an office outside the college or university, since a professional setting such as that enhances the candidate's credibility and, again, maximizes any remaining goodwill between the parties.

Resolve contract and fallback options at the outset. One type of initial employment agreement provides for the incoming president to serve at the pleasure of the board. This provides the transitioning chief executive with no false expectation of a right to continued employment, and it virtually eliminates legal recourse to sue. A second type of arrangement is a term contract. The new president is hired for a definite time period, and he or she is virtually guaranteed employment for that time period, with one key exception: termination for cause. Cause in the legal sense means conduct that is sufficiently egregious to justify termination of a contract.[20]

Some outgoing presidents genuinely enjoy teaching more than administrative duties. Thus, in certain situations, returning the individual to a faculty position can be the right decision for both the institution and the outgoing president. In other circumstances, faculty resistance may make such a transition less practical or even impossible. If a candidate is seriously interested in teaching postpresidency, an explicit guarantee of a teaching position should be included in the original contract. This should apply even if the president originally came up "through the ranks," by moving from a tenured faculty position through administrative positions to the presidency. Without an explicit statement, it can be argued that a candidate waives all rights to tenure when she or he moves into the administrative sphere. When the time arrives, if it is decided that a return to the faculty is not going to be possible, this option can serve as a bargaining chip in negotiating a more favorable severance package.

Know when the deal is a deal. No matter who conveys the job offer, the successful candidate does not have a contractually binding offer of employment until the following actions have taken place.

1. The board has voted to approve the appointment and the minutes have been adopted.
2. The final terms and conditions of an employment contract have been agreed upon.
3. The chair or other board representatives have been delegated authority to enter into a contract or appointment.
4. The proposed contract has been reviewed by counsel, if deemed necessary by the board.
5. The contract has been executed by all parties, i.e., the new president and the chair of the board.

As noted at the outset of this chapter, the environment for presidential transitions has changed over the past decade such that college or university counsel has increasingly become an important factor in the process. The framework provided here argues for a strategic and pragmatic approach to transitions, with attorneys and legal advisers serving as members of the transition team for both proactive and preventive purposes.

CHAPTER FOURTEEN

Partners in Transition: The President's Spouse as Overlooked Power Base

Thomas J. Trebon and Scottie Trebon

Although significant attention inevitably is given to the president of a college or university during the transition process, often his or her spouse receives far less than adequate recognition and support. Whether one is seeking best practices in the nonexistent literature on the topic or assessing actual practice, one finds that the focus remains exclusively on the leader, incoming or outgoing. In the standard transition scenario, the spouse is vaguely considered, at best, and yet still referenced as an important element in a "presidential partnership." Typically, the spouse is attended to less as a partner than for the level of support she or he must now extend to the president.

Clearly, the landscape regarding gender and marital status has changed significantly among college and university presidents since 1980, as the percentages of single men and women, as well as married females, holding office have steadily increased. Additionally, more spouses are involved in their own professional lives separate from that of the president. Cumulatively, these changes add to the complexity and challenge for the institution, the president, and the spouse during a transition of leadership. Given the continuing large percentage of presidents who arrive, or depart, with a spouse, these changes also are important enough to address in a broad study of the presidential transition process such as this one.

On the issue of the spouse during a presidential transition, we have identified no book chapters, essays, or case studies. Even brief references of substance are scant. One is left to infer the real roles of the spouse during the transition process based on interpretations of what is written about the president. Thus, what follows are observations based on our own experiences of transition; comments by other presidents and their spouses during transition periods, reported directly by them or by those involved in the transition events; and our work with numerous colleagues over the years for the Council of Independent Colleges in the development of its comprehensive workshop for presidential spouses at its annual Presidents Institutes.

While significant emphasis in a discussion such as this should be given to the incoming president and spouse, hardly anything has been said about the leader and family who are transitioning out of the presidency. The "new" brings interest, offers excitement, and suggests positive change; "outgoing" often reminds us of the past, of problems, and of perceived mistakes. We have found no written information whatsoever regarding the presidential spouse during an outgoing transition and few comments from those involved in such situations. It is certainly appropriate to focus attention on both the incoming and outgoing families, but the lessons offered here mostly concern the spouse during the transition *into* a presidency. We acknowledge, though, that some of the ideas suggested for engaging the president's spouse may well apply to the end of a presidential term as well.

1. *From the earliest reasonable stage in the selection process, provide to the spouse, as well as to the presidential candidate, a broad spectrum of information regarding the community context of the institution.* Significant information regarding an *institution* is regularly made available to candidates, but typically, the focus of materials provided is too narrow. Comments from many presidents and their spouses indicate that very little is provided regarding the community context of the institution and its resources. Information regarding public services, schools, medical services, occupational opportunities, the physical environment, comparative expense data, arts and entertainment, clubs, and community organizations can be very valuable to both partners, especially the spouse. Sources readily available on the Internet—Chamber of Commerce listings, for example—enable the couple to search for specific information of interest. While the presidential candidate will focus his or her attention on the institutional information, the spouse will often take responsibility to research the community within which the institution rests. Providing a significant level of detail about these areas signals an institution that values an authentic "presidential partnership" concept.

2. *Include the spouse on visitations to the campus, during the selection process and after the naming of the new president.* The move to a new institution, and even a move within an institution to its presidency, involves entering a significantly different context—physically, socially,

and interpersonally. There are new faces, new obligations, new events to attend, and new opportunities to represent the institution. Numerous examples in our research indicate that direct involvement of the spouse in learning more about the institution, the community in which it is located, and the scope of experiences in which the family will be involved were critically important to the decision the president made, in partnership with the spouse, about leading the institution. A number of institutions also confirmed that it was important for the spouse to be integrally involved in key stages of the transition process, because this provided both college representatives and community representatives the opportunity to identify specific strengths that the spouse could bring to assist the new president.

3. *Identify an institutional colleague for the spouse who will be able to respond to questions, provide ongoing information regarding the college and the community, and serve as a trusted contact before and after arrival.* For the new president and spouse, having such a mentor and colleague can be most helpful in the transition process. The president has "built-in" assistance, as many individuals will be readily available to answer her or his questions and provide advice. For the spouse, a contact person can be asked to address numerous questions, from the practical to the more personal. One excellent model for this is provided by the Council of Independent Colleges, which systematically links new presidents and their spouses at their annual professional institutes with a colleague who has greater familiarity with the roles and responsibilities involved in that office.

Whether the new president is moving into a new city or moving up within the same institution, his or her spouse will find the ready availability of a colleague who can speak with extensive experience regarding the community and the institution to be helpful and, when needed, comforting. These same contact and networking opportunities are equally valuable to same-sex spouses, who are even more overlooked in presidential transition planning. In the case of Charles Middleton's arrival as chief executive of Roosevelt University in Chicago in 2002, the institution approached this issue with honesty and sophistication, in his view: "During the interview process, my partner, John, and I were impressed by the Board's granting him the same considerations that were given to spouses of other candidates and doing so forthrightly on its own initiative early in the process. Later, as I was negotiating the contract and subsequently during the transition process, it was particularly reassuring that John had routine independent contact with University leaders and others to ensure that things were going well for him personally."[1]

Best Practices

- Provide a broad spectrum of information to the spouse about the campus community throughout the search process.
- Include the spouse on visits to the campus and during the selection process.
- Identify an institutional colleague to serve as a trusted contact for the spouse.
- Provide several structured opportunities for the spouse to meet persons representing a cross section of the community.
- Involve the spouse integrally in planning transition details.
- Provide additional assistance for spouses who will work outside the home.

4. *Provide structured opportunities for the spouse, separately from the president, to meet persons from various sectors of the community.* In concert with the president, there will be innumerable opportunities for the spouse to meet members of the campus and extended communities during the transition period. On this subject, the literature on modern college and university presidents is replete with cautions regarding the tendency for the president and spouse to be drawn into every imaginable campus activity over the first few months of residency. In fact, joint appearances at these functions, even for a brief time, will be anticipated and expected. Similarly, involvement in the community by both, and even by the spouse alone to represent the institution, will potentially mean attendance at a very large number of social occasions. On this issue, several colleagues have suggested that it will also be important to identify specific opportunities for the spouse to meet a variety of persons in the community *aside from* clearly representative commitments. Several spouses indicated that building a network of friends, which is a challenge to anyone moving into a new environment, can be daunting and eventually isolating when one's spouse (the president) is a major figure in the community. Opportunities for structured, yet informal, gatherings and associations can provide the president's spouse with important introductions to build on in developing her or his own circle of immediate associates.

5. *Involve the spouse in planning transition details.* There are a great many details involved in the transition process, from welcoming receptions to deciding on needed changes to the presidential residence. Many spouses, especially those who do not have full-time careers of their own, might well have greater interest in and time for participation

Emerging Trends

- Providing the spouse with a defined set of professional responsibilities and placing him or her on the college or university payroll.
- Providing equal considerations and support to same-sex spouses during the transition.
- Encouraging personal time away from the position for the spouse and the president starting within the first six months of service.

in some transition matters than the new president will have as a result of the press of business. Furthermore, involvement in some activities provides opportunities for the spouse to learn more about the institution and its traditions as well as develop helpful contacts for future projects. One college noted that involvement of the spouse in transition events provided a separate "face" of the president and the opportunity for the community to view the new chief executive as a partner in a key relationship as well as the next leader of their institution.

6. *If the spouse expects to work outside the home, provide frequent and ongoing assistance well in advance of the move to the new institution.* The number of spouses of presidents who will pursue careers and work experiences outside the home continues to increase. Although there are still a number of spouses who are not employed outside the home, particularly in rural and small institutions, the majority of instances we have researched have involved external employment by the spouse. As part of the transition, institutions may consider extending various forms of support and assistance in this regard. Spouses who received such help reported a welcome sense of institutional support for their goals and interests. Unfortunately, there was not a significant number of these cases in our research. Where there are opportunities for the spouse to transfer professionally to a position of interest, providing contact information and referrals can be instrumental. There continue to be examples of spouses who are employed by the institution itself. When this occurs, the president and the spouse need to be continually attentive for any perceptions of undue spousal power and influence that may have to be addressed or explained.

7. *Encourage the spouse and the president to take personal time during the first six months of leadership to step away from the initial workload and social schedule.* Presidents and spouses interviewed often con-

veyed the same message. Regular opportunities for the couple to take a break away from the institution, and even away from the local community, were viewed as critically important throughout the presidency but especially during the first six months after arrival. Options included adding an extra day or two for personal time when the couple travels on behalf of the institution and initially designing vacation time so that contact with the executive offices was minimal. At one institution, the president and spouse's vacation plans were included in general comments to the college community, in part to indicate that wellness needs to be considered important to all.

The literature on presidential tenures and the stages of a presidency documents a growing level of interest in what seems to be an ever-expanding set of obligations and expectations. While there has been little to nothing of substance written about the roles of the presidential spouse, it is clear that these roles are also growing in importance and complexity, especially during periods of presidential transition. The practices outlined above speak to the need for a deeper, more specific examination of this overlooked power base, as well as more extensive study of the roles of the presidential spouse in the larger topic of institutional leadership.

CHAPTER FIFTEEN

Knowing the End of the Beginning: A Conceptual Approach to Presidential Transition

James Martin and James E. Samels

Presidential transitions are messy, challenging, and inevitable, and each one can provoke hundreds of questions that do not fall neatly into even broadly designed chapters on subjects like public relations, governance, and board involvement. Often, the most challenging questions emerge at the edges of a transition, and for this reason we are closing this study of what is coming to be known as "transition management" with a concise methodology to approach some of the basic concepts involved and a comprehensive flowchart highlighting necessary actions and decisions, from the earliest confidential discussions to public statements, the search, and finally, to that moment when the transition fades into the fully launched presidency of the next chief executive officer. The chapter closes with a presentation of the benchmarks by which participants can gauge "the end of the beginning" and know that the transition process has concluded.

The following summary concepts define the core of the transition process relative to the *departing president,* the *incoming president,* and the *institution as a whole.*

—For departing presidents, *view recognition as closure.*

—For incoming presidents, *avoid overreactions.*

—For the institution as a whole, *treat transition as a strategic moment.*

View recognition as closure. When asked about the most important element in helping a departing president plan a transition, Ronald Remington, former president of the thirty-three-thousand-student Community College of Southern Nevada (and the only individual to hold administrative leadership posts at every community college in the Nevada state system) advised: "Celebrate that individual's contributions to the institution in a public and high profile way. The point is not simply to pay courtesy to an outgoing chief executive but, on a deeper level, to provide sometimes the first opportunity for an institution collectively to consider and enter into the complexities of its own transition process. In this sense, recognition and reward for the outgoing president can also provide a form of closure within the broader transition experience."[1]

In recognizing the contributions of its former leader, no matter how short or long the tenure, a college or university "takes responsibility" for its future by "structuring its first steps forward without this central authority figure."[2] In this way, a carefully designed ending acts as the gateway to the new beginnings implicated below.

Avoid overreactions. Terrence Gomes, interviewed in June 2003, one week after his appointment to the presidency of Roxbury Community College in Boston, one of the most resource-challenged community colleges within the Massachusetts state system, captured this concept in just two sentences: "I was appointed to bring change to Roxbury Community College—but not change that ignores our journey to this point. This institution has a bright future, but that brightness depends, in part, on how we respect those who have gone before."[3] Gomes offers a clear illustration of the second basic concept behind effective presidential transitions: Avoid overreactions and the "pendulum syndrome" by which an institution, in the process of searching for its next president, decides that it needs a completely new and "fresh" approach with a candidate at the other end of the leadership spectrum from the exiting president, no matter how valued and effective that individual was.

By traveling down this path, institutions voluntarily cut themselves off from many talented candidates simply because they are too much like the departing leader. This sometimes desperate search for a "new voice" or "new vision" can weaken the search process and its eventual results. In contrast, the most effective interview teams remain centered in looking for the candidates who can most capably lead the institution forward.

Treat transition as a strategic moment. Presidential transition should be viewed as an event in the life of an institution that is greater than the choice of its next leader. Whether the new president is an outsider with a strong agenda for change or a long-term member of the faculty or administration chosen for reasons of stability and continuity, the transition process offers strategic opportunities, typically overlooked in the past, to continue to refine the curriculum, enhance student life, and rethink board priorities—just three illustrations among many possibilities.

Transition events now occur more frequently on all campuses. Similar to the regional accreditation process, presidential turnover has become a much more familiar activity for everyone on campus over the past quarter century, and as this familiarity has grown, so have the percentages of faculty and administrators who view leadership change as a set of opportunities to be shaped beyond the search process.

The three groups most important to accomplishing strategic objectives during a transition are the board, the vice presidents and other cabinet members, and the leadership of the faculty. These three groups hold enough power to make the transition event into a strategic planning activity, whether stated or implied. Traditionally, many on campus have responded negatively to new or significant assignments during a search process. However, with the incursion of hundreds of market-sensitive, for-profit competitors and corporate universities; the escalating expectations of student consumers; and the potentially adverse impact of even one or two months of operational uncertainty at many colleges, leaders of numerous institutions are beginning to think differently about the meaning and scope of a transition process. For planners on fragile, resource-poor campuses, issues of time and money can so severely condition a pending transition that those on the leadership team may be *forced* to broaden the process into an accompanying matrix of strategic action steps.

Whatever the institution's history, reputation, and endowment, a change in its executive leadership increasingly means more than simply a new president. An irony of succession is that those institutions that have the most resources can be the most conservative in their search perspectives, while those with the smallest endowments are sometimes the most entrepreneurial. At some universities, academic reputation, ranking, and niche will be the themes of its leadership change. For others, fund-raising and institutional advancement will drive the process. For those in the resource-challenged group mentioned above, fiscal instability may finally prevent the school from securing a nationally recognized candidate who can inspire confidence about its future. Such are the challenges of transition in the current higher education environment.

The flowchart in figure 15.1 summarizes the stages of presidential transition discussed in this book and encapsulates much of the advice offered.

	PHASE I	PHASE II	PHASE III
Initial discussions and decisions between president and board chair	Agree on wordings for public statements	Press release on search team and/or appointment of interim president, if needed	Press release on search update and upcoming meetings for community to meet candidates
Reasons for transition:	Press release on transition	Orientation of interim president, if needed	Deadline for candidate nominations and applications
Standard Examples: 1. Different position 2. Retirement 3. Board termination or nonrenewal	Board requests transition plan from cabinet	Executive Committee of Board continues to meet regularly on transition issues	Decide on institutional position and procedures for any internal candidates
Nonstandard Examples: 1. Sudden illness or death 2. Threatened vote of no confidence 3. Scandal, compromising activities, or personal reasons	Agree on single campus spokesperson for transition issues	Stabilize the cabinet	Initial review of candidate dossiers
Note: Nonstandard reasons can alter this flow chart	Decide yes/no regarding executive search firm	Cabinet continues to meet regularly on transition issues	Campus and community opportunities to recognize contributions of departing president
	Decide yes/no regarding interim president	Board forbids "midnight appointments"	Ongoing meetings of transition team
	Call for independent financial audit	Board holds last-minute pledges of credit to scrutiny	
	Board reviews departing president's contract for relevant stipulations and severance	Advertising and calls for nominations begin	
	Ensure involvement of faculty, students, staff, and alumni in search process	Board creates vehicles to communicate directly on transition issues, as needed	
	Board chair notifies regional accrediting agency and state higher education authorities of pending transition	Board begins informational briefings with major donors, as needed	
	Board finalizes scope of search plan and recruiting strategies	Ongoing meetings of transition team	
	Creation of transition team to oversee institutional operations, as needed		
	Board and cabinet interviews of interim presidential candidates, if needed		

Figure 15.1. Flow Chart for a Presidential Transition

PHASE IV	PHASE V	PHASE VI	PHASE VII
Identification of semifinalist candidates	Press release announcing 3 to 5 finalist candidates	Press release announcing appointment of next president	Press release on start of new presidency and schedule of related community events
Telephone/airport interviews of semifinalist candidates	Comprehensive on-campus interviews of finalist candidates	Receive from cabinet members briefing books for new president on status of their areas	Arrival of next president
Search committee review of responses from interviews with semi-finalist candidates	Inclusion of candidates' spouses in key interview activities	Schedule meeting(s), as appropriate, between departing and incoming president	Continuation of various transition team responsibilities, if needed
Reference checks on semifinalist candidates	Further reference checks on finalists	Form committee to plan scope and timing of inaugural activities	Introductions of president to key campus and external community members, regional accreditors, and state higher education leaders
Check-in and coordination by board and transition team on cabinet members' initiatives and work product, as needed	Search committee representatives visit home campuses of finalists	Receive from chief student affairs officer calendar of events for new president to attend for the coming year	Immediate briefing by cabinet on status of budget and any campus "hot spots"
Ongoing meetings of transition team	Search committee sends final ranked/unranked recommendations to board	Departure of former president or interim president	President's first official meetings with faculty, staff, students, and alumni
	Board representatives meet with and negotiate, as needed, with first-choice candidate	Final meetings of transition team	Integration and orientation of president's spouse to his/her institutional responsibilities
	Appointment of next president by board		President's first meetings with key donors coordinated by advancement office
	Dissolution of presidential search committee		
	Ongoing meetings of transition team		

Knowing the End of the Beginning: Ten Indicators

The following ten indicators, which gauge the conclusion and, more indirectly, the success of a transition's signature elements, are supplied in order to help governing boards and transition management teams design a coherent and accountable transition process—and to know when that process is completed.

For many on campus, it can be difficult to sense the moment when a presidential transition ends. Stereotypically, the conclusion of the process has been viewed as the end of a traditional honeymoon. Every new president still experiences some grace period, but the length and breadth of that honeymoon now varies from institution to institution, and its overall duration is clearly shortening on many outcome-driven campuses. There are, however, several identifiable benchmarks that clearly signal the inevitable shift from president-in-transition to established leader. It should be noted also that the conclusion of each transition begins a new cycle, which will also end in a transition, such that senior administrative and faculty leaders would be wise to record and preserve the lessons from each transition for use as they prepare for the next one.

While the new president officially becomes chief executive officer with her or his appointment by the board, in practice, the president has fully arrived when he or she supplants the predecessor in the collective consciousness of the institution.

1. *When the new leadership team is in place.* It is easy to argue that, in the name of continuity and harmony, it is best to allow individuals to work in the same capacity they enjoyed under the previous administration. While this can be effective, in many instances a new president will need a core group of trusted advisers and cabinet members whose commitment and loyalty arise from both merit and selection. That does not mean that a new president should risk disrupting the operations of the institution by demoting or removing all of the administrators and leaders from the previous administration. Instead, the president's ability to cull team members from among those already at the institution, coupled with her or his abilities as a recruiter of new, outside talent, signal that this individual has moved well beyond the "get to know you" phase of a presidency.

2. *When the board will no longer follow the new president over the cliff.* In its construction of a list of qualifications and its influence over the search process, the board provided a very public statement of its institutional vision. The selection of a provost as president, for example, sug-

Ending the Transition: Managing the Campus

- Do not underestimate the value of walking around: Take a daily walk around campus and leave the entourage at home. Faculty, staff, and especially students can provide interesting and informative insights when they are not speaking through senior staff interpreters.
- Assume that internal and external communities know little about the state of the college or university: Do not rely on other offices to get the presidential message out. Issue newsletters, create an interactive Web page for the president's office, and deliver periodic or semester-based "State of the Institution" addresses.
- Be good to the town, and it will be good to the gown: One of the best ways to invest in the internal campus community is to invest in its *external* one. Build up a bank of good currency by being courteous and visible neighbors. Remember, faculty and staff are also members of that larger community that serves as host to the institution.
- Enhance student engagement: If campus ambassadors, tour guides, and office interns are not students and alumni, they should be. Colleges and universities, at their most basic levels, belong to the students that they serve.

gests in no uncertain terms that the trustees view the institution's academic priorities, from new curriculum to issues of academic quality and reputation, as paramount. Likewise, the selection of a candidate with demonstrated capital campaign experience demonstrates the primacy of fund-raising to institutional mission.

Whatever the particular skills and agenda of the new president, the board typically gives the new leader a wide berth to maneuver in the first few months. It is the decision by the board members to reengage and assert themselves that signals a general acceptance that the transition period is now complete. Rigorous scrutiny of the new president by trustees does not necessarily represent a challenge to his or her authority. Instead, it can signify that the president has entered a new phase of leadership and is more equipped to handle the candid, tough discussions with board members that occur at most institutions, no matter what the size or mission.

3. *When the faculty tell the new leader what they really think at Senate meetings.* Presidents have ended their transitional periods when faculty members, either individually or through committees and collective bargaining units, begin to voice opinions and concerns regarding the

direction of the institution. From issues of academic freedom to larger institutional questions about outcomes assessment, presidents must be prepared to hear what the faculty think, and often.

Differing campus climates will dictate the nature and level of communication between faculty and administration, as will the new president's approach to issues of faculty concern. The fact that both senior and junior professors are willing to be candid and expressive in their communications with the president demonstrates an end to transitional thinking.

4. *When the first cycle of the next strategic plan has been completed.* This accomplishment puts the end of the transition beyond the traditional first one hundred days of a presidency; in fact, the typical length of a strategic plan may put this benchmark one to three years after the inauguration. That said, nothing acquaints a leader with an institution like an in-depth self-assessment and fair-minded evaluation of strengths, opportunities, threats, and weaknesses.

Perhaps more than any other benchmark, successful completion of the strategic planning cycle tells the entire community that the president has fully arrived as the new chief executive leader. Through a strategic plan, a president becomes so familiar with all aspects of an institution, as well as their points of intersection and conflict, that it is a natural step to close the door on more tentative, transitional decision making.

5. *When the new president knows the real story of the institution, that is, where the bodies are buried.* Presidents need to know the *real* story of their institutions, and it is accurate to say that the transition has ended when they grasp the most efficient ways of getting things accomplished, particularly in educational policy and financial planning areas.

6. *When the media exposure is earned.* Being new is not news. When the new president attracts media attention, the institution also receives welcome publicity, and the community is enriched by the (generally) positive, high-level exposure. Press can be a double-edged sword, however, as missteps make good copy, and journalists are less apt to withhold tough questions as the months of a new president's first year tick by. Positive, negative, or somewhere in between, earned media exposure for a president is another signal that the transition period is over. No self-respecting media outlet will waste ink or air time on a president who has not established a leadership imprint. At that point, additional "listening tours" and "no comment" responses will not suffice.

Final Advice for Presidents in Transition

Former University of Akron president Norman Auburn has made several suggestions for new leaders to follow as they establish themselves:

- Do not violate tradition.
- Be a good—and politely skeptical—listener.
- Get the best ideas.
- Find out in whom you can safely confide.
- Don't make promises you cannot keep.[4]

7. *When the structural deficit has been eliminated.* Turning a surplus is a proven way to ensure the continued existence of high-quality programs and professorships while simultaneously pleasing the board, often comprised of men and women with a keen understanding of the financial bottom line. The inability to advance the financial security of an institution and, if applicable, leave precious endowment funds alone can be a quick way for the president to enter a new transition: looking for a job elsewhere.

8. *When institutional advancement capacity is developed.* Connecting with alumni and convincing them that a new vision for their alma mater not only celebrates the institutional legacy they hold dear but also ensures that the college will be a viable and attractive option for their children and grandchildren is key to building development capacity. Alumni will open their wallets in both modest and larger ways to support a president who effectively courts them. As such, a president who earns their loyalty through creativity and courage will wield substantial increased power on and off campus.

9. *When a new building has been financed, designed, and constructed.* Be it the product of an aggressive capital campaign or simply the culmination of a campus master-planning process, the successful construction of the first building during a president's tenure becomes a perpetual reminder that the transition period is over. He or she has literally left a mark on the campus. Whether it turns out to be a field house, an enterprise center, or a science laboratory, the results are tangible and can be immediately recognized and accepted.

10. *When a new degree program has been launched.* The key is to mount online a first *complete* degree or certificate program. Too often,

questions of information technology in a college curriculum are framed in either-or constructs, making the erroneous claim that traditional liberal arts and sciences will suffer with the expansion of information technology options on campus. Presidents who are able to marry these complementary but often competing areas of campus power and influence will gradually find their decision making and leadership styles noticed on other campuses. Finally, securing one or more high-profile partners in a strategic alliance will provide a powerful external showcase for the new degree program and its faculty.

Final Thought

Most college and university trustees have had only isolated experience with the overlapping complexities of a presidential transition, much less a sense of how to manage its elements strategically. Yet, when viewed from a board's overall fiduciary and stewardship perspectives, the transition process involves a great deal more than the simple search for a successor. For those boards with a shared vision, transitions offer rare opportunities for tough-minded introspection and meaningful involvement in shaping the future of the institution.

Notes

Preface

1. George Keller, telephone interview by James Martin and James Samels, 10 September 2001.

Chapter 1. A New Model of Transition Management

1. John W. Moore with Joanne M. Burrows, *Presidential Succession and Transition: Beginning, Ending, and Beginning Again,* AASCU Special Report (Washington, DC: American Association of State Colleges and Universities, 2001), 1.

2. Ibid., 2.

3. James L. Fisher, Martha W. Tack, and Karen J. Wheeler, *The Effective College President* (New York: American Council on Education and Macmillan, 1988), 43.

4. Kathryn Mohrman, "A Lame Duck President Looks Back," *Chronicle of Higher Education,* 25 April 2002, Career Network section online; available at www.chronicle.com (accessed April 2002).

5. Richard T. Ingram and associates, *Governing Independent Colleges and Universities: A Handbook for Trustees, Chief Executives, and Other Campus Leaders* (San Francisco: Jossey-Bass, 1993), 340.

6. Jean Dowdall, Robert H. Perry, Maria M. Perez, Darryl G. Greer, and William A. Weary, "Roadblocks on the Road to Diversity: Five Presidential Experts Respond to a *Trusteeship* Query on Why There Are Not More Females and Minorities Leading American Colleges and Universities Today," *Trusteeship* 10, no. 3 (May–June 2002): 13.

7. Commission on the Academic Presidency, *Renewing the Academic Presidency: Stronger Leadership for Tougher Times* (Washington, DC: Association of Governing Boards of Universities and Colleges, 1996), 6.

8. Michael D. Cohen and James G. March, *Leadership and Ambiguity: The American College President,* A General Report Prepared for the Carnegie Commission on Higher Education (New York: McGraw-Hill, 1974), 191.

9. Judith Block McLaughlin, ed., *Leadership Transitions: The New College President,* New Directions for Higher Education, no. 93 (San Francisco: Jossey-Bass, 1996), 1.

10. Jamilah Evelyn, "Community Colleges Face a Crisis of Leadership," *Chronicle of Higher Education,* 6 April 2001, A36.

11. Erica Kelly, "The Changing of the Guard," *Community College Week,* 27 May 2002, 7.

12. See ibid. See also Evelyn, "Community Colleges Face a Crisis," A36.

13. Katherine Shek, "College President and Faculty Retirements Loan," *Community College Times,* 17 April 2001, 10.

14. Ibid.

15. Ann Korschgen, Rex Fuller, and John Gardner, "The Impact of Presidential Migration," *AAHE* [American Association for Higher Education] *Bulletin* 53, no. 6 (2001): 3.

16. Art Padilla and Sujit Ghosh, "Turnover at the Top: The Revolving Door of the Academic Presidency," *Presidency* 3 (winter 2000): 32, 34.

17. Commission on the Academic Presidency, *Renewing the Academic Presidency,* 9.

18. Daniel Perlman, "Paradoxes of the Presidency," *AAHE* [American Association for Higher Education] *Bulletin* 42 (1989): 4, 3.

19. Anne Diffily, "Tales of Gregorian," *Brown Alumni Monthly,* October 1988, 35.

20. Carol Lucey, interview by the authors, 25 June 2002.

21. Debra Murphy, interview by the authors, 24 June 2002.

22. Michael Arnone, "International Consortium Readies Ambitious Distance Education Effort," *Chronicle of Higher Education,* 28 June 2002, A28.

23. Mary Louise Fennell and Catherine Cook, "Capital Gains: Surviving in an Increasingly For-Profit World," *Presidency* (winter 2001): 29.

24. Corporate University Exchange, Inc., *Executive Summary: 1999 Survey of Corporate University Future Directions* (n.p., 1999), 1.

25. Christopher Jencks and David Riesman, *The Academic Revolution* (Garden City, NY: Doubleday, 1968), 17.

26. Perlman, "Paradoxes of the Presidency," 3.

27. Karen Arenson, "The Moral Compass on Campus," *New York Times,* 10 June 2001, 33.

28. William D. Rezak, "Leading Colleges and Universities as Business Enterprises," *AAHE* [American Association for Higher Education] *Bulletin* 53, no. 2 (October 2000): 6.

29. Rudolph Weingartner, *Fitting Form to Function: A Primer on the Organization of Academic Institutions* (Phoenix: American Council on Education and Oryx Press, 1996), xi.

30. Frank Newman and Lara K. Couturier, "The New Competitive Arena: Market Forces Invade the Academy," *Change* 33, no. 5 (September–October 2001): 12.

31. Bruce T. Alton and Kathleen L. Dean, "Why Presidents Think the Grass Is Greener," *Trusteeship* 10, no. 3 (May–June 2002): 23.

32. Michael Skapinker, "Business Heads for Too Much Room at the Top," *Financial Times,* 23 April 2002, 12.

33. Piper Fogg and Julianne Basinger, "Review: Shelf Date," *Chronicle of Higher Education,* 19 April 2002, A8.

34. Eric Hsu, "First Movers, Fast Followers," *Microsoft Executive Circle* 2, no. 2 (summer 2002): 47.

35. Michael Riccards, interview by the authors, 18 June 2002.

36. Philip G. Altbach, "Knowledge and Education as International Commodities: The Collapse of the Common Good," *International Higher Education*, no. 28 (summer 2002): 2.

37. Diffily, "Tales of Gregorian," 35.

38. Ronald Remington, interview by the authors, 26 June 2002.

39. Stanley Bergen, interview by the authors, 16 July 2002.

40. Julianne Basinger, "When a President Quits Early, the Damage Can Linger On," *Chronicle of Higher Education*, 27 July 2001, A22.

41. Cohen and March, *Leadership and Ambiguity*, 192–93.

42. Steven Muller, "The University Presidency Today: A Word for the Incumbents," in *Leaders on Leadership*, ed. James L. Fisher and Martha W. Tack, New Directions for Higher Education, no. 61 (San Francisco: Jossey-Bass, 1988), 24, 25.

43. Clara M. Lovett, "The Dumbing Down of College Presidents," *Chronicle of Higher Education*, 5 April 2002, B20.

44. Knight Higher Education Collaborative, "Inside Out," *Policy Perspectives* 10, no. 1 (2001): 2.

45. Mclaughlin, *Leadership Transitions*, 1.

46. Sylvan Lashley, interview by the authors, 24 December 2002.

47. Clara Lovett, "Dumbing Down," B20.

48. John Ekarius, interview by the authors, 15 July 2002.

49. Lorna D. Edmundson and Gwendolyn E. Jensen, "The Ten Commandments of Presidential Transition," paper presented at the annual meeting of the National Institute of the Association of Governing Boards, Boston, April 23, 2002, 1.

Chapter 2. Presidents Who Leave, Presidents Who Stay

1. Marlene Ross and Madeleine Green, *The American College President* Washington, DC: American Council on Education, 2000; executive summary available at www.acenet.edu/programs/president-study (accessed August 2002).

2. Muller, "University Presidency Today," 24–25.

3. Perlman, "Paradoxes of the Presidency," 3.

4. Altbach, "Knowledge and Education," 2.

5. Diffily, "Tales of Gregorian," 35.

Chapter 4. Passing the Baton

1. S. Finkelstein and D. C. Hambrick, *Strategic Leadership: Top Executives and Their Effects on Organizations* (Minneapolis: West Publishing, 1996).

2. Cohen and March, *Leadership and Ambiguity.*

3. Finkelstein and Hambrick, *Strategic Leadership.*

4. Association of Governing Boards, *Bridging the Gap between State Government and Public Higher Education* (Washington, DC: Association of Governing Boards of Universities and Colleges, 1998).

5. Finkelstein and Hambrick, *Strategic Leadership.*

6. Clark Kerr, "Holding the Center—Presidential Discontent," in *Perspectives on Campus Tensions: Papers Prepared for the Special Committee on Campus Tensions*, ed. D. Nichols (Washington, DC: American Council on Education, 1970), 137–62.

7. Cohen and March, *Leadership and Ambiguity.*

8. See Marlene Ross and Madeleine F. Green, *The American College President* (Washington, DC: American Council on Education, 1998); W. K. Selden, "How

Long Is a College President?" *Liberal Education* 46 (1960); M. R. Ferrari, *Profiles of American College Presidents* (East Lansing: Michigan State University School of Business, 1970).

9. Ross and Green, *American College President* (1998).

10. Cohen and March, *Leadership and Ambiguity,* 164.

11. Kerr, "Holding the Center."

12. Padilla and Ghosh, "Turnover at the Top."

13. This and the following section are based on A. Padilla and S. Ghosh, "On the Tenure of University Presidents," *On the Horizon* 8 (1999); and Padilla and Ghosh, "Turnover at the Top."

14. Ross and Green, *American College President* (1998).

15. R. F. Vancil, *Passing the Baton* (Boston: Harvard Business School Press, 1987).

16. R. Ehrenberg, J. Cheslock, and J. Epifantseva, "Paying Our Presidents: What Do Trustees Value?" *Review of Higher Education* 25 (2001): 30.

17. Association of Governing Boards, *Bridging the Gap.*

18. Finkelstein and Hambrick, *Strategic Leadership.*

19. For baseball teams, see M. Allen, S. Panian, and R. Lotz, "Managerial Succession and Organizational Performance: A Recalcitrant Problem Revisited," *Administrative Science Quarterly* 24 (1979). For semiconductor firms, see W. Boeker and J. Goodstein, "Performance and Successor Choice; The Moderating Effects of Governance and Ownership," *Academy of Management Journal* 36 (1993). For a cross section of large companies in various industries, see A. Cannella and M. Lubatkin, "Succession as a Sociopolitical Process: Internal Impediments to Outsider Selection," *Academy of Management Journal* 36 (1993).

20. W. Gamson and N. Scotch, "Scapegoating in Baseball," *American Journal of Sociology* 70 (1964).

21. Robert F. Carbone, *Presidential Passages* (Washington, DC: American Council on Education, 1981).

22. H. W. Stoke, *The American College President* (New York: Harper and Row, 1959).

23. Finkelstein and Hambrick, *Strategic Leadership,* 191.

Chapter 5. The Role of the Board in Presidential Transition

Epigraph: William Bridges, *Managing Transitions: Making the Most of Change* (Reading, MA: Addison-Wesley, 1991), 6.

1. E. K. Fretwell Jr., *The Interim Presidency: Guidelines for University and College Governing Boards* (Washington, DC: Association of Governing Boards of Universities and Colleges, 1995). See also Edward J. Kormondy and Kent M. Keith, "The Salvaging President: Institutions That Fall on Hard Times Often Hire an Experienced Former President to Act as a Non-Traditional Leader of Change: Here's How They Succeed," *Trusteeship* 9, no. 3 (May–June 2001): 24–27.

2. Jean Dowdall, "The President's House," *Chronicle of Higher Education,* 3 June 2002.

3. William A. Weary, *Essentials of Presidential Search (AGB Board Basics: Board Leadership)* (Washington, DC: AGB, 1998); Charles B. Neff and Barbara Leondar, *Presidential Search: A Guide to the Process of Selecting and Appointing College and University Presidents* (Washington, DC: AGB, 1992); William A. Weary, *Guidelines for Selecting a Presidential Search Consultant and Directory of Search Consulting*

Firms, 3d ed. (Washington, DC: AGB, 2002); Richard A. Hogarty, "UMass Selects a New President: Elements of a Search Strategy," *New England Journal of Public Policy* (fall–winter 1992): 9–35; Alice S. Huang, "Marriage Counseling for Boards: Today More Than Ever, the President's Spouse Is Apt to Have Valuable Skills the Institution Should Tap: Boards Should Formally Recognize the Partner's Roles and Contributions," *Trusteeship* 7, no. 6 (November–December 1999): 29–32; Judith Block McLaughlin and David Riesman, *Choosing a College President: Opportunities and Constraints* (Princeton, NJ: Carnegie Foundation for the Advancement of Teaching, 1990). This section of the chapter obviously is not meant to substitute for all of the detail found in the above resources.

4. See www.chronicle.com and www.careernetwork.com (accessed August 2003).

5. Nick Estes, "State University Presidential Searches: Law and Practice," *Journal of College and University Law* 26, no. 3 (winter 2000): 485–509.

6. Weary, *Guidelines.*

7. Neff and Leondar, *Presidential Search,* 90–91 (contains a sample charge); Weary, *Guidelines,* 11 (contains a sample code).

8. University System of Maryland, Adelphi, MD. See Web site on chancellor search at www.usmd.edu (accessed August 2002). For an institutional agenda by itself—not turned into a leadership statement—see Auburn University, Auburn, AL, "Auburn University's Agenda," Web site for Auburn, "Special Reports," at www .auburn.edu (accessed August 2003).

9. William A. Weary, "Describe a Clear Vision," in Dowdall et al., "Roadblocks on the Road to Diversity," 18.

10. Moore with Burrows, *Presidential Succession and Transition,* 13. See also Ross and Green, *American College President* (2000).

11. Robert H. Atwell, Madeleine F. Green, and Marlene Ross, *The Well-Informed Candidate: A Brief Guide for Candidates for College and University Presidencies* (Washington, DC: American Council on Education, 2001).

12. Julianne Basinger, "No Long-Term President and No Prospects," *Chronicle of Higher Education,* 9 March 2001. See also Basinger, "When a President Quits Early."

13. See University of Toledo, Toledo, OH, Web site on presidential search: www.utoledo.edu (accessed August 2002).

14. Moore with Burrows, *Presidential Succession and Transition,* 11–13.

15. Robert H. Atwell and Jane V. Wellman, *Presidential Compensation in Higher Education: Policies and Best Practices* (Washington, DC: AGB, 2000).

16. Ibid.

17. Moore with Burrows, *Presidential Succession and Transition,* 22.

18. Julianne Basinger, "For Presidents and Boards, a Handshake Is No Longer Enough," *Chronicle of Higher Education,* 24 May 2002.

19. Atwell and Wellman, *Presidential Compensation,* 7–9.

20. Sara Hebel, "IRS Clarifies Law on Pay for Leaders of Nonprofit Groups," *Chronicle of Higher Education,* 19 January 2002.

21. Richard T. Ingram and William A. Weary, *Presidential and Board Assessment in Higher Education: Purposes, Policies, and Strategies* (Washington, DC: AGB, 2000).

22. Merrill Pellows Schwartz, *A National Survey of Board Performance Assessment Policies and Practices,* AGB Occasional Paper, no. 35 (Washington, DC: AGB,

1998); Barbara E. Taylor, "Assessing Board Performance," in *Governing Public Colleges and Universities: A Handbook for Trustees, Chief Executives, and other Campus Leaders,* ed. Richard T. Ingram and Associates (San Francisco: Jossey-Bass, 1993), 361–76; also in *Governing Independent Colleges and Universities: A Handbook for Trustees, Chief Executives, and Other Campus Leaders,* ed. Richard T. Ingram and Associates (San Francisco: Jossey-Bass, 1993), 344–60. Numerous associations and consultants provide board assessment services.

23. Lorna D. Edmundson and Gwendolyn E. Jensen, "The Ten Commandments of Presidential Transition," *Chronicle of Higher Education,* 26 February 2002. Also see Huang, "Marriage Counseling for Boards"; and McLaughlin, *Leadership Transitions.*

Chapter 6. A Proactive Model for Presidential Transition

1. American Council on Education and Association of Governing Boards of Universities and Colleges, *Deciding Who Shall Lead: Recommendations for Improving Presidential Searches* (Washington, DC: American Council on Education and Association of Governing Boards of Universities and Colleges, 1986).

2. Clark Kerr, *Presidents Make a Difference: Strengthening Leadership in Colleges and Universities* (Washington, DC: Association of Governing Boards of Universities and Colleges, 1984), 14.

3. Allison Noonan, "Introductions All Around," *Case Currents* 19 (November–December 1993): 44–48.

4. See Alan E. Guskin, "Soft Landings for New Leaders," *Trusteeship* 4 (January–February 1996).

5. Ibid., 16.

6. George Vaughan, *Balancing the Presidential Seesaw: Case Studies in Community College Leadership* (Washington, DC: Community College Press, 2000), 20.

7. See Kevin E. Drumm, "Difficulties in Leadership Transition: A Case Study of a Community College Presidency" (Ph.D. diss., New York University, 1995).

8. See McLaughlin and Riesman, *Choosing a College President.*

9. American Council on Education and Association of Governing Boards of Universities and Colleges, *Deciding Who Shall Lead.*

10. Noonan, "Introductions All Around," 44.

11. See Lee Bolman and Terrence Deal, *Reframing Organizations: Artistry, Choice, and Leadership* (San Francisco: Jossey-Bass, 1991).

12. Patricia Stanley, President's Inauguration Address, Frederick Community College, 11 November 1998.

Chapter 7. When Presidents Leave Suddenly

1. Thomas N. Gilmore, *Making a Leadership Change* (San Francisco: Jossey-Bass, 1986), 11.

2. Richard F. Chait, Thomas P. Holland, and Barbara E. Taylor, *Improving the Performance of Governing Boards* (Washington, DC: American Council on Education and Oryx Press, 1996), 8.

3. James L. Fisher, quoted in Arthur Levine, *Higher Learning in America* (Baltimore: Johns Hopkins University Press, 1993), 227.

4. *Chronicle of Higher Education,* 21 February 1997.

5. David Leslie and E. K. Fretwell, *Wise Moves in Hard Times: Creating and Managing Resilient Colleges and Universities* (San Francisco: Jossey-Bass, 1996), 240.

Chapter 8. Presidential Turnover and the Institutional Community

1. Edmundson and Jensen, "Ten Commandments of Presidential Transition," *Chronicle of Higher Education,* 26 February 2002.

2. Ned J. Sifferlen, "Celebrating Presidential Leadership Transitions," *Leadership Abstracts* 11, no. 5 (1998), available from www.league.org/publication/abstracts/leadership/labs0598.htm (accessed March 2002).

3. Ibid.

4. Moore with Burrows, *Presidential Succession and Transition,* quoted in Basinger, "When a President Quits Early."

5. Basinger, "When a President Quits Early."

6. Jennifer Jacobson, "Waiting for a President," *Chronicle of Higher Education,* 19 September 2001, Career Network section, available from www.chronicle.com/jobs/2001/09/2001091901c.htm (accessed February 2002).

7. Kit Lively, "A 'Rent-a-President' Service Helps Colleges in Transition," *Chronicle of Higher Education,* 28 May 1999, Money and Management section, A35, available from www.chronicle.com (accessed February 2002).

8. Jacobson, "Waiting for a President."

9. Jeannette T. Wright, "Conditions for Effectiveness," in *Leaders on Leadership: The College Presidency,* ed. James Fisher and Martha Tack (San Francisco: Jossey-Bass Inc., 1988), 89.

10. Eric Wahlgren, "Passing the Baton Peacefully," *Business Week Online,* 5 March 2001, available at www.businessweek.com:/print/careers/ma . . . /ca2001035_048.htm (accessed March 2002).

11. Philip A. Glotzbach, "Conditions of Collaboration: A Dean's List of Dos and Don'ts," *Academe* (May–June 2001); available at www.aaup.org/publications/Academe/01mj/mj01glot.htm (accessed August 2002).

12. Edmund W. Moomaw, "Participatory Leadership Strategy," in *Leadership Roles of Chief Academic Officers,* ed. David G. Brown (San Francisco: Jossey-Bass Inc., 1984), 25.

13. Burton R. Clark, "Collegial Entrepreneurialism in Proactive Universities," *Change* 32, no. 1 (January–February 2000): 10, accessible via Academic Search Elite: AN 2757084.

14. James L. Fisher and James V. Koch, *Presidential Leadership: Making a Difference* (Phoenix: Oryx Press, 1996).

15. Paula M. Krebs, "Wheaton Does Diversity," *Academe* (September–October 2000), available at www.aaup.org/publications/Academe/00so/SO00Kreb.htm (accessed August 2002).

16. Clark, "Collegial Entrepreneurialism."

17. Julianne Basinger, "Private Sources Play More of a Role in Paying Public-University Chiefs," *Chronicle of Higher Education,* 30 November 2001, Money and Management section, available at www.chronicle.com/weekly/v48/i14/14a02401.htm (accessed August 2002).

18. Claire Gaudiani, "Developing a Vision," in McLaughlin, *Leadership Transitions,* 61.

19. Judith Block McLaughlin, "Entering the Presidency," in McLaughlin, *Leadership Transitions,* 11.

20. Ibid., 13.

21. Basinger, "When a President Quits Early."

22. Gaudiani, "Developing a Vision," 63–64.

23. Kathryn Mohrman, "Making It Less Lonely at the Top," *Chronicle of Higher Education,* 17 December 2001, Career Network section, available at www.chronicle.com/jobs/2001/12/200112170c.htm (accessed March 2002).

24. Ted Marchese, "Restructure?! You Bet!: An Interview with Change Expert Alan E. Guskin," *Bulletin,* 2 September 1998.

25. Quoted in Basinger, "When a President Quits Early."

26. John W. Nason, *Presidential Search: A Guide to the Process of Selecting and Appointing College and University Presidents* (Washington, DC: Association of Governing Boards of Universities and Colleges, 1980).

27. Frank Rhodes, "The Art of the Presidency," *Presidency* (spring 1998): 1–2.

28. Gaudiani, "Developing a Vision," 61.

29. Ibid., 65.

30. Basinger, "When a President Quits Early."

Chapter 9. When Colleges Should, and Should Not, Use Executive Search Firms

1. For a guide to presidential searches that favors broad committee involvement, see Theodore J. Marchese, *The Search Committee Handbook: A Guide to Recruiting Administrators* (Washington, DC: American Association for Higher Education, 1989). Also see Neff and Leondar, *Presidential Search,* 6. For a different perspective, see James L. Fisher, *The Board and the President* (New York: American Council on Education and Macmillan, 1991), 45.

2. Melanie Corrigan, *The American College President* (Washington, DC: American Council on Education, 2002), 45–46.

3. Milton Greenberg, "A Reality Check on Presidential Searches," *Trusteeship* 10, no. 5 (September–October 2002): 16.

4. Ibid., 15.

5. Corrigan, *American College President,* 44.

6. McLaughlin and Riesman, *Choosing a College President,* 225.

7. Stephen A. Garrison, *Institutional Search: A Practical Guide to Executive Recruitment in Nonprofit Organizations* (New York: Praeger, 1989), 141.

8. McLaughlin and Riesman, *Choosing a College President,* 225.

9. Garrison, *Institutional Search,* 141.

10. "Bosses for Sale," *Economist* 3 (5 October 2002): 57.

11. McLaughlin and Riesman, *Choosing a College President,* 228.

12. Author's communication with the Roundtable, 2002.

13. Association of Governing Boards, *Presidential Search Guidelines and Directory* (Washington, DC: Association of Governing Boards of Universities and Colleges, 2002).

14. See FutureStep Web site, www.futurestep.com (accessed October 2002).

15. See LeadersOnLine Web site, www.leadersonline.com (accessed October 2002).

16. Rakesh Khurana, "Finding the Right CEO: Why Boards Often Make Poor Choices," *MIT Sloan Management Review,* fall 2001, 94.

17. McLaughlin and Riesman, *Choosing a College President,* 213.

18. Corrigan, *American College President,* 37.

19. Ibid., 53.
20. Estes, "State University Presidential Searches," 485.
21. Ibid., 486.

Chapter 10. The Interim President

The authors wish to express their thanks to Dr. Jody Koenig, assistant professor of speech and communication studies, San Francisco State University, for her helpful comments and editorial work. Also, we are grateful to Wendy Koenig, president of the Association of Vermont Independent Colleges, for her helpful editorial work.

1. This handbook is written by Thomas H. Langevin and may be obtained by writing to him at 41 San Pedro Drive, Lady Lake, FL 32159.
2. This report came from the former interim president in spring 2002 and was augmented by Allen Koenig in July 2002.
3. Chairman of the board of trustees to the authors, 19 September 1998.
4. This case history was condensed from a letter from the former interim president to Thomas H. Langevin, 12 June 2002.
5. This case history was developed by the former interim president, with the assistance of Allen Koenig, spring–summer, 2002.
6. The former interim president provided much of this account of the interim presidency at this community college on 15 July 2002. The concluding paragraph was written by Allen Koenig, based on his knowledge of the situation at the college.
7. Thomas H. Langevin developed these case histories based upon conversations with the interim presidents in spring 2002.

Chapter 11. Leaks Kill

1. See Estes "State University Presidential Searches."
2. Margarita Bauzá, "U-M Hires Jet for Search," *Detroit News,* 5 July 2002, 6.
3. Theodore Marchese, interview by the author, 10 July 2002, Washington, DC, tape recording.
4. Heidi Templeton, telephone interview by the author, 6 June 2003.
5. Marchese interview, 10 July 2002; telephone interview, 6 June 2003.

Chapter 12. Weathering the Storm

1. McLaughlin, "Entering the Presidency."
2. William R. Harvey, "Successful Fund Raising at a Historically Black University: Hampton University," in *Successful Fund Raising for Higher Education,* ed. Frank H. T. Rhodes (Phoenix: Oryx Press, 1997), 149.
3. Gifts to an academic medical center can occur in a relatively short time frame because of the "grateful patient" phenomenon, but more often than not, such commitments are designated for the work of a particular investigator, a reflection of a special relationship.
4. Roger L. Williams, telephone interview by the author, 19 June 2002.
5. Michael J. Worth and James W. Asp II. *The Development Officer in Higher Education: Toward an Understanding of the Role,* ASHE-ERIC Higher Education Report, no. 4 (Washington, DC: George Washington University, 1994).
6. Frederick E. Balderston, *Managing Today's University: Strategies for Viability, Change, and Excellence* (San Francisco: Jossey-Bass, 1995), 81.
7. Janet Clarke, interview by the author, 28 June 2002.

8. Donald Kennedy, interview by the author, 24 June 2002.

9. Dan West, telephone interview by the author, 18 June 2002.

10. Ibid.

11. Van Zandt Williams, telephone interview by the author, 17 June 2002.

12. Ibid.

13. West interview.

14. Richard F. Seaman, "Employment," in *The Ethics of Asking: Dilemmas in Higher Education Fund Raising,* ed. Deni Elliott (Baltimore: Johns Hopkins University Press, 1995).

15. Roger Williams interview.

16. James L. Fisher, "The President and the Professionals," in *Presidential Leadership in Advancement Activities,* ed. James L. Fisher, New Directions for Institutional Advancement, no. 20 (San Francisco: Jossey-Bass, 1980).

17. Seaman, "Employment."

18. Robert R. Lindgren, interview by the author, 17 June 2002.

19. William E. Stone, telephone interview by the author, 19 June 2002.

20. Robert Birnbaum, *How Academic Leadership Works: Understanding Success and Failure in the College Presidency* (San Francisco: Jossey-Bass, 1992).

21. The expectations of the trustees and institutional leadership may also play a key role here. If the former president was perceived as spending too much time away from campus, it may be necessary to project an inward orientation, and vice versa.

22. Roger Williams interview.

23. Nancy Gray, telephone interview by the author, 18 June 2002.

24. Clarke interview.

25. Lindgren interview.

26. Gray interview.

27. Kennedy interview.

28. Birnbaum, *How Academic Leadership Works,* 328.

29. David Riesman, "Afterword: Reflections on the College Presidency," in McLaughlin, *Leadership Transitions,* 86.

Chapter 13. Shaky Ground in Troubled Times

1. James Martin and James E. Samels, *First among Equals: The Role of the Chief Academic Officer* (Baltimore: Johns Hopkins University Press, 1997).

2. Beverly W. Miller, "Traditions in Transition," paper presented at the 18th Annual Law & Higher Education Conference, Clearwater Beach, Florida, 13–15 February 1997.

3. Neff and Leondar, *Presidential Search,* 17 and Exhibit C, 98–101.

4. Ross and Green, *American College President,* cited in Atwell, Green, and Ross, *Well-Informed Candidate,* 1.

5. Neff and Leondar, *Presidential Search,* 87.

6. Estes, "State University Presidential Searches," 485, 503.

7. Ibid., 485–86.

8. Ibid., 485, 487.

9. See Estes, "State University President Searches," citing the following cases: *Arizona Board of Regents v. Phoenix Newspapers, Inc.,* 806 P.2d 348 (Ariz. 1991) (requiring disclosure of names of 17 candidates interviewed in confidence); *Board of Regents of the Univ. Sys. of Ga. v. Atlanta Journal*, 378 S.E.2d 305 (Ga. 1989) (re-

quiring board to produce names of all candidates for presidency of Georgia State University); *Hubert v. Harte-Hanks Tex. Newspapers, Inc.*, 652 S.W.2d 546 (Tex. Ct. App. 1983) (requiring Texas A&M to disclose names of 171 candidates).

10. The following analysis is drawn from Neff and Leondar, *Presidential Search*, 92–94. Also see Exhibit B, 92–94, in the same book.

11. Richard Ingram, "Searching for Reason in Presidential Compensation," *Trusteeship* 5, no. 4 (July–August 1997): 6.

12. Julianne Basinger, "The Growing $500,000 Club: 27 Private-College Presidents Earned More than Half a Million in Compensation in 2000–1," *Chronicle of Higher Education*, 22 November 2002.

13. Comments and information about housing matters are based on *Presidential Housing and Tax Reform, a Guide for Chief Executives* (Washington, DC: American Association of State Colleges and Universities and National Association of College and University Attorneys, 1987).

14. IRC s.119(a) and *Presidential Housing and Tax Reform.*

15. Stanley Koplik, interview by the authors, 12 June 1998.

16. *Winchell v. United States*, 564 F.Supp. 131 (D. Neb. 1983); aff'd without opinion, 725 F.2d 689 (8th Cir. 1983).

17. *Commissioner v. Kowalski*, 434 U.S. 77 (1977).

18. Fretwell, *The Interim Presidency*, 33–35.

19. Ingram, "Searching for Reason," 7.

20. See *Black's Law Dictionary*, rev. 4th ed., which defines cause as follows:

> As used with reference to the removal of an officer or employee, "cause" means a just, not arbitrary, cause; one relating to a material matter, or affecting the public interest. *Brokaw v. Burk*, 89 N.J. Law 132, 98 A.11, 12; a cause relating to and affecting administration of office and of substantial nature directly affecting public's rights and interests. *State ex rel. Rockwell v. State Board of Education*, 213 Minn. 184, 6 N.W.2d 251, 260, 143 A.L.R. 503. Conduct indicating unworthy or illegal motives or improper administration of power; *Voorhees v. Kopler*, 239 App. Div. 83, 265 N.Y.S. 532, 533; *Tappan v. Helena Federal Savings & Loan Assn. Of Helena, Ark.*, 193 Ark. 1023, 104 S.W.2d 458, 459; *Zurich General Accident & Liability Ins. Co. v. Kinsler*, 12 Ca.2d 98, 81 P.2d 913, 95; misfeasance or nonfeasance, *Schoonover v. City of Viroqua*, 244 Wis. 615, 12 N.W.2d 912, 914.

Chapter 14. Partners in Transition

1. Charles Middleton, interview by James Martin, 29 December 2002.

Chapter 15. A Conceptual Approach to Presidential Transition

1. Ronald Remington, interview by the authors, 21 May 2003.
2. Ibid.
3. Terrence Gomes, interview by the authors, 4 June 2003.
4. Fretwell, *Interim Presidency*, 37

Bibliography

Allen, M., S. Panian, and R. Lotz. "Managerial Succession and Organizational Performance: A Recalcitrant Problem Revisited." *Administrative Science Quarterly* 24 (1979): 167–80.

Altbach, Philip G. "Knowledge and Education as International Commodities: The Collapse of the Common Good." *International Higher Education,* no. 28 (summer 2002): 2–5.

Alton, Bruce T., and Kathleen L. Dean. "Why Presidents Think the Grass Is Greener." *Trusteeship* 10, no. 3 (May–June 2002): 19–23.

American Council on Education and Association of Governing Boards of Universities and Colleges. *Deciding Who Shall Lead: Recommendations for Improving Presidential Searches.* Washington, DC: American Council on Education and Association of Governing Boards of Universities and Colleges, 1986.

Arenson, Karen. "The Moral Compass on Campus." *New York Times,* 10 June 2001, 33.

Arnone, Michael. "International Consortium Readies Ambitious Distance Education Effort." *Chronicle of Higher Education,* 28 June 2002, A28.

Association of Governing Boards. *Bridging the Gap between State Government and Public Higher Education.* Washington, DC: Association of Governing Boards of Universities and Colleges, 1998.

———. *Presidential Search Guidelines and Directory.* Washington, DC: Association of Governing Boards of Universities and Colleges, 2002.

Atwell, Robert H., Madeleine F. Green, and Marlene Ross. *The Well-Informed Candidate: A Brief Guide for Candidates for College and University Presidencies.* Washington, DC: American Council on Education, 2001.

Atwell, Robert H., and Jane V. Wellman. *Presidential Compensation in Higher Education: Policies and Best Practices.* Washington, DC: Association of Governing Boards of Universities and Colleges, 2000.

Axelrod, Nancy R. *Chief Executive Succession Planning: The Board's Role in Securing Your Organization's Future.* Washington, DC: BoardSource, 2002.

Balderston, Frederick E. *Managing Today's University: Strategies for Viability, Change, and Excellence.* San Francisco: Jossey-Bass, 1995.

Bartlett, Thomas, and Scott Smallwood. "Peer Review: Reed College Runs an Open Book Search." *Chronicle of Higher Education,* 14 December 2001.

Basinger, Julianne. "For Presidents and Boards, a Handshake Is No Longer Enough." *Chronicle of Higher Education,* 24 May 2002.

——— "The Growing $500,000 Club: 27 Private-College Presidents Earned More than Half a Million in Compensation in 2000–1." *Chronicle of Higher Education,* 22 November 2002.

———. "No Long-Term President and No Prospects." *Chronicle of Higher Education,* 9 March 2001.

———. "Private Sources Play More of a Role in Paying Public-University Chiefs." *Chronicle of Higher Education,* 30 November 2001, Money and Management section. Available at www.chronicle.com/weekly/v48/i14/14a02401.htm.

———. "When a President Quits Early, the Damage Can Linger On." *Chronicle of Higher Education,* 27 July 2001, A22. Also available at www.chronicle.com/weekly/v47/i46/46a02201.htm.

Basinger, Julianne, and Piper Fogg. "Peer Review: Harassment Accusation Causes an Abrupt Exit at Northern Arizona U." *Chronicle of Higher Education,* 23 November 2001.

Basinger, Julianne, and Scott Smallwood. "Peer Review: Northern Arizona U. Faculty Derides Choice for Chief Executive." *Chronicle of Higher Education,* 15 June 2001.

Bauzá, Margarita. "U-M Hires Jet for Search." *Detroit News,* 5 July 2002.

Bessire, Henry E. "Fund Raising." In *A Princeton Companion,* ed. Alexander Leitch. Princeton, NJ: Princeton University Press, 1978.

Bianco, A., and L. Lavelle. "The CEO Trap." *Business Week,* 11 December 2000, 86–92.

Birnbaum, Robert. "The Dilemma of Presidential Leadership." In *American Higher Education in the Twenty-First Century: Social, Political, and Economic Challenges,* ed. Philip G. Altbach, Robert O. Berdahl, and Patricia J. Gumport. Baltimore: Johns Hopkins University Press, 1999.

———. *How Academic Leadership Works: Understanding Success and Failure in the College Presidency.* San Francisco: Jossey-Bass, 1992.

Boeker, W., and J. Goodstein. "Performance and Successor Choice: The Moderating Effects of Governance and Ownership." *Academy of Management Journal* 36 (1993): 172–86.

Boggs, George R., and Cindra J. Smith. "When Boards Change: The Presidential Response." In Weisman and Vaughan, *Presidents and Trustees in Partnership.*

Bolman, Lee, and Terrence Deal. *Reframing Organizations: Artistry, Choice, and Leadership.* San Francisco: Jossey-Bass, 1991.

"Bosses for Sale." *Economist* 3 (5 October 2002): 57–58.

Bridges, William. *Managing Transitions: Making the Most of Change.* Reading, MA: Addison-Wesley, 1991.

Cannella, A., and M. Lubatkin. "Succession as a Sociopolitical Process: Internal Impediments to Outsider Selection." *Academy of Management Journal* 36 (1993): 763–93.

Carbone, Robert F. *Presidential Passages.* Washington, DC: American Council on Education, 1981.

Chait, Richard F., Thomas P. Holland, and Barbara E. Taylor. *Improving the Perfor-*

mance of Governing Boards. Washington, DC: American Council on Education and Oryx Press, 1996.

Cheshire, Richard D. "Strategies for Advancement." In *Presidential Leadership in Advancement Activities,* ed. James L. Fisher. New Directions for Institutional Advancement, no. 20. San Francisco: Jossey-Bass, 1980.

Clark, Burton. "Collegial Entrepreneurialism in Proactive Universities." *Change* 32, no. 1 (January–February 2000). Accessible via Academic Search Elite: AN 2757084.

Clark, Charles S. "Is the Press a Trustee's Friend or Foe?" *Trusteeship* 10, no. 2 (March–April 2002): 15–19.

Cohen, Michael D., and James G. March. *Leadership and Ambiguity: The American College President.* A General Report Prepared for the Carnegie Commission on Higher Education. New York: McGraw-Hill, 1974.

Commission on the Academic Presidency. *Renewing the Academic Presidency: Stronger Leadership for Tougher Times.* Washington, DC: Association of Governing Boards of Universities and Colleges, 1996.

Corporate University Exchange, Inc. *Executive Summary: 1999 Survey of Corporate University Future Directions.* (N.p., 1999).

Corrigan, Melanie. *The American College President.* Washington, DC: American Council on Education, 2002.

Cox, D. R., and D. Oakes. *Analysis of Survival Data.* London: Chapman and Hall, 1984.

Davis, Gary. "Orientation and Professional Development of Trustees." In Weisman and Vaughan, *Presidents and Trustees in Partnership.*

DeFelice, Jonathan, O.S.B., John J. Reilly Jr., and Paul A. Dowd. "Successful Fund Raising at a Religious-Based College: Saint Anselm College." In Rhodes, *Successful Fund Raising for Higher Education.*

Diffily, Anne. "Tales of Gregorian." *Brown Alumni Monthly,* October 1988, 27–35.

Dowdall, Jean. "The President's House." *Chronicle of Higher Education,* 3 June 2002.

Dowdall, Jean, Robert H. Perry, Maria M. Perez, Darryl G. Greer, and William A. Weary. "Roadblocks on the Road to Diversity: Five Presidential Experts Respond to a *Trusteeship* Query on Why There Are Not More Females and Minorities Leading American Colleges and Universities Today." *Trusteeship* 10, no. 3 (May–June 2002): 13–18.

Drumm, Kevin E. "Difficulties in Leadership Transition: A Case Study of a Community College Presidency." Ph.D. diss., New York University, 1995.

Edmundson, Lorna D., and Gwendolyn E. Jensen. "The Ten Commandments of Presidential Transition." Paper presented at the annual meeting of the National Institute of the Association of Governing Boards, Boston, 23 April 2002.

———. "The Ten Commandments of Presidential Transition." *Chronicle of Higher Education,* 26 February 2002, Career Network section. Also available at www.chronicle.com/jobs/2002/02/2002022601c.htm.

Ehrenberg, R., J. Cheslock, and J. Epifantseva. "Paying Our Presidents: What Do Trustees Value?" *Review of Higher Education* 25 (2001): 15–37.

Estes, Nick. "State University Presidential Searches: Law and Practice." *Journal of College and University Law* 26, no. 3 (winter 2000): 485–509.

Evelyn, Jamilah. "Community Colleges Face a Crisis of Leadership." *Chronicle of Higher Education,* 6 April 2001, A36.

Fennell, Mary Louise, and Catherine Cook. "Capital Gains: Surviving in an Increasingly For-Profit World." *Presidency* (winter 2001): 29.

Ferrari, M. R. *Profiles of American College Presidents*. East Lansing: Michigan State University School of Business, 1970.

Ficklen, Ellen. "Presidency as Platform: Use Campus Inaugurations to Set the Tone for What's to Come." *Currents* 28, no. 5 (May–June 2002).

Finkelstein, S., and D. C. Hambrick. *Strategic Leadership: Top Executives and Their Effects on Organizations*. Minneapolis: West Publishing, 1996.

Fisher, James L. *The Board and the President*. New York: American Council on Education and Macmillan, 1991.

———. "The President and the Professionals." In *Presidential Leadership in Advancement Activities,* ed. James L. Fisher. New Directions for Institutional Advancement, no. 20. San Francisco: Jossey-Bass, 1980.

Fisher, James L., and James V. Koch. *Presidential Leadership: Making a Difference.* Phoenix: Oryx Press, 1996.

Fisher, James L., Martha W. Tack, and Karen J. Wheeler. *The Effective College President.* New York: American Council on Education and Macmillan, 1988.

Fogg, Piper, and Julianne Basinger. "Review: Shelf Date." *Chronicle of Higher Education,* 19 April 2002, A8.

Footlick, Jerrold K. "A Steady Hand during a Presidential Crisis." *Trusteeship* 8, no. 5 (September–October 2000): 15–19.

Forman, Robert G. "The Potential in Alumni Stewardship." In *Presidential Leadership in Advancement Activities,* ed. James L. Fisher. New Directions for Institutional Advancement, no. 20. San Francisco: Jossey-Bass, 1980.

Francis, Norman C. "Fund Raising at a Developing Institution." In *Presidential Leadership in Advancement Activities,* ed. James L. Fisher, New Directions for Institutional Advancement, no. 20. San Francisco: Jossey-Bass, 1980.

Fredrickson, J. W., D. C. Hambrick, and S. Baumrin. "A Model of CEO Dismissal." *Academy of Management Review* 13 (1988): 255–70.

Freeland, Richard M. "Academic Change and Presidential Leadership." In *In Defense of American Higher Education,* ed. Philip G. Altbach, Patricia J. Gumport, and D. Bruce Johnstone. Baltimore: Johns Hopkins University Press, 2001.

Fretwell, E. K., Jr. *The Interim Presidency: Guidelines for University and College Governing Boards*. Washington, DC: Association of Governing Boards of Universities and Colleges, 1995.

Gamson, W., and N. Scotch. "Scapegoating in Baseball." *American Journal of Sociology* 70 (1964): 69–72.

Garrison, Stephen A. *Institutional Search: A Practical Guide to Executive Recruitment in Nonprofit Organizations*. New York: Praeger, 1989.

Gaskin, Fred. "At the Millennium." In Weisman and Vaughan, *Presidents and Trustees in Partnership*.

Gaudiani, Claire. "Developing a Vision." In McLaughlin, *Leadership Transitions.*

———. "Vision, Lemon Spritzers, and Saying Thank You: A New Job Description for College Presidents." Paper prepared for discussion with the Connecticut College, 1992. Available at www.clairegaudiani.com/speeches/lemon.html.

Gephart, R. P., Jr. "Status Degradation and Organizational Succession: An Ethnomethodological Approach." *Administrative Science Quarterly* 23 (1978): 553–81.

Gilmore, Thomas N. *Making a Leadership Change.* San Francisco: Jossey-Bass, 1986.

Glotzbach, Philip A. "Conditions of Collaboration: A Dean's List of Dos and Don'ts." *Academe* (May–June 2001). Available at www.aaup.org/publications/Academe/01mj/mj01glot.htm.

Gordon, Milton A., and Margaret F. Gordon. "Finding a Balance." In McLaughlin, *Leadership Transitions.*

Greenberg, D. "Small Men on Campus." *New Republic,* June 1998, 16–21.

Greenberg, Milton. "A Reality Check on Presidential Searches." *Trusteeship* 10, no. 5 (September–October 2002): 14–16.

Grusky, O. "Corporate Size, Bureaucratization, and Managerial Succession." *American Journal of Sociology* 67 (1961): 261–69.

Gumport, Patricia J. "Public Higher Education." In *In Defense of American Higher Education,* ed. Philip G. Altbach, Patricia J. Gumport, and D. Bruce Johnstone. Baltimore: Johns Hopkins University Press, 2001.

Guskin, Alan E. "Soft Landings for New Leaders." *Trusteeship* 4 (January–February 1996): 12–16.

Hahn, Robert. "Demystifying the Presidency." In McLaughlin, *Leadership Transitions.*

Hambrick, D. C. "Environment, Strategy, and Power within Top Management Teams." *Administrative Science Quarterly* 26 (1981): 253–61.

Hambrick, D. C., and G. D. S. Fukutomi. "The Seasons of a CEO's Tenure." *Academy of Management Review* 16 (1991): 719-42.

Harris, R. G. *The Potential Effects of Deregulation upon Corporate Structure, Merger Behavior, and Organizational Relations in the Rail Freight Industry.* Washington, DC: Public Interest Economics Center, 1979.

Harvey, William R. "Successful Fund Raising at a Historically Black University: Hampton University." In Rhodes, *Successful Fund Raising for Higher Education.*

Hebel, Sara. "IRS Clarifies Law on Pay for Leaders of Nonprofit Groups." *Chronicle of Higher Education,* 19 January 2002.

Hiller, Jennifer. "Dobelle Mum on Overall UH Plan." *Honolulu Advertiser,* 15 July 2001. Available at www.the.honoluluadvertiser.com/article/2001/Jul/15/In/In13a.html.

Hogarty, Richard A. "UMass Selects a New President: Elements of a Search Strategy." *New England Journal of Public Policy* (fall–winter 1992): 9–35.

Hsu, Eric. "First Movers, Fast Followers." *Microsoft Executive Circle* 2, no. 2 (summer 2002): 47.

Huang, Alice S. "Marriage Counseling for Boards: Today More Than Ever, the President's Spouse Is Apt to Have Valuable Skills the Institution Should Tap: Boards Should Formally Recognize the Partner's Roles and Contributions." *Trusteeship* 7, no. 6 (November–December 1999): 29–32.

Ingram, Richard T. "Searching for Reason in Presidential Compensation." *Trusteeship* 5, no. 4 (July–August 1997).

Ingram, Richard T., and associates. *Governing Independent Colleges and Universities: A Handbook for Trustees, Chief Executives, and Other Campus Leaders.* San Francisco: Jossey-Bass, 1993.

Ingram, Richard T., and William A. Weary. *Presidential and Board Assessment in*

Higher Education: Purposes, Policies, and Strategies. Washington, DC: Association of Governing Boards of Universities and Colleges, 2000.

Jacobson, Jennifer. "Inaugural Hoopla: Price, Precedent, and Personality." *Chronicle of Higher Education,* 14 November 2001, Career Network section.

———. "Waiting for a President." *Chronicle of Higher Education,* 19 September 2001, Career Network section. Available at www.chronicle.com/jobs/2001/09/2001091901c.htm.

James, D. R., and M. Soref. "Profit Constraints on Managerial Autonomy: Managerial Theory and the Unmaking of the Corporate President." *American Sociological Review* 46 (1981): 1–18.

Jencks, Christopher, and David Riesman, *The Academic Revolution.* Garden City, NY: Doubleday, 1968.

Keller, George. "Governance: The Remarkable Ambiguity." In *In Defense of American Higher Education,* ed. Philip G. Altbach, Patricia J. Gumport, and D. Bruce Johnstone. Baltimore: Johns Hopkins University Press, 2001.

Keller, Morton, and Phyllis Keller. *Making Harvard Modern: The Rise of America's University.* New York: Oxford University Press, 2001.

Kelly, Erica. "The Changing of the Guard." *Community College Week,* 27 May 2002, 7.

Kerr, Clark. *The Great Transformation in Higher Education.* Albany: SUNY Press, 1991.

———. *Higher Education Cannot Escape History: Issues for the Twenty-First Century.* Albany: SUNY Press, 1994.

———. "Holding the Center—Presidential Discontent." In *Perspectives on Campus Tensions: Papers Prepared for the Special Committee on Campus Tensions,* ed. D. Nichols. Washington, DC: American Council on Education, 1970.

———. *Presidents Make a Difference: Strengthening Leadership in Colleges and Universities.* Washington, DC: Association of Governing Boards of Universities and Colleges, 1984.

———. *The Uses of the University.* Reprint, Cambridge, MA: Harvard University Press, 2001.

Kerr, Clark, and Marian L. Gade. *The Guardians: Boards of Trustees of American Colleges and Universities.* Washington, DC: Association of Governing Boards of Universities and Colleges, 1989.

———. *The Many Lives of Academic Presidents.* Washington, DC: Association of Governing Boards of Universities and Colleges, 1986.

Khurana, Rakesh. "Finding the Right CEO: Why Boards Often Make Poor Choices." *MIT Sloan Management Review,* fall 2001, 91–95.

Kirkland, Travis P., and James L. Ratcliff. "Community College Presidents—Selection and Appointment." *Community College Review* 21, no. 4 (spring 1994): 3–10.

Knight Higher Education Collaborative. "Inside Out." *Policy Perspectives* 10, no. 1 (2001).

Kopecek, Robert J., and Susan K. Kubik. "Successful Fund Raising at a Two-Year Community College with a Foundation: Northampton County Area Community College." In Rhodes, *Successful Fund Raising for Higher Education.*

Kormondy, Edward J., and Kent M. Keith. "The Salvaging President: Institutions

That Fall on Hard Times Often Hire an Experienced Former President to Act as a Non-Traditional Leader of Change: Here's How They Succeed." *Trusteeship* 9, no. 3 (May–June 2001): 24–27.

Korschgen, Ann, Rex Fuller, and John Gardner. "The Impact of Presidential Migration." *AAHE* [American Association for Higher Education] *Bulletin* 53, no. 6 (2001): 3.

Kossan, Pat, and Bill Hart. "NAU President's Abrupt Resignation Stuns Campus." *Arizona Republic,* 13 November 2001.

Krebs, Paula M. "Wheaton Does Diversity." *Academe* (September–October 2000). Available at www.aaup.org/publications/Academe/00so/SO00Kreb.htm.

Leatherman, Courtney. "A Costly Breach of Presidential 'Etiquette.'" *Chronicle of Higher Education,* 1 September 1993.

———. "New York Regents Vote to Remove 18 of 19 Adelphi U. Trustees." *Chronicle of Higher Education,* 21 February 1997.

Leslie, David W., and E. K. Fretwell. *Wise Moves in Hard Times: Creating and Managing Resilient Colleges and Universities.* San Francisco: Jossey-Bass, 1996.

Levine, Arthur. *Higher Learning in America, 1980–2000.* Baltimore: Johns Hopkins University Press, 1993.

Lively, Kit. "A 'Rent-a-President' Service Helps Colleges in Transition." *Chronicle of Higher Education,* 28 May 1999, Money and Management section, A35. Available at www.chronicle.com.

Lovett, Clara M. "The Dumbing Down of College Presidents." *Chronicle of Higher Education,* 5 April 2002, B20.

Mace, M. L. *Directors: Myth and Reality.* Cambridge, MA: Harvard Business School, Division of Research, 1971.

Magner, Denise. "'Never Tranquility,' Says New Johns Hopkins Chief." *Chronicle of Higher Education,* 22 May 1991.

Marchese, Theodore J. "Research That Matters: Boards and Presidential Transitions." *Trusteeship* 9, no. 5 (September–October 2001): 34–35.

———. "Restructure?! You Bet!: An Interview with Change Expert Alan E. Guskin." *Bulletin,* 2 September 1998.

———. *The Search Committee Handbook: A Guide to Recruiting Administrators.* Washington, DC: American Association for Higher Education, 1989.

Martin, James, and James E. Samels. *First among Equals: The Role of the Chief Academic Officer.* Baltimore: Johns Hopkins University Press, 1997.

Martin, Roger H. "Establishing Key Relationships." In McLaughlin, *Leadership Transitions.*

McLaughlin, Judith Block. "Entering the Presidency." In McLaughlin, *Leadership Transitions.*

———, ed. *Leadership Transitions: The New College President.* New Directions for Higher Education, no. 93. San Francisco: Jossey-Bass, 1996.

McLaughlin, Judith Block, and David Riesman. *Choosing a College President: Opportunities and Constraints.* Princeton, NJ: Carnegie Foundation for the Advancement of Teaching, 1990.

Mercer, Joye. "When a College's Head Leaves during a Major Fund Drive." *Chronicle of Higher Education,* 16 June 1995.

Miller, Beverly W. "Traditions in Transition." Paper presented at the 18th Annual

Law and Higher Education Conference, Clearwater Beach, FL, February 13–15, 1997.

Miller, D. "Some Organizational Consequences of CEO Succession." *Academy of Management Journal* 36 (1993): 644–59.

Mohrman, Kathryn. "A Lame Duck President Looks Back." *Chronicle of Higher Education,* 25 April 2002, Career Network section online. Available at www.chronicle.com.

———. "Making It Less Lonely at the Top," *Chronicle of Higher Education,* 17 December 2001, Career Network section. Available at www.chronicle.com/jobs/2001/12/2001121 70c.htm.

Moomaw, Edmund W. "Participatory Leadership Strategy." In *Leadership Roles of Chief Academic Officers,* ed. David G. Brown. San Francisco: Jossey-Bass, 1984.

Moore, John W., with Joanne M. Burrows. *Presidential Succession and Transition: Beginning, Ending, and Beginning Again.* Washington, DC: American Association of State Colleges and Universities, 2001.

Morita, J. G., T. W. Lee, and R. T. Mowday. "The Regression-Analog to Survival Analysis: A Selected Application to Turnover Research." *Academy of Management Journal* 36 (1993): 1430–64.

Muller, Steven. "Presidential Leadership." In *The Research University in a Time of Discontent,* ed. Elinor G. Barber and Stephen R. Graubard. Baltimore: Johns Hopkins University Press, 1993.

———. "The University Presidency Today: A Word for the Incumbents." In *Leaders on Leadership: The College Presidency,* ed. James L. Fisher and Martha W. Tack. New Directions for Higher Education, no. 61. San Francisco: Jossey-Bass, 1988.

Nason, John W. *Presidential Search: A Guide to the Process of Selecting and Appointing College and University Presidents.* Washington, DC: Association of Governing Boards of Universities and Colleges, 1980.

Neff, Charles B., and Barbara Leondar. *Presidential Search: A Guide to the Process of Selecting and Appointing College and University Presidents.* Washington, DC: Association of Governing Boards of Universities and Colleges, 1992. Reprint, 1997. Page citations are to the 1992 edition.

Newman, Frank, and Lara K. Couturier. "The New Competitive Arena: Market Forces Invade the Academy." *Change* 33, no. 5 (September–October 2001): 10–17.

Nielsen, Norm, and Wayne Newton. "Board-President Relations: A Foundation of Trust." In Weisman and Vaughan, *Presidents and Trustees in Partnership.*

Noonan, Allison. "Introductions All Around." *Case Currents* 19 (November–December 1993): 44–48.

Padilla, Art, and D. Baumer. "Big-time College Sports: Management and Economic Issues." *Journal of Sport and Social Issues* 18 (1994): 123–43.

Padilla, Art, and Sujit Ghosh. "On the Tenure of University Presidents." *On the Horizon* 8 (1999): 5.

———. "Turnover at the Top." *Presidency* 3, no. 1 (winter 2002): 30–37.

Perlman, Daniel. "Paradoxes of the Presidency." *AAHE* [American Association for Higher Education] *Bulletin* 42 (1989): 3–6.

Pfeffer, J. "The Ambiguity of Leadership." *Academy of Management Review* 2 (1977): 104–12.

———. *Power in Organizations.* Marshfield, MA: Pitman, 1981.

Pfeffer, J., and W. M. Moore. "Average Tenure of Academic Department Heads: The Effects of Paradigm, Size, and Departmental Demography." *Administrative Science Quarterly* 25 (1980): 387–406.

Pfeffer, J., and G. R. Salancik. *The External Control of Organizations: A Resource Dependence Perspective.* New York: Harper and Row, 1978.

Presidential Housing and Tax Reform, a Guide for Chief Executives. Washington, DC: American Association of State Colleges and Universities and National Association of College and University Attorneys, 1987.

Ray, Joseph M. "Reflections on Presidential Transition (in the Middle of the Stream)." *Public Administration Review* 30 (March–April 1970): 125–28.

Rezak, William D. "Leading Colleges and Universities as Business Enterprises." *AAHE* [American Association for Higher Education] *Bulletin* 53, no. 2 (October 2000): 6.

Rhodes, Frank H. T. "The Art of the Presidency." *Presidency* (spring 1998): 1–6.

———, ed. *Successful Fund Raising for Higher Education.* Phoenix: Oryx Press, 1997.

Riesman, David. "Afterword: Reflections on the College Presidency." In McLaughlin, *Leadership Transitions.*

Rosovsky, Henry. *The University: An Owner's Manual.* New York: Norton, 1990.

Ross, John, and Carol Halstead. *Public Relations and the Presidency: Strategies and Tactics for Effective Communications.* Council for Advancement and Support of Education Books, 2001.

Ross, Marlene, and Madeleine F. Green. *The American College President.* Washington, DC: American Council on Education, 2000.

———. *The American College President.* Washington, DC: American Council on Education, 1998.

Salancik, G. R., and J. Pfeffer. "Effects of Ownership and Performance on Executive Tenure in U.S. Corporations." *Academy of Management Journal* 23 (1980): 653–64.

Saroff, J. R. "Is Mobility Enough for the Temporary Society? Some Observations Based upon the Experience of the Federal Executive Institute." *Public Administration Review* 34 (1974): 480–86.

Schmidt, Peter. "Seeking in the Shade: Public Colleges and News Media Increasingly Clash over Sunshine-Law Issues." *Chronicle of Higher Education,* 5 October 2001.

Schwartz, Merrill Pellows. *Annual Presidential Performance Reviews (AGB Board Basics: Board Leadership).* Washington, DC: Association of Governing Boards of Universities and Colleges, 2001.

———. *A National Survey of Board Performance Assessment Policies and Practices.* AGB Occasional Paper, no. 35. Washington, DC: Association of Governing Boards of Universities and Colleges, 1998.

———. *A National Survey of Presidential Performance Assessment Policies and Practices.* AGB Occasional Paper, no. 34. Washington, DC: Association of Governing Boards of Universities and Colleges, 1998.

Seaman, Richard F. "Employment." In *The Ethics of Asking: Dilemmas in Higher Education Fund Raising,* ed. Deni Elliott. Baltimore: Johns Hopkins University Press, 1995.

Selden, W. K. "How Long Is a College President?" *Liberal Education* 46 (1960): 5–15.

Shafer, Mark. "Give and Take: New President Scraps His Inaugural Festivities in Favor of Scholarships." *Chronicle of Higher Education,* 2 November 2001.

———. "NAU President under Attack—Campus' New Chief Defends His Skills." *Arizona Republic,* 14 June 2001.

Shapiro, Harold T. "University Presidents—Then and Now." In *Universities and Their Leadership,* ed. William G. Bowen and Harold T. Shapiro. Princeton, NJ: Princeton University Press, 1998.

Shek, Katherine. "College President and Faculty Retirements Loan." *Community College Times,* 17 April 2001, 10.

Sherman, Michael J. "How Free Is Free Enough? Public University Presidential Searches, University Autonomy, and State Open Meeting Acts." *Journal of College and University Law* 26, no. 4 (2000): 665–700.

Sifferlen, Ned J. "Celebrating Presidential Leadership Transitions." *Leadership Abstracts* 11, no. 5 (1998). Available at www.league.org/publication/abstracts/leadership/labs0598.htm.

Skapinker, Michael. "Business Heads for Too Much Room at the Top." *Financial Times,* 23 April 2002, 12.

Stanley, Patricia. President's inauguration address. Frederick Community College, Frederick, MD, 11 September 1998.

Stanley, Patricia, and Lee J. Betts. "A Model for Presidential Transition." *Trustee Quarterly* (winter 2000): 24–28.

Stoke, H. W. *The American College President.* New York: Harper and Row, 1959.

Sweet, David E. "Minding Our Own 'Business.'" In *Presidential Leadership in Advancement Activities,* ed. James L. Fisher. New Directions for Institutional Advancement, no. 20. San Francisco: Jossey-Bass, 1980.

Taylor, Barbara E. "Assessing Board Performance." In Ingram and associates, *Governing Public Colleges and Universities.*

Tumminia, Philip A., and Lori D. Marshall. "Successful Fund Raising at a Medium-Sized Public University with a Foundation Rowan University." In Rhodes, *Successful Fund Raising for Higher Education.*

Vancil, R. F. *Passing the Baton.* Boston: Harvard Business School Press, 1987.

Vaughan, George. *Balancing the Presidential Seesaw: Case Studies in Community College Leadership.* Washington, DC: Community College Press, 2000.

Wahlgren, Eric. "Passing the Baton Peacefully." *BusinessWeek Online,* 5 March 2001. Available at www.businessweek.com:/print/careers/ma . . . /ca2001035_048.htm.

Weary, William A. *Essentials of Presidential Search (AGB Board Basics: Board Leadership).* Washington, DC: Association of Governing Boards of Universities and Colleges, 1998.

———. *Guidelines for Selecting a Presidential Search Consultant and Directory of Search Consulting Firms.* 3d ed. Washington, DC: Association of Governing Boards of Universities and Colleges, 2002.

Weingartner, Rudolph. *Fitting Form to Function: A Primer on the Organization of Academic Institutions.* Phoenix: American Council on Education and Oryx Press, 1996.

Weisman, Iris M., and George B. Vaughan, eds. *Presidents and Trustees in Partner-*

ship: New Roles and Leadership Challenges. New Directions for Community Colleges, no. 98. San Francisco: Jossey-Bass, 1997.

Wharton, Donald P., and Kathleen A. Corak. "Faring Forward: The Strategic Planning Process as Talisman during Periods of Institutional Transition." Paper presented at the annual meeting of the Society for College and University Planning, Minneapolis, August 1992.

Whittier, H. Sargent, Jr.. "Presidential Commitment to Educational Fund Raising." In *Presidential Leadership in Advancement Activities,* ed. James L. Fisher. New Directions for Institutional Advancement, no. 20. San Francisco: Jossey-Bass, 1980.

Worth, Michael J., and James W. Asp II. *The Development Officer in Higher Education: Toward an Understanding of the Role.* ASHE-ERIC Higher Education Report, no. 4. Washington, DC: George Washington University, 1994.

Wright, Jeannette T. "Conditions for Effectiveness." In *Leaders on Leadership: The College Presidency,* ed. James Fisher and Martha Tack. San Francisco: Jossey-Bass, 1988.

Zajac, E. J., and J. D. Westphal. "Who Shall Succeed? How CEO/Board Preferences and Power Affect the Choice of New CEOs." *Academy of Management Journal* 39 (1996): 64–90.

Zaleznik, A., and M. F. R. Kets de Vries. *Power and the Corporate Mind.* Boston: Houghton Mifflin, 1975.

Contributors

JAMES MARTIN has been a member of the Mount Ida College faculty since 1979. Now a professor of English, he served for more than fifteen years as the college's vice president for academic affairs and provost. Under a Fulbright Fellowship, he studied mergers in the University of London system. He is also an ordained United Methodist minister.

With his writing and consulting partner James E. Samels, Martin has coauthored two previous books published by the Johns Hopkins University Press: *Merging Colleges for Mutual Growth* (1994) and *First among Equals: The Role of the Chief Academic Officer* (1997). He has also cowritten a column on college and university issues, "Higher Ed101," for the *Boston Business Journal* since 1993. Martin and Samels cohosted the nation's first television talk program on higher education issues, *Future Shock in Higher Education,* from 1994 to 1999 on the Massachusetts Corporation for Educational Telecommunications (MCET) satellite learning network. A graduate of Colby College (A.B.) and Boston University (M.Div. and Ph.D.), Martin has written articles for the *Chronicle of Higher Education,* the *London Times,* the *Christian Science Monitor,* the *Boston Globe, University Business, Trusteeship,* and *Case Currents,* and *Planning for Higher Education.*

JAMES E. SAMELS is the founder and CEO of both the Education Alliance and the Samels Group, a full-service higher education consulting firm. He is also the founding partner of Samels Associates, a law firm serving independent and public colleges and universities and nonprofit and for-profit higher education organizations. Samels has served on the faculties of the University of Massachusetts and Bentley College and has been a guest lecturer at Boston University and Harvard University. Prior to his appointment at the University of Massachusetts, Samels served as the deputy and acting state comptroller in Massachusetts and as special assistant attorney general, Massachusetts Community College counsel, and general counsel to the Massachusetts Board of Regents. Samels holds a bachelor's degree in political science, a master's degree in public administration, a juris doctor degree, and a doctor of education degree. He has written and cowritten a number of scholarly articles, monographs, and opinion editorials appearing in the *Chronicle of Higher Education, Trusteeship,* the *Christian Science Monitor,* the *Guardian* of London, the *Boston Globe,* the *Boston Herald,* the *Boston Business Journal,* the *Journal of Higher Education Management,* and *Planning for Higher Education.* He is the coauthor, with James Martin, of *Merging Colleges for Mutual Growth* (1994) and *First among Equals: The Role of the Chief Academic Officer* (1997). Samels has consulted on projects and presented research papers at universities, colleges, schools, and ministries of education in China, Canada, Great Britain, France, Korea, Sweden, Thailand, and Turkey.

LEE J. BETTS is president emeritus of Frederick Community College, Frederick, Maryland. Previously he served as president of Muscatine Community College, Muscatine, Iowa, and, concurrently, as vice chancellor of staff and student development for the Eastern Iowa Community Colleges. He also facilitated the development of the Servicemembers Opportunity Colleges consortium, which provides educational opportunities for active-duty military service personnel through more than one thousand affiliated colleges and universities. Betts is an Honorably Retired minister in the Presbyterian Church (USA), having served as a pastor and a hospital and prison chaplain in Massachusetts, Ohio, and Florida.

CHARLES BROWN started in institutional advancement in 1979 as a member of the annual giving staff at Princeton University, where he worked for nine years. He also served in senior positions in the nonprofit practice of A. T. Kearney Executive Search, the Solomon R. Guggenheim Museum, and the Johns Hopkins University. Brown joined Stanford University in 2000 as director of medical development, and he is now the director of the Campaign for Stanford Medicine.

JEAN A. DOWDALL, vice president in the education practice of Witt/Kieffer, is a search consultant specializing in senior executive searches for colleges, universities, foundations, and other nonprofit organizations. In that capacity she has carried out more than thirty searches for presidents and chancellors. She has served as a dean of arts and sciences (West Chester University), a vice president (Arcadia University), and a president (Simmons College). She is the author of "Moving Up," a column that appears monthly on the Web site of the *Chronicle of Higher Education,* offering advice about searches and professional development for institutions and candidates.

E. K. FRETWELL JR. has worked in system leadership positions for more than forty years. He is currently chancellor emeritus of the University of North Carolina at Charlotte, which he headed for ten years, and before that he was president of State University of New York College at Buffalo. He has served as interim president of the University of Massachusetts five-campus system and interim president of the University of North Florida. He taught at Teachers College, Columbia University, and at the University of California at Berkeley. Fretwell's writings include *The Interim Presidency* (1995) and (with David Leslie, senior author) *Wise Moves in Hard Times: Creating and Managing Resilient Colleges and Universities* (1996).

VARTAN GREGORIAN is president of Carnegie Corporation of New York. Prior to his current position, which he assumed in 1997, Gregorian served for nine years as president of Brown University. Having taught at San Francisco State College, the University of California at Los Angeles, and the University of Texas at Austin, he joined the University of Pennsylvania faculty in 1972, becoming its provost in 1978. For eight years (1981–89), Gregorian served as a president of the New York Public Library.

Gregorian is the author of *Emergence of Modern Afghanistan, 1880–1946,* and he currently serves on the boards of the Institute for Advanced Study at Princeton, the Human Rights Watch, the Museum of Modern Art, and the McGraw-Hill Companies. In 1989 the American Academy of the Institute of Arts and Letters awarded him its Gold Medal for Service to the Arts, and in 1998 President Clinton awarded him the National Humanities Medal.

ALLEN E. KOENIG is senior consultant and partner-in-charge of the higher education practice of R. H. Perry & Associates, Inc. (Executive Search Consultants, Washington, D.C., and Columbus, Ohio). He joined the firm in 1993 after cofounding (with Thomas H. Langevin) the Registry for College and University Presidents during the previous year. Through a collaborative agreement between Perry and the Registry, Koenig specializes in public and independent higher education presidential searches and interim presidential placements. From 1979 to 1989, he served as president of Emerson College in Boston and from 1989 to 1991 as president of Chapman University in Orange, California. In 1989 he was honored by Governor Michael Dukakis in his "State of the State Address" as one of the ten outstanding citizens of Massachusetts.

THOMAS H. LANGEVIN is chairman and CEO of the Registry for College and University Presidents, a firm he cofounded with Allen E. Koenig in 1992. In this endeavor, he has been instrumental in making more than sixty placements of interim presidents and senior administrators in colleges and universities. Through Thomas H. Langevin & Associates, Inc., which he established in 1978, he has done strategic planning, curriculum consultation, and presidential and board assessments. Langevin served as president of Capital University in Columbus, Ohio, from 1969 to 1979.

STEVEN MULLER is president emeritus of the Johns Hopkins University, a fellow of the Foreign Policy Institute, and a distinguished professorial lecturer at the Paul H. Nitze School of Advanced International Studies of the Johns Hopkins University in Washington, D.C. He served as president of the Johns Hopkins University from 1972 to 1990. He is a member of the American Association of Rhodes Scholars, the Council on Foreign Relations, and the International Institute for Strategic Studies. Formerly, Muller served as a member and chairman of the Association of American Universities and as founding chairman of the National Association of Independent Colleges and Universities.

ARTHUR PADILLA is a professor in the College of Management at North Carolina State University, where he has won awards for undergraduate teaching excellence. He returned to his alma mater after working as a senior officer in the headquarters of the sixteen-campus University of North Carolina. He has also served as secretary of the university and assistant to the chancellor at North Carolina State University. Shortly after completing his doctoral dissertation, which won an award from the U.S. Department of Labor, Padilla served as a fellow at the Brookings Institute. He has written extensively about the management of higher education and of multicampus universities, both in professional journals and in the *Washington Post,* the *New York Times,* and the *Chronicle of Higher Education.*

JOHN ROSS, principal author of *Public Relations and the Presidency: Strategies and Tactics for Effective Communication,* (CASE,

2001), provides strategic communications counsel and services to educational institutions as well as to associations and nonprofit organizations. His specialties are leadership in analysis of client communications, development and implementation of strategic communications plans, and national media relations campaigns. Founder of RossWrites, a strategic higher education communications firm, he has served as a senior media relations–public relations officer at Tusculum College, Plymouth State College, Dickinson College, the University of Miami, and the University of Cincinnati. He is the winner of a gold medal for news and information from CASE and a former vice president of the national Education Writers Association.

PATRICIA STANLEY became president of Frederick Community College in January 1998. Formerly, she served as administrator for the economic development and vocational education division of the California Community College chancellor's office for the 107-college system. She is a 2002 appointee to the American Association of Community Colleges board of directors and was recently elected by her peers to serve as president of the Maryland Council of Community College CEOs.

THOMAS J. TREBON is currently president of Carroll College in Helena, Montana. His teaching and research interests have focused on international studies, with particular emphasis on the politics of developing nations, especially sub-Saharan Africa. He spent a year in the United Kingdom as a Fulbright Scholar. Thomas Trebon's service in teaching and academic leadership has included St. Norbert College as vice president for academic affairs and Sacred Heart University as provost. As part of their shared experiences in academic service, Thomas and Scottie Trebon have been active participants and leaders in efforts of the Council of Independent Colleges. SCOTTIE TREBON served as a member of the Deans Spouse Task Force for the Council of Independent Colleges for several years and participated in a number of national conference panels. Thomas Trebon received the Dean's Award from CIC in 1997.

WILLIAM A. WEARY is president of Fieldstone Consulting, Inc., a firm that helps develop strategies for boards and administrations of colleges, universities, schools, and other nonprofit groups. He has taught European history at Amherst and Bowdoin Colleges and has headed the upper schools of Abington Friends School in Philadelphia and the Dalton School in New York City. Weary has led the workshops on presidential and board assessment for the National Conference of Trusteeship of the Association of Governing Boards of Universities and Colleges. As a consultant to AGB, Weary wrote its *Essentials of Presidential Search* and *Guidelines for Selecting a Presidential Search Consultant* and, in 2000, with AGB's president, published *Presidential and Board Assessment in Higher Education: Purposes, Policies, and Strategies.*

NANCY L. ZIMPHER became chancellor of the University of Wisconsin-Milwaukee in 1998, having previously served as the executive dean of the Professional Colleges and dean of the College of Education at the Ohio State University. Zimpher has served in various administrative positions while engaging in research and development efforts concerned with improving the preparation of teachers, especially teachers in urban contexts. She is an active participant at both national and international conferences on these issues.

Index